Washington Water Power, Main Office Personnel, 1908. (Courtesy of NWMAC, L97-69.23)

SPOKANE'S STORIES

28 STORIES

OF THE PEOPLE, PLACES AND EVENTS THAT HAVE SHAPED SPOKANE

SPOKANE'S STORIES

28 STORIES
OF THE PEOPLE, PLACES AND EVENTS THAT HAVE SHAPED SPOKANE

by
Blythe J. Thimsen

Edited by
Pia I. Longinotti

Creative Design by
David J. Crary, Cedar Bay Studio

Up Escalator Publications
Spokane, Washington, 2014

Published in Spokane, Washington
by Up Escalator Publications

Printed in Visalia, California
by Jostens, Inc.

ISBN: 978-0-692-31591-0
Library of Congress Control Number: 2014918895

Cover photo: Color reproduction postcard of Middle Falls of Spokane River photograph.
Thorough research done, with no known original copyright determined.
Any information on photo may be sent to blythe@blythethimsen.com
Author photo, on back cover, by Kelly Tareski Photography

To my parents, Jeff and Marcy Thimsen, who gave to me a love of history, the encouragement to write, and endless support.

"Have I not commanded you? Be strong and courageous. Do not be frightened, and do not be dismayed, for the Lord your God is with you wherever you go."
~ Joshua 1:9

Contents

Introduction

IT WAS MY FAVORITE TIME OF THE DAY. TEETH BRUSHED, face washed and pajamas on, as a child, I would grab a book, put my glasses on and settle in for my 30 minutes of reading before turning out the light each night. During that half hour, I would get lost in whatever world I was reading about, forgetting everything around me, and seeing only the words on the page coming to life in my mind. As the years passed, my schedule and time frame changed, but the love of reading never went away.

In 2004, I became the editor of *Spokane Coeur d'Alene Living*, the city lifestyle magazine for Spokane and the surrounding areas. Having spent most of my life in Spokane, I thought I knew a lot about this great city, but it wasn't until I began researching our city's history, that my eyes were opened to the incredible treasure we have in our community. Researching for work, I would get lost in the stories, newspaper clippings and accounts of Spokane's earliest days. My love of reading combined with a newfound interest in the history of our community led to the vision for this book: A compilation of my work, some of it previously published, some of it new, and a chance to dive deeper into well-known topics, and get lost in the details. Though there are so many stories to share, for this volume, I've selected 28 of the most impactful people, places and events that helped shape Spokane into the city it is today.

Presenting the history of any place is a bit like sewing a patchwork quilt, with scraps and pieces of fabric coming from a variety of people, voices and sources. I appreciate all of the local historians and writers who have gone down a similar road before me, whose works, used as references and citations, have added to the colorful and rich texture of this historic patchwork quilt you hold in your hands.

Spokane has some incredible stories tucked into its past. With stories of bold steps, daring defeats, life altering tragedies and divinely appointed blessings, this is a town that has seen it all. Add to it a hearty dose of zesty personalities, strong characters and determined individuals, and it is easy to get lost in the rich and riveting history of Spokane. This town has a story to tell; it has many stories to tell. These are *Spokane's Stories.*

- Blythe

(Note: When Spokane officially became an incorporated city in 1881, it went by the name Spokan Falls. The "e" was added in 1883, changing the name to Spokane Falls. In 1891, "Falls", well, fell off, and it became simply Spokane. In this book, references to the city were done by the appropriate name based upon the time period. So if you see "Spokane Falls" and "Spokane" peppered throughout each story, it is not a mistake; rather, it is an appropriate representation of what the name was at that time.)

1

The Father of Spokane

James N. Glover

James N. Glover, formal pose. (Courtesy of Northwest Room, Spokane Public Library (NWR - SPL))

"Being the man who laid the foundation of this prosperous city, and who built his home where no other white man had realized the enormous advantages and great future of Spokane Falls, he has during the succeeding years of his life done everything to make this city the great metropolis of the Northwest."

- Spokane Falls and Its Exposition

Maxwell

Spokane & Walla Walla, Wash.

PARENTS HAVE A RESPONSIBILITY OF SETTING AN EXAMPLE FOR THEIR CHILDREN, guiding them as they grow, helping them to establish and reach goals, and preparing for their future. James N. Glover never had any children of his own, but he is still known as a father; specifically, he is known as the "father of Spokane." Through his example, perseverance, determination and guidance, he laid the groundwork that transformed Spokane Falls from a small cluster of people to the great city we now call home.

On the evening of May 11, 1873, Glover, along with his friend and business partner, J.N. Matheny, arrived on horseback in the area which became known as Spokane Falls. They had set out from Salem earlier that year, lured by the "glowing descriptions of the beauties and possibilities of the Palouse and Spokane regions." Once his eyes fell upon the roaring falls, with their fine white mist arching into the air, Glover's heart and soul were captivated. He had found his home and wanted to build this area into a great city.

At the time, the only inhabitants of the area were the Spokane Indians, a handful of families who had erected meager homes, and two squatters who had laid claim to the area, J.J. Downing and S.R. Scranton.

Glover offered to purchase the squatters rights from both men for $2,000 each. Downing accepted the offer, but Scranton refused to sell. Having secured ownership of half the site, Glover and Matheny returned to Salem to get supplies for survival in what was an uncharted area. They came back to Spokane Falls in 1874, and found the squatter's outpost deserted. Downing had left upon Glover's purchase, and Scranton, who had refused to sell, had been on the run from the law and had taken up in a hideout nearby. Determined to own the rights to the area, Glover found Scranton's hideout and again offered to purchase his half of the area for $2,000. Scranton took the offer. According to records, this made Glover, Matheny and an individual named Yeaton the sole possessors of the town site. It is believed that Yeaton began homesteading in Spokane Falls during the year that Glover and Matheny were back in Oregon, and it was decided he should have partial rights to the town site as well.

Together, Glover, Matheny and Yeaton ventured into the milling and general merchandise business. "About November 1, 1873, we opened Spokane's first store. The trade, however, was far from rapid in coming to us," wrote Glover in *Reminiscences of James N. Glover.*

Trade was slow in coming, as the town was small and isolated. Eventually Matheny and Yeaton decided they did not want to keep their families in the small and struggling region, so Glover bought out their shares in 1877, giving him ownership of 160 acres of land. Most of this land was where the heart of current day downtown Spokane is located, between Division and Monroe, with some of the land located on the north side of the river, but most of it on the south side.

As the first permanent white settler in the area, Glover had a good relationship with the Spokane Indian tribe, and most of the trade done in his store was with them. In 1877, the Nez Perce Indian tribe came to Spokane Falls to join the Spokane Tribe in powwows. It was said that the Nez Perce were in a "warring mood" which was terrifying for the white inhabitants of the area. The whites all gathered together and sought sanctuary in James Glover's store and home, where they were barricaded for several days.

James and Esther Glover in their parlor. (Courtesy of NWR - SPL)

As the powwows continued, the Nez Perce became more of a threat. Glover would not give into the layer of fear that was blanketing the community, though. As the father of the community, he realized he needed to step in and intercede for the people of Spokane Falls. He called a council with the oldest chiefs of the Spokane Indians and, not pulling any punches, he told them the Nez Perce needed to be gone by noon on the following day or he would call for U.S. soldiers to come and kill them.

It must have taken nerves of steel for Glover to stand before the chiefs and tell

Wagons in front of Glover's First National Bank. (Courtesy of NWMAC, L2003-14.496)

them this, especially because he was bluffing. He didn't have access to any soldiers and would not have been able to get them to Spokane Falls in enough time even if he knew where they were. The Nez Perce did not know this though, and based on their great fear of the "Brass Buttons" as they called soldiers, they took the threat seriously. With memories still fresh in their minds of Gen. George Wright, who, in 1858, captured and killed 900 horses belonging to local tribes, as punishment for the Steptoe incident, and in order to restore control, they were not interested in facing a similar situation.

Just as Glover must have been holding his breath, waiting to see if the Nez Perce would really leave, an unexpected arrival of the Second Regiment, led by Gen. Frank Wheaton, occurred. It was pure coincidence; Glover had no clue they were in the area, and they did not know of the situation that was brewing in town. With the arrival of the regiment, however, Glover's ranking as someone important and with immense amounts of power was sealed forever, both for the Indians and for the people of Spokane Falls. That notion became permanently associated with him.

Though the incident with the Indians ended well and without bloodshed, it reinforced Glover's belief that there needed to be a permanent military presence in the area, so he personally approached Gen. William T. Sherman, and on behalf of Spokane Falls, presented the case for a military fort to be built nearby. Fort Sherman, in Coeur d'Alene, Idaho, was the resulting fort.

"That was the dawning of a bright day for me and for the city of Spokane. Thereafter, I felt that the future of the city on this western frontier was assured and I knew it would have to come right around the wonderful falls," said Glover after learning Fort Sherman would be built in Coeur d'Alene.

With a military presence, more people were willing to live in the area, and the city continued to grow. By 1881, Glover had been elected to the city council, and he was later elected mayor in 1884, helping guide and grow the city he loved. "What's good for Spokane is good for me," was Glover's personal motto.

Along with Glover's business and political success, he was well on the road to financial success as well. In 1882, he helped incorporate First National Bank, where he was the principle stockholder, as well as serving as bank president for ten years. Spokane Falls was becoming a successful city.

Glover Mansion, 1908. (Courtesy of Washington State Digital Archives (WSDA))

When the Panic of 1893 led to a run on First National Bank, Glover was said to have used some of his own assets in order to pay customers. As a president and a major stockholder, Glover lost over $1,500,000 in the crisis. A weaker man would have packed up and left, searching again for an easier life in a larger city, but Glover knew he could recover, and he worked hard, gaining back most of that money in his lifetime.

The generosity which Glover demonstrated during the Panic of 1893 permeated into all areas of his life, as he was known as one of the kindest, most helpful and generous men you would ever meet.

"He was a square shooter if ever there was one," said his sister-in-law, Mrs. Edwin A. Smith, in a newspaper report. "He was kind and considerate to everyone, never holding a grudge and never knowingly offending anyone. I don't think there ever was a man more loved and respected by his fellows."

He often gave of his own personal finances to help people start their own businesses. It was said, "He would do anything for a friend, and Spokane was one of the best friends he had."

Glover so wanted Spokane to grow and be a strong, successful and populated city that he would sell at low prices – or even give away – his own land holdings if it was to someone who would help the city thrive.

"In one instance he gave forty acres to Frederick Post (for whom Post Falls was named) if he would locate a grist mill here, which he did," stated an undated clip of the *Spokesman-Review.*

Glover was in the upper echelons of society of the rapidly growing Spokane. He was often seen walking about town in his silk top hot, fine cut clothing, walking stick and silk ties. As the town grew and prospered, so did his businesses and those of his peers. It is no stretch of the imagination to think about the fancy dinners and grand parties that took place in his mansion, or the homes of his friends. What may be difficult to imagine is that these parties, when hosted by Glover, were void of any alcohol. Though considered by many to be liberal, one area where Glover did not extend a liberal notion was that of drinking. In fact, Glover was in favor of a "bone dry law" outlawing liquor for Spokane.

Not knowing Glover's stand on alcohol, one of his grocery suppliers in Portland, Oregon, who kept him stocked in his merchandise store, wanted to thank him for being such a long-term, loyal customer, so they told him they were sending him a present in his next shipment. He looked forward with curiosity to seeing what they sent him. When the next shipment came from them he opened it up and found a barrel of whiskey tucked in as his present.

Glover was horrified. He told the following story to N.W. Durham, of Spokane, who later recounted it to the *Spokesman-Review*. "I was at once considerably alarmed, for I got to fearing what might happen if the wild young fellows, or the Indian bucks, should find that I had this liquor. I had always stoutly refused to sell it, although I could have built up quite a business in it because it was greatly in demand. Other grocers did make a lot out of it, but I knew it was bad for the boys, and refused. I worried about that barrel of booze until I decided to hide it away. I built a sort of false partition to the store and boarded the barrel up inside. It was there for several years and I had in fact almost forgotten about it."

A specific event jogged Glover's memory. For many years he had been burdened by the worry that the squatter's right which he bought didn't extend to the riverbank. It was a constant stress because he worried he would find out he didn't own all of his land and that part of it was railroad property. He had asked the railroad's engineers about it several times, and desired to have the land surveyed. Finally, the engineers looked into it and found out Glover's land extended all the way to the river, and that the railroad did not own it. They knew it was of great concern to Glover, so they were eager to go give him the good news.

"I thought about ten years of my life had rolled off my shoulders," Glover later shared. "Then, by golly! I thought about that barrel of whiskey that had been there all these years, getting mellow, and of the fine boys that had done this thing for me, and I reached for my ax! Those boys had a fine time that night. Oh yes, I had a fine time too!"

Not all of Glover's times had been so fine, though. He later said that 1877, and the years following, after Matheny and Yeaton departed Spokane Falls, were the loneliest in his life. "The prospects were pretty dark for me after my partners had gone," he wrote in *Reminiscences of James N. Glover*, "but I determined to stay on, for I still believed that someday there would be an important city here. I had sunk about $12,000 here and I was unwilling to give up and acknowledge myself beaten."

What is interesting is that though he may have been lonely, he wasn't alone. In all of the newspaper clippings, books, and stories of James Glover, there is rarely if ever a mention of his *first* wife, Susan T. Glover. One wouldn't even know he was married, except for the court documents that describe the marriage and petition for divorce.

At one point in the 1870s James and Susan were the only full time inhabitants of Spokane Falls. The census of 1878, 1880 and 1885 lists Susan as "wife," and her occupation as "housekeeper."

In 1888, famed Spokane Falls architect Kirtland K. Cutter built the Glover Mansion, a baronial mansion with twenty-two rooms, leaded glass, intricate carving and curving arches, located on seven acres. On the main floor of the home a stained glass portrait of Susan remains, today.

Their marriage was not a happy one, and Susan Glover returned to Oregon on August 28, 1891, three days before James Glover filed official Complaint for Divorce papers.

As unfortunate as divorce is nowadays, in the late 1800s it was downright shameful, which might explain why Glover's divorce was never mentioned publicly. The depth of animosity between the two is evident in their legal papers: "There was in fact, no compatibility whatsoever between the plaintiff (James N. Glover) and defendant (Susan T. Glover), but they were wholly unsuited and incongenial, the one with the other. This incongeniality which existed between the parties was so extreme, that it rendered cohabitation and social intercourse between them repulsive beyond endurance on the part of the other and in fact impossible."

Only one day after their divorce was granted, on April 2, 1892, Glover married Esther Emily Leslie in Kootenai County, Idaho. Records from the county show a second marriage between Glover and Leslie dated October 12, 1892. It is believed that Glover and his second wife were concerned about the legality of their marriage because it occurred so closely on the heels of his divorce. To ensure their marriage was legal, they wed again six months later. They would be happily married for twenty-nine years.

With her divorce settlement of a horse and carriage, $1,000 a month from her ex-husband, and a house worth $3,000 in Salem, Susan returned to Oregon. After a short time back there, she returned to Spokane. By the 1900 census, Susan Glover was listed as a resident of Eastern Washington Hospital for the Insane. In 1921, she died at Eastern Washington Hospital of pneumonia with senility as a contributing factor. She was buried the next day at the Eastern State Hospital Cemetery.

A long-lingering, unnamed disease plagued Glover in his last years. Confined to a chair, his doctors recommend he take to his bed, but he refused. He told Esther if he were to go into his bedroom, he knew he would never

Mr. and Mrs. James Glover in the same spot in the Glover Mansion where James Glover spent his last year of life. (Courtesy of WSDA)

come out. Instead, he had a special chair set up for him by his living room window and he sat and slept in there for over a year, so he could look out on the scenery of his beautiful Spokane.

Glover died in his home on January 18, 1921, with his wife Esther, and his brother Samuel, by his side. Samuel had lived with Glover for thirty years. A few months before Glover's death, Samuel returned to the family's land in Salem, Oregon. Before he left for his travels, Samuel and James both agreed their one wish was to make sure they saw each other again; therefore, when Samuel received a telegraph that his brother had fallen ill, he boarded a train in Oregon and came home. He was able to see his brother, and spend time with him for two days before James passed away.

When he died, the body of Glover, who had been Spokane's first Mason, lay in state at the Masonic Temple, while people of the community filed past to view. Uniformed guard members of the Knights of Templar guarded his body. His death put the city in mourning and was front-page news for the January 19, 1921 issue of the *Spokesman-Review.*

"There passed before the coffin for a last look at the face of the man they had all known and loved through the years, men and women who have felt the kindly generosity of Mr. Glover, old pioneers who feel in his passing a real grief and those who knew him as cheery, friendly neighbor and friend in later years."

When he arrived, Spokane Falls was nothing more than a few people, but Glover put his heart, soul, finances and unwavering determination into building up the city. This father of Spokane led by example with his hard work, kind treatment of others and devotion to civic pride, showing future generations what the city of Spokane Falls, later to be called Spokane, could be.

Herbert Gaston, author of *J. N. Glover and the Beginning of Spokane Falls* offered this observation about Glover. "The founding of Spokane differed very materially from the founding of most other cities, and nearly all those who have watched its growth or become acquainted with the history of its progress bear testimony to the fact that neither was an accident. Spokane did not happen, nor did it just grow in the ordinary sense – it was founded and was built – with deliberation, with foresight and with unbounded energy. It stands today a monument to unflagging faith and to pluck which no disaster was great enough permanently to discourage, and to none more truly a monument than to 'Uncle Jimmy' Glover." ●

2

Spokane's Loose Cannon

A.M. Cannon's Impact on Spokane

WHEN HE WAS BORN TO A POOR FAMILY IN ILLINOIS IN 1837, THERE WAS NO way to know that Anthony McCue Cannon's (A.M. Cannon) life would be full of adventure and fortunes made and lost, nor that he would play a pivotal role in the growth of a little town in the Washington Territory named Spokane Falls. That is exactly what was in store for Cannon though, and it was with his hard work, high expectations and brazen arrogance, that Spokane Falls prospered and grew, becoming the city we know today.

A.M. Cannon in his older years. (Courtesy of Washington State Digital Archives)

Mrs. A.M. (Jennie F.) Cannon. (Courtesy of NWMAC, L87-96)

Wayward and full of wanderlust, Cannon set his sights on the Pacific Northwest. When he arrived in Portland, Oregon, Cannon met Jane Pease, who went by the name Jennie, and whom he would soon marry. A widow and single mother of five, Jennie taught sewing to Chinese workers in Portland, while Cannon sold Singer sewing machines across Oregon. It may be said this sewing connection brought them together, stitching their two lives together into one. In 1878, seven years after her first husband's death, Jennie and Cannon married. While Cannon was testy, arrogant and brazen, Jennie had a warm heart and was known for her nurturing spirit.

Cannon was known to live, play and work hard – hard enough that he received a doctor's order to take time off and travel in order to rest his weary self. Leaving his wife and children behind for a while, Cannon set out, and in 1878, his travels took him to Spokane Falls.

Cannon and his traveling partner, J.J. Browne, arrived when the town was nothing more than a glorified village, with a smattering of crudely constructed homes. Despite the sparse population (James Glover was already here and running his general store), Cannon saw the potential in building a town in such a well-suited location. He knew the railroad that was soon to arrive, as well as the opportunities for travel and transportation via the river, would bring both people and money to Spokane Falls, ensuring its success, as well as his.

Pooling their money, Cannon and Browne mustered up $3,200, which they paid to James Glover, thus purchasing half of the town. They then divided that half of the town into two sections: Browne's Addition and Cannon's Addition.

"Cannon already owed $4,000 in Portland. But at 55, rheumatic, patriarchal in a flamboyant white beard, he scorned a picayune debt if he saw a chance to make real money. He was impatient, testy and inclined to splurge," wrote John Fahey in *Requiem for a High Roller*.

When Cannon bought his portion of Spokane Falls, he got Glover's store as part of the purchase price. After securing the deal, he sent for Jennie and her five children, who made their way to Spokane Falls and took up residence in a lean-to attached to the store.

Keeping his eyes open for opportunities, Cannon began storing money for railroad workers in a vault in the store. At that time, there was only one bank in Eastern Washington, and it was located in Walla Walla. Tapping into a need, Cannon launched the Bank of Spokane Falls, in 1879. All it took was a handcrafted sign that read "Bank of Spokane Falls: A.M. Cannon" on the front door. Forget a business license or any official paperwork; with a finely printed script and well-hung sign, the bank was officially open for business. Cannon had no capital when he opened the bank, and it was rumored he had to borrow $1,000 from a "lady friend" to get it started.

Cannon's Bank of Spokane Falls, 1889. (Courtesy of NWMAC, L97-1.141)

In 1881, the Northern Pacific Railroad finally arrived in Spokane Falls, and with it Cannon saw an opportunity to help himself, as well as the town, prosper. He would travel to Cheney, where the railroad made a stop, greet passengers and recruit them to live in Spokane Falls, instead of Cheney. This was a move that served him well as he also sold land to those whom he convinced to move to Spokane Falls; therefore, he lined his pockets and built up his bank account while also building up the population of the town.

He proved to be an effective salesman, recruiting many people to Spokane Falls, where they bought land and made him a wealthy man. His wealth became visible to his fellow citizens when he built his own home, as described in John Fahey's *Requiem for a High Roller:*

One of Cannon's competitor banks. (Courtesy of NWMAC, L86-1394)

"(In 1883) Cannon outdid himself. He built a twenty-two-room house in gabled Queen Anne style near his shanty. It had spindled friezes, two-and-a-half stories and a turret rising above. With parquet floors, tapestries, leaded windows, the house was indeed extravagant, heated by warm air and lit by gas – the first in Spokane Falls. The grand house also had the town's first bathtubs, mahogany boxes lined with tin. But with not enough water for a garden, the house stood in brown weeds for several years. Finally, a water system was installed which enabled Cannon to landscape a full block, erect a fountain in the front yard and place a live seal in its pool, a form of animal life few in Spokane Falls had seen before. Jennie Cannon set a Steinway grand piano in the living room…that is how the Cannons lived."

A political career seemed like the next step, as it often is for prominent wealthy men in a community. When Spokane Falls incorporated in 1881, Cannon was appointed to one of seven city council spots. From there, he was elected Spokane Falls' third mayor, serving from 1885-1887.

Being a man of great importance in the city, Cannon's arrogance often showed, as he demanded to be treated in a certain manner. On April 6, 1892 (exactly thirteen years to the day before his death), Cannon and his son-in-law, B.H. Bennett were "Arrested and brought before J.S. Gray, Justice of the Peace for examination on a charge of committing the crime of assault with intent to murder," according to a court document of the Territory of Washington. They were held on $1,000 bail. The cause of the arrest was explained in the following article, which appeared in the April 1, 1882, edition of the *Spokan Times*, the first newspaper in Spokane.

A sketch of the Cannon's grand home. (Courtesy of NWMAC, L86-1395)

"A.M. Cannon and B.H. Bennett, of the bank in this city, called at the residence of Francis H. Cook last evening, and finding he had not returned from town, wanted to know where he was, saying they might meet him. The visit was occasioned by articles published in the Times, to which Mr. Cannon took exceptions. At

1884 view of the north side of Riverside Avenue, where much of Cannon's business — and antics —took place. (Courtesy of NWMAC, L2003-14-656)

10 o'clock, to-day Cannon and Bennett entered the Times office on the second floor, while none were present but Mr. and Mrs. Cook, with a babe in the cradle. Cannon demanded retraction, and swore Mr. Cook must sign papers [not then shown] or he would kill him. The editor did not do so, and Cannon drew a revolver to carry out his threat. Mr. Cook took up an iron side-stick (used in the office) and induced Cannon to put away his revolver; whereupon Bennett drew a revolver, stating that he was going to take part in the affair, even while Mrs. Cook pleaded with him to desist. As Bennett was trying to shoot, Cook took up another iron and knocked the weapon out of his hand. Cannon's aim was again being taken, with Mrs. Cook in line, when Mr. Cook knocked the revolver out of his hand and across the room. Bennett, by this time had regained his weapon, but his left hand was stricked (sic) down by Mr. Cook. Cannon, who had regained his deadly weapon on the opposite side of the room, raised it to fire; but Mr. Cook threw a missile that hit him just as he was pulling trigger, the weapon discharging and the bullet passing through the stovepipe, glancing to the ceiling. After this the blows fell rapidly, blood was scattered over the room, a case of type was pied, and the men closed in close embrace. Mrs. Cook had rushed downstairs, and a crowd began to gather. By this time Mr. Cook had regained his feet, and the assaulting party had ceased their efforts. After regaining the street, and after Mr. Cook had given up his piece of printing material, Cannon again threatened to kill Mr. Cook, but bystanders interfered. Warrants for the arrest of Cannon and Bennett have been issued; but neither will be able to be out, perhaps, for weeks. Both are under the care of physicians, and the scalp wounds they received, which are very severe, have been sewed up. Mr. Cook was not injured, but was somewhat tired."

Townsfolk sitting near Cannon's store. (Courtesy of NWMAC, L88-27.16)

The case was soon settled, with neither Cannon nor Bennett serving time, and Cannon was soon back to developing the community and his personal wealth. According to Fahey, "Before 1890, nearly every civic enterprise [in Spokane Falls] involved Cannon in some way."

One example was the Spokane and Palouse Railway, of which Cannon was in charge. He also was part of the Northwestern & Pacific Mortgage Co., with his friend and fellow townsman, a Dutchman named Herman A. Van Valenburg, who formed the company in 1885. This was an extremely profitable company that made more than 550 loans in four years, worth $1.1 million. With eight to twelve percent interest charged on each loan, it was a cash cow for Van Valenburg and Cannon. Due to the success of the business, Dutch investors from Amsterdam became

A.M. Cannon's traveling partner, and look alike, JJ Browne. (Courtesy of Northwest Room, Spokane Public Library (NWR, SPL))

intrigued and put up a great deal of money to be a part of the company, making it an international venture. As a result, the name was changed to Northwestern & Pacific Hypotheekbank, and Cannon was appointed to one of only two bank director positions in the U.S. for the company.

According to Fahey, it was Northwestern & Pacific Hypotheekbank that helped fund much of the rebuilding in Spokane Falls following Spokane's Great Fire of 1889, which destroyed nearly the entire city.

Though the fire was devastating for the city, it provided a way for Cannon to prosper. After the fire, one of Cannon's brothers, (much of his extended family had moved to Spokane Falls by that point) Aniel Cannon, was supervising the rebuilding of the Auditorium Theatre, which was to become a jewel of the city. Seizing his desire to make Spokane Falls an enviable place to live, Cannon instructed his brother to go all out for the Auditorium.

"The Auditorium suited Cannon fine: he preferred the gaudy and ornate," wrote Fahey. "Its ninety-foot entry hall from Post flickered with gas torches illuminating Turkish rugs and plaster statues in niches. Stained glass windows played colored lights across the box office. One window showed facing portraits of Cannon and Browne."

Good times were not to last, though. The Panic of 1893 hit Cannon particularly hard. The Bank of Spokane Falls faced a run, as depositors demanded their money in fear. In order to cover the depositors, Cannon turned to other bankers for help, but they were not willing to lend him any money. He owed $80,000 to Hypotheekbank on the Bank of Spokane Falls' building. It was a marble building with a Corinthian roof held up by pillars and accessorized with two marble reclining lions by which depositors and customers would have to pass as they climbed the steps from the street. All of Cannon's land was held as collateral for other loans. Simply stated, he was over-extended. As a result of the financial crisis and his debt, he lost his job at Northwestern & Pacific Hypotheekbank.

The greatest loss for Cannon was not his job, his land nor his wealth. It was the loss of his wife, Jennie. According to the September 8, 1893, issue of the *Spokane Chronicle* in an article announcing her death, "In June 1892, Jennie underwent a very severe surgical operation which confined her to her bed for some time…in November, Dr. Ludlam of Chicago was called to this city and the operation was repeated."

Jennie suffered from a mysterious condition for nearly a year, confined to her house and then her bed. Her final weeks were fitful, with the last days spent slipping in and out of consciousness. She was said to manage a lucid moment or two, during one of which she offered a few words to one of her sisters who had come to Spokane Falls to sit by her bedside.

Jennie died in 1893, leaving Cannon financially broken as well as brokenhearted. The sympathy others felt for him dissipated when, six weeks after Jennie's death, Cannon suddenly and secretly married a young widow named Eleanor. The lack of an appropriate mourning period was considered scandalous, and Cannon's friends and family disowned him, horrified by his actions. Remarried at age 66, six weeks after his wife died, Cannon was abandoned by friends, family and society.

If it was love that lead him to marry Eleanor, it was short-lived because he soon left her and her children in Spokane Falls and headed east for New York. That was a brief stop before continuing on to South America, where he was on a hunt for some new venture that would net him instant and intense wealth. He never found it though, and he never again saw his beloved Spokane Falls, nor his new wife; Cannon died alone on April 6, 1895, in his hotel room in New York City, after returning from South America.

Cannon's death was a sad end to a life that had much adventure, success and failure. He was arrogant and self-serving, and yet at the same time, created the foundation for a strong city. He was a proud and arrogant man, and yet one to whom we owe our thanks, for the city he helped to build. ●

A.M Cannon, 1879, (Courtesy of NWMAC, L93-66.71)

3

Deposits of Success

Spokane's Early Banks

IN 1878, WHEN SPOKANE FALLS BOASTED ROUGHLY 100 CITIZENS, MOST PURCHASES were made in trade or with small amounts of cash. A.M. Cannon, a new arrival to the city, ran a general store with his brother in a small wood building, and from his perch, Cannon had a front row seat to observe the growth of Spokane Falls. When the impending arrival of the Northern Pacific Railway was announced, Cannon began considering ways to capitalize on Spokane Falls' success. It was then that he became aware of the absence of a bank in the town.

The Marble Bank Building. (Courtesy of NWMAC, L85-79-191)

"I have started a bank," declared Cannon after placing a sign on his general store that read: Bank of Spokane Falls. "You know I haven't got a dollar, but my sister-in-law has $1,000 to loan me," he stated to friends. "There is no business for a bank, but the Northern Pacific is coming this way with its grade and construction, and there will be all sorts of time-checks to cash, and I thought I might as well get in and be ready to take care of it."

As the railroad arrived and the population increased, Cannon's bank grew to the point that it could no longer be contained in the back of his general store. Eventually, it found a home at the corner of Wall and Riverside. The success of the bank, however, was no match for the hunger of fire that consumed the bank building on the

First National Bank. (Courtesy of NWMAC, L2003-14.496)

night of August 4, 1889, when Spokane Falls was engulfed in the flames of what became known as The Great Fire. As the city rebuilt after the fire, buildings of great beauty were erected, buildings of brick and stone, which demonstrated the expectation that they would last for years to come.

One such building was the Marble Bank, which was constructed entirely of Vermont marble and was located on the same lot as The Crescent Building, which once housed The Crescent department store. Built in 1892, the Marble Bank building was originally constructed as the new home of the Bank of Spokane Falls; however, the bank failed before it moved into the building, a victim of the financial Panic of 1893, which swept across the country, creating fear and devastation, closing many banks.

"Because Cannon was one of Spokane's most enterprising men and was at that time its leading financier, the impact of these [bank] failures upon the public was tremendous," wrote economics professor Claude A. Campbell, in *Old National Bank of Spokane: The Pioneer "Big Bank" of Spokane and the Inland Empire.*

Though Cannon's bank wouldn't be housed in it, the Marble Bank building went on to house many of Spokane's financial institutions throughout the years. "This building was a twelve-carat diamond set in the center of Spokane's belt buckle," wrote historian Robert Hyslop, about the Marble Bank. "Even though it was built on the site of the pre-fire Cannon's Block with his bank [Bank of Spokane Falls] in the corner, it was not called by his or its name, as both were in ill-repute by the time the building was finished."

Cannon was the first banker in Spokane, but he certainly was not the only one. Realizing the financial success a good bank could bring to the pockets of the owners, soon other enterprising men followed suit.

The second bank to make its debut in Spokane was First National Bank, which was started in 1882 by James N. Glover, F. Rockwood More and Horace L. Cutter. "They saw a future for Spokane Falls as the first railroad had just completed its through lines, settlers were taking up the rich Palouse farmland and the rush to the newly discovered gold camps in the nearby Coeur d'Alenes was underway," wrote Joel E. Ferris in *Early Day Banks and Bankers.*

Traders National Bank of Spokane Falls. (Courtesy of NWR, SPL)

While the Bank of Spokane Falls was started with a mere $1,000, First National Bank was considerably more solid, with a $50,000 investment of capital. Glover, one of the founders of First National Bank, was the owner and landlord of the building rented by A.M. Cannon to house his general store and bank. When Cannon had decided to start his bank in 1878, it was while Glover was out of town on travels. It was said that Glover was rather shocked to see the presence of a bank in his building when he returned.

Cannon and Glover were both marked with an entrepreneurial streak and were shrewd businessmen who were fond of finding ways to enhance their wealth, secure their positions and line their pockets with a few extra coins, so it is not hard to imagine Glover was put out to discover that his renter had opened a bank in his building without notifying him; it may have been a further injustice to see this bank succeed and to see Cannon beating Glover to the punch and making money. Whether Glover was following in great footsteps or was a ruthless businessman who, concerned for his own financial success, was willing to sacrifice a friendship and compete against Cannon in pursuit of a great business opportunity cannot be firmly determined.

Northwestern & Pacific Mortgage Co., formed in 1885 by Dutchman Herman A. Van Valenburg, was an extremely profitable company. Dutch investors from Amsterdam soon invested, making it an international venture. The name was changed to Northwestern & Pacific Hypotheekbank, and A.M. Cannon was appointed to one of only two bank director positions in the U.S. for the company.

Four years after opening, and with a strong business to support it, Glover's First National Bank was successful enough to enable him to build a three-story building at the corner of Riverside and Howard. Alas, a strong financial start and enough deposits and customers to fund a three-story building did not guarantee success when the financial panic of 1893 hit. Like its predecessor, the Bank of Spokane Falls, First National Bank succumbed to the financial strains of the time and collapsed. "Failure and liquidation worked the end of many – and in fact most – of the early day banks," wrote Ferris. "The Panic of 1893 thinned their ranks."

There were some banks that did survive. Old National Bank was one of only three out of seven national banks

Old National Bank postcard. (Courtesy of NWR, SPL)

in Spokane that weathered the panic of 1893. Founded eighteen years after the first settlers arrived in Spokane, two years after Washington became a state and twelve years after the first bank opened its doors in the area, Old National Bank developed a long history in Spokane.

Before Old National Bank, there was Pacific Bank, which was chartered before The Great Fire of 1889. S.S. Glidden, who had already made himself a great success in the mines of North Idaho, joined with several of his associates to charter Pacific Bank in 1889, but soon thereafter, they decided they'd like to convert it in to a national bank. In 1891, they secured a charter for Old National Bank of Spokane. It had capital stock of $250,000 and officially began operating on December 22, 1891. Realizing there was power in numbers, Old National Bank's management took steps to acquire banking connections with individuals and financial institutions throughout the U.S. This meant that while its focus was on local banking, Old National Bank was able to "issue drafts to all ports of the world." Suddenly, Spokane's banking power had expanded beyond the banks of the river.

After successfully seeing Old National Bank through the Panic of 1893 and watching Spokane's and Old National Bank's profits increase dramatically over the ensuing years, Glidden was ready to retire from banking altogether. He didn't want to leave his beloved bank in the hands of just anyone, though. He found favor in two brothers, James C. and John Twohy, who owned Twohy Brothers Railway Contractors, and suggested they purchase controlling interest in Old National Bank. Interested in the opportunity, they wanted the input of a trusted expert before they took such a big risk. They asked their brother, D.W. Twohy, who was the president of Northwestern National Bank of West Superior, Wisconsin, to travel to Spokane to look at all aspects of the offer and advise them on whether it was a wise deal. After careful consideration, he not only gave them his brotherly stamp of approval, but D.W. got in on the deal as well. James C. Twohy purchased controlling interest in the bank and appointed D.W. as president. A mystery exists though,

Washington Trust Bank's original building. (Courtesy of NWMAC, L87-1-101)

as the purchase price was never revealed, and John Twohy was not part of the purchase.

While banks in Spokane were recovering after the Panic of 1893, a long-established bank from neighboring Sprague, Washington, was about to break on to the scene.

George S. Brooke was the first manager and sole employee of the Bank of Fairweather & Brooke, located in Sprague, Washington. Having worked at Oregon Steamship and Navigation Company in Portland, Oregon, with H.W. Fairweather, Brooke was recruited by Fairweather to come to Sprague to start a bank with him. The Bank of Fairweather & Brooke opened May 6, 1882, in Sprague Washington. "Opening its doors consisted mostly of moving bolts of calico and barrels of nails aside to make room for a desk and a safe, for the Bank of Fairweather & Brooke was located in the rear of the general store," wrote Norman E. Kilgore. "Business was lively during the first few months. About the time the bank opened, the Northern Pacific Railway completed its division headquarter shops at Sprague. The great Northwest Country was just beginning to come alive."

The sense of liveliness was nipped in the bud when fire struck on a cold winter night in January 1884. While the store burned, the bank's safe in the back of the store survived and the contents avoided destruction, meaning the bank could stay in business.

By July 1885, the bank, back on its feet and in a newly constructed two-story building, took out a national charter, changing its name to First National Bank of Sprague, with $50,000 capital. Though the bank survived the rough economic times endured by the town, it could not survive a second fire, this one ripping through the town in 1885. Having been through two fires and witnessing the Northern Pacific Railway relocate to Spokane, First National Bank of Sprague decided to close its doors in Sprague and reopen in Spokane, where the money was. One weekend, tended to by four unarmed guards, two horses pulled a weighted-down wagon of over 11,000 pounds containing the bank's safe, in which was $1,500,000, from Sprague to Spokane.

The following business day, the Spokane location was open and ready for clients. There was only one glitch: there was already a First National Bank in Spokane, the one that Glover had opened in 1882. In order to sidestep the problem, in 1896, Congress passed a special act changing the bank's name to Fidelity National, which it kept until 1929. The original charter, Charter #3528, was kept, meaning it was the same bank with a new name. In 1929, Fidelity National merged with Union Trust Company, increasing its capital to $500,000, and changing its name to First National Trust and Savings Bank. In 1934, the name changed once more, becoming First National Bank of Spokane, bringing it almost full circle in its name.

Christmas Club at First National Savings, ca. 1930. (NWMAC, L87-1.44154-30)

Not too many years after First National Bank moved to Spokane, one of the region's greatest local banks – a financial pillar of the community that still

Old National Bank employees, ca. 1930s (Courtesy of NWR, SPL)

stands strong today – made its debut.

Washington Trust Bank was organized by J. Grier Long, Romie L. Webster and Martin B. Connelly in 1902, and opened its doors on November 3, 1902. The original bank was located in a one-room office at 115 Mill Street, which is now Wall Street, between The Crescent, and Pacific Telephone and Telegraph Co. Rather than pulling up in cars, customers could hitch their horses and wagons to the posts out front. This was a time when, "The Crescent, next door was advertising men's all wool sweaters for 89 cents, and Old Crow was selling for $1.25 a bottle. The population of Spokane was 36,848 and there were nearly 700 students in the only high school in Spokane. Coffee was selling eight pounds for a dollar and you could get a full set of teeth for five dollars," according to a story in the *Spokane Chronicle.*

The founders of Washington Trust knew the people of Spokane deserved a bank they could trust and that would see the value not just in their money, but also in them. According to an article in a 1902 issue of the *Spokane Chronicle,* "J. Grier Long selected the name Washington Trust because 'in the name of Washington I have always trusted' he said."

Trust is something the bank earned from its customers. During the worst days of the Depression, when many nervous patrons fled to their banks to drain their accounts and curl their fingers tightly around the tangible security of their cash, "Washington Trust was the only bank in the city to keep its doors open and continue paying out withdrawals to customers," noted a history story written about the bank in the *Spokane Chronicle.*

Part of Washington Trust Bank's success comes from years of wise leadership. Connelly was the first and third president of the bank, with Long serving as the second president, until his death in 1914. Connelly devoted a total of twenty-seven years to the presidency of the bank. In 1919, E.H. Stanton sold his business, Stanton Packing Co., and used the $1 million from the sale to purchase fifty-one percent of Washington Trust's outstanding stock. Thus began a banking dynasty with several generations of Stantons involved with the bank.

One thing that was common in all of the men behind these earliest of banks in Spokane was their spirit of adventure, not just in blazing a trail for the financial vision of Spokane, but also for their own lives. Many had ventured to Spokane from back east, riding across the plains, encountering Indians, blazing trails, searching after financial success in the gold rush of California, the riches of mining and the profits of lumber. After tasting success in other areas, they made Spokane their home and were willing to take entrepreneurial risks. They believed the future of Spokane was something you could bank on. ●

4

Father Joseph Cataldo

The Man Who Built Gonzaga

LONG BEFORE THERE WAS A KENNEL CLUB, A LAW SCHOOL, FAMED ALUMNUS BING Crosby or the existence of NCAA Basketball, Gonzaga University was simply an idea in the mind of its founder, Fr. Joseph Cataldo.

Born in 1837, in The Kingdom of Two Sicilies, it would not have been easy to guess that Joseph Cataldo would one day envision and bring to fruition a school the likes of Gonzaga. A sickly child, he spent most of his youth

Gonzaga's first student body, 1888, (Courtesy of Gonzaga University, University Archives & Special Collections (USAC))

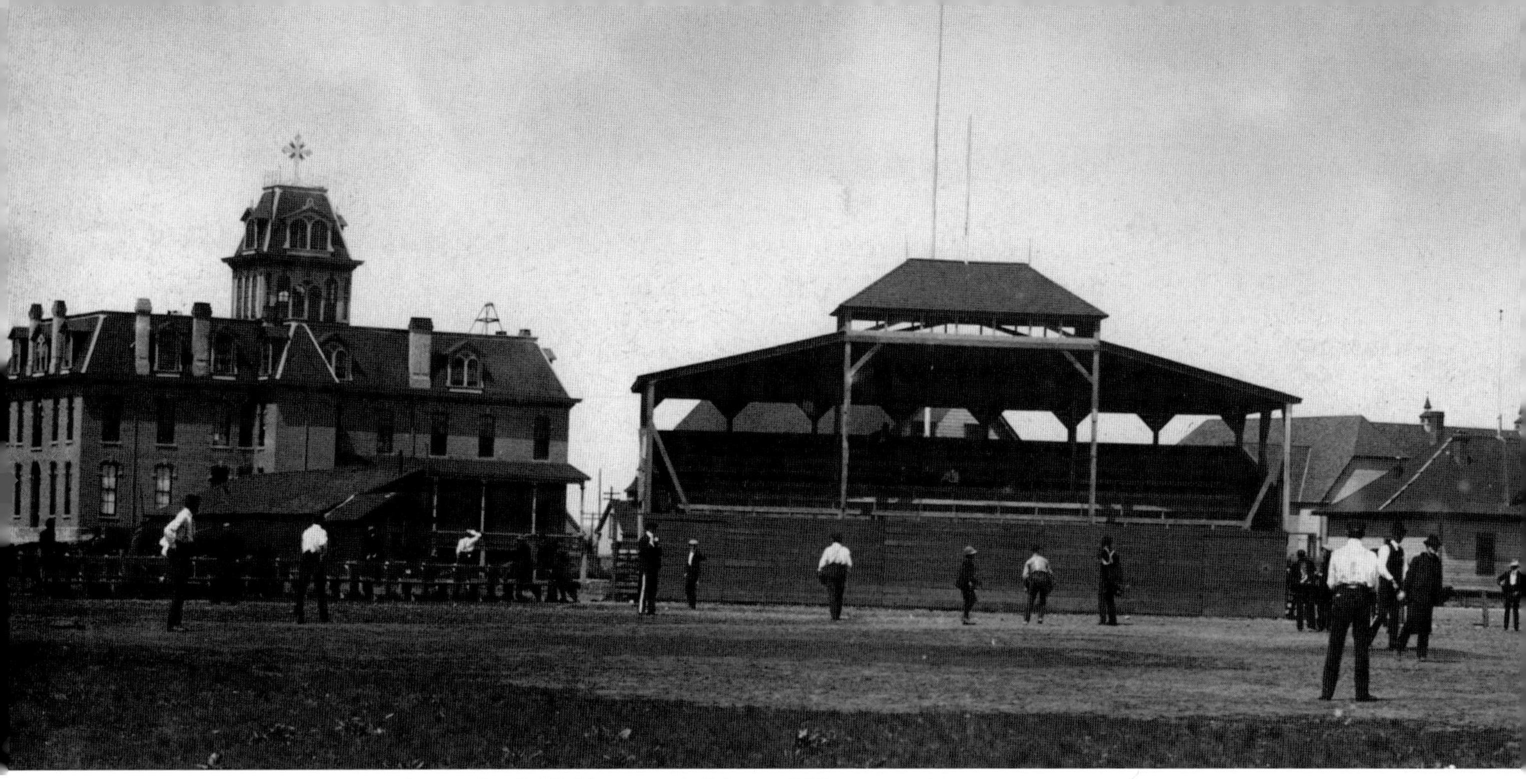

Gonzaga baseball field and main building, ca. 1900. (Courtesy of Gonzaga University, USAC)

frail and suffering from ill health. At one point in his early childhood, he was so sick that he was pronounced dead and the preparations for his funeral were put into motion. Before they could lay him in the ground, however, he rallied. Despite continued illness and frailty, Cataldo had a clear mission in his mind: to become a Jesuit. At the age of fifteen, Joseph Cataldo boldly approached the Jesuit Novitiate in Palermo, Sicily, and asked for admission into the Jesuit Order. He was accepted on the 22nd of December, 1852.

After his training, Cataldo asked to be sent on a foreign mission and was assigned to the Rocky Mountain Mission, pending further studies. When he arrived in the U.S, he again became very sick and was sent to a warmer climate in order to recover. After traveling through Panama, he arrived at Santa Clara College in Santa Clara, California, where he stayed until he was finally able to travel to Walla Walla, where provisions were procured for his trip to Spokane Falls.

According to Fr. Cataldo's journals, "We traveled some few miles up the [Spokane] river, and there we found a Camp of Seltis (or Selteees), the Chief of the Coeur d'Alene Indians whose mother was a Spokane. Seltees said many things about the Spokane Indians and added 'that the Spokane Indians should be attended by the Fathers, because several of them were well disposed towards the Catholic Religion.' I took that word in my heart, and began to think, to pray and then to speak about the Spokane Indians." It is said that from that day forward, the Spokane Indians were Fr. Cataldo's favorites. Eventually, Fr. Cataldo was made General Superior, meaning he was in charge of overseeing the entire Rocky Mountain Mission area, which included the Spokane Indians.

Fr. Cataldo had been interested in opening a school for some time, but he became increasingly passionate about the idea after the Protestants opened one in 1880, in Forest Grove, Oregon. Worried that the school would draw men away from Spokane Falls, and they would be converted to Protestantism, Fr. Cataldo quickly ordered a small schoolhouse to be built at St. Michael's Mission, where both Indians and white students would attend.

In 1880, government land was available to whites, either as homestead land or as preemption claims. By the time Fr. Cataldo and his colleagues began looking for available parcels, homesteaders had taken most of the desirable land. They did, however, find a section of railroad land, which was available. Fr. Cataldo wrote in his journals that the land "was all that we could desire for a central establishment for all our missions, being about equidistant North and South from Colville and Lewiston: East and West from Helena, Montana, and Yakima."

For 936 "hard silver dollars," Fr. Cataldo purchased 320 acres, 280 of which were on land and forty of which were water acres on a portion of the Spokane River that was not navigable. He hoped that someday a school would occupy this property.

With the swelling tide of settlers, Spokane Falls was increasing in population, and within this population boom was a steadily growing Catholic community. On October 1, 1881, a group of capitalists in Spokane Falls wrote

a letter to Fr. Cataldo, urging him to consider building a Jesuit college in town. The letter argued that Spokane Falls was the perfect location for a school. The group also offered $2,650 of support for the college if it was built exactly to their specifications, if construction was started and completed on the dates of their choice, and if it was modeled after Santa Clara University, in California.

Despite the offer, the financing never came to fruition. There was much debate and tension regarding whether the school, and the Jesuits in general, should be there to serve the Indians or for the white people. By 1882, the offer of funds for the school had disappeared.

Without the previously offered funds, in 1883, Fr. Cataldo moved ahead with the school, assigning Fr. Joset to oversee the beginning of the construction. Fr. Joset was older and didn't have much interest in the establishment of the school, though. So, while Fr. Cataldo was tending to his responsibilities as General Superior, not much work was done. That all changed in May of 1883, when Fr. Grassi was brought to Spokane Falls from Yakima. With enthusiasm and a vision, he had the foundation of the building completed by October of 1883.

It was a long process completing the building, though, because Fr. Cataldo insisted that it be built of brick, which was difficult to keep in stock. The lengthy process was tracked by the townspeople and in the newspaper, which stated, "The building is unquestionably the most commanding and imposing one in the Northwest. The probable cost when completed will be considerably over $30,000."

Construction in Spokane Falls continued and the finished school was named Gonzaga, in honor of St. Aloysius Gonzaga, who came from a noted family in Italy and was recognized as the patron saint of youth. A glowing description and review of the Gonzaga building appeared in the January 1, 1887 *Morning Review*. "The second floor contains eight rooms for the professors, two very large class rooms, the library which is already well started, the bath and toilet rooms. The attic divided into two large dormitories for the boys with a sleeping capacity in each for twenty students…The sanitory [sic] arrangements are excellent, and all the modern improvements in the way of baths and toilets are applied."

Set to open September 15, 1887, the Jesuits created a prospectus to mail to potential students. Printed by the Spokane Printing Company, the twelve-page brochure announced the opening of the much awaited school and explained the requirements for admission. "Applicants for admission must know how to read and to write and not be under ten years of age. Each student on entering should be supplied with, at least, two suits of clothes for daily wear, and one for Sundays, six shirts and collars, (some night shirts), six pairs of socks, six handkerchiefs, four pairs of drawers, four undershirts, six towels, six napkins, two or three neckties, two or three pairs of shoes or boots, a pair of rubbers, an overcoat; besides brushes, combs and other toilet articles." The cost for room, board and ten months of school was $250.

Gonzaga University main building, 1892-1897. (Courtesy of Gonzaga University, USAC)

The prospectus was boldly mailed out before the school had furnishings or a faculty. Conveniently, at the same time, a Jesuit college in Prairie du Chien, Wisconsin, was closing and offered to donate their furnishings, stationery, desks, beds and bedding to Gonzaga, charging them only for the shipping of the supplies.

As the beginning of September 1887, loomed closer, the townspeople and Jesuits were anxiously awaiting the opening day. The students were also excited, coming from both near and far. The excitement was so much for three students that they mistakenly arrived weeks early for the school term. Their names were never recorded in order to "shield them from the shame of their folly." During those weeks before classes began, these boys were allowed to roam the campus, spending time with the milk cows and the horses. The campus also had chickens, a garden of vegetables and grain to tend to, and an empty prairie stretched to the north, perfect for exploring.

Fr. Cataldo, S.J. formal pose, ca. 1878.
(Jesuit Oregon Province Archives, GU image ID #816.01)

On September 14, 1887, the first student officially registered: Constantine Aloysius McHugh, from Helena, Montana. Three more registered the next day: Richard Ganahl, from Spokane Falls; Samuel Hannon, from San Francisco; and Stanislaus Healy, from Fort Sherman, Idaho. Then three more came: Frank Healy, from Fort Sherman; Lawrence Corbett, from Salem, Oregon; and Charles Dowd, from Lewiston, Idaho.

By the end of the first year, twenty students had registered and attended school. It was a modest start, but a start none the less. Today, there are over 6,000 students enrolled at Gonzaga University. State of the art buildings fill what were once empty fields, and the school is known around the country and the world for its excellent reputation. Yet before all this came to be, it all started with the dream of a man named Fr. Cataldo. ●

5

Fort Spokane

The Military Makes Its Mark

Fort Spokane at the confluence of rivers. (Courtesy of NWMAC, L94-24.27)

WITH BUSY STREETS, HOUSING DEVELOPMENTS THAT STRETCH neighborhoods into the horizon and beyond, and a bustling downtown, it is hard to picture Spokane as a tiny town with nothing but wilderness in the surrounding area. Such was the case, however, in the early 1880s when Fort Spokane, one of the last of the frontier Army posts to be established in the Pacific Northwest, was created north of Spokane Falls. While its years were few and the memories are nearly forgotten, Fort Spokane played an important part in the history of our region. According to David H. Chance, author of *Sentinel of Silence*, a historic review of Fort Spokane, "In the 1880s, Fort Spokane was considered to be the Army's most important post in the Department of the Columbia, then the official military designation for the Pacific Northwest."

Established as Camp Spokane on October 21, 1880, the fort was formed when a garrison of the 2nd Infantry withdrew from Camp Chelan, which was determined to be a poorly situated and "unhealthful" post.

If the goal was to establish a better camp, it was not an overnight success. Brigadier General Nelson A. Miles, commander of the Department of the Columbia, visited Camp Spokane in 1881, but what he found was not impressive. He noted that what awaited him at Camp Spokane was nothing more than "log huts covered with boards and canvas" as well as tents serving as the housing for the four companies occupying the camp. It was in such poor shape that after seeing the conditions, Miles sent two companies to Fort Coeur d'Alene in order to have adequate shelter for the winter of 1881 to 1882.

Soldiers in formation on the fields at Fort Spokane. (Courtesy of NWMAC, L84-24)

Camp Spokane was declared a military reservation on January 12, 1882, and the name was quickly changed to Fort Spokane on February 11, 1882. Throughout the years, Fort Spokane was home to troops from the 2nd, 4th and 16th Infantries, as well as the 2nd Cavalry. The head of five companies of 2nd Infantry and one troop of 2nd Cavalry, Lieutenant Colonel Henry Clay Merriam, was the first military leader stationed at Fort Spokane.

Minimum funds were spent on Fort Spokane the first year it was in existence, which is why Brigadier General Miles found it in such poor shape. He recommended $40,280.07 be appropriated for construction of a permanent post that would be large enough for six to eight companies and cavalry. Twelve years of construction resulted in a fort with over forty-five buildings.

Fort Spokane was established by the military General Order No. 2, in response to situations in the area involving Indian tribes. The Nez Perce War of 1877 and Bannock Campaign of 1878 had established a need for a military presence to monitor actions between the whites and Indians.

Members of Salish Tribe at Spokane, 1883. (Courtesy of NWMAC, L84-423.51.3)

By 1884, there were fifteen Indian reservations inhabited by over 10,600 Indians. Oftentimes, relations between the Indians who had been moved from their lands and the whites who settled in the area were strained.

A sign, which stands today at the Fort Spokane site explains how and why the location was selected. "…the fort was ideally situated near both the Colville and Spokane Indian reservations for the protection of settlers from possible Indian raids and to prevent the encroachment by whites on Indian lands."

According to *Sentinel of Silence*, Indian uprisings led the Army to believe there could be trouble in the area and a military presence was necessary. "The Nez Perce in 1877 and the Bannocks and Paiutes during the next year had led the Army on humiliating chases through the mountains and had been brought to bay only when exhausted from keeping their families with them. The next trouble spot looked as though it might be the northern Columbia Plateau…"

Additionally, there was no treaty signed by the Indians who had been relocated to the Colville Reservation; therefore, there were concerns that without a legal reason for them to stay on the reservation, they may decide to move out onto the lands. Because of these situations it was considered necessary to have a military presence in the area. The Army was meant to serve as a buffer between the whites and the Indians; to keep the Indians from resisting the takeover of their lands, and to keep the whites from overreacting to, or instigating, problems.

The soldiers from Fort Spokane were involved with a few skirmishes with Indians throughout the years. One such occurrence involved a group of Chelan Indians who did not want to follow the agreement that took their reservation from them in exchange for $1,000 per person and their agreeing to the survey of their lands. As a result of their stubbornness, soldiers from Fort Spokane got involved as this passage from *Sentinel of Silence* describes. "The Chelan inability to come to terms with the white law, indeed even to understand concepts so alien to their way of life, resulted in troops being sent in 1890 from Fort Spokane. Chief Long Jim and his followers were apprehended by the forty-five men of Company A with two Indian Scouts. The Chelans were forcibly removed from their homes and sent east to the Colville Reservation to join the crowded, sick and starving Indians from many tribes who were by then living at Nespelem."

For the most part though, the soldiers at Fort Spokane enjoyed a peaceful life in a beautiful part of the country. Fort Spokane encompassed 640 acres of wilderness and was located 400 feet above the Spokane River, one mile above its confluence with the Columbia.

With a sawmill, workshop, grainery, laundry, hospital, bakery and other comforts, the officers and enlisted men that called the fort home were blessed with many amenities. An elaborate reservoir and water supply system, fed by a large spring and a pump that pulled water from the river, was used to irrigate their crops and held 150,000 gallons of water.

The fort included six barracks (two on each side of the guard house), which were wooden, two-story structures built in 1884 for about $3,000 each. The top floors served as a dorm for thirty-three men, while the first floors housed a kitchen, mess hall, day rooms, orderly rooms and housing for the cooks and the company clerk. Only two bathtubs were provided for each company, though – something that caused great concern for the post surgeon.

A sawmill was one of the first buildings built at the fort. It was needed to produce the lumber that was used for the other buildings. The mill cut between 6,000 and 7,000 feet of lumber per day when it ran at full capacity. (It burned to the ground on May 6, 1884, but was quickly replaced.)

The buildings that were a part of Fort Spokane were sturdy and handsomely constructed of wood and brick. In 1893, the post hospital was built for $11,337, which made it the most expensive building at Fort Spokane.

The buildings were constructed by soldiers as well as local craftsmen, who found it exciting to be a part of the building of an army fort. In a January 1981 article in *Rawhide Press,* Jerome Peltier wrote, "The late Walter Plough, Wenatchee, was the contractor, brick mason and plasterer who built the guard house in 1893. He enlisted the services of young Walter, age 10, in its building. Walter was told to collect broken glass to mix with cement so prisoners could not dig their way out of jail. Walter wrote: 'I took my wagon to the garbage dump and picked up old bottles, the smashed them for the floor. My grandfather paid me ten cents a load.'"

There was other work for the soldiers to do; when not building the fort, they often were working on projects such as road building. Fort Spokane troops helped to create roads, including a military road to Cheney, a road from the fort to the middle of the Colville Valley and from the Columbia River to the mouth of the Colville River. They also reopened the trail between Kettle Falls and the Okanogan Valley.

Fort Spokane, 1894. (Courtesy of NWMAC, L84-423.32.2)

"In addition to their extraordinary duties, the troops were put to work in the construction of military roads and the establishment of military telegraph lines. These not only added to the efficiency of the military, but also greatly benefited the citizens," wrote Brigadier General Miles in his journals.

A report from Van Buren Hubbard, Post Surgeon, to the Adjunct General, U.S. Army, dated January 23, 1893, described life at the fort from his perspective.

> *The food of the troops is in good quantity and quality, with the exception of fresh beef, which during the past seven months has been exceedingly poor and tough, owing to the severity of the winter...*
>
> *There are two bathtubs to each company. This is manifestly inadequate for securing personal cleanliness in full company, especially as the water of Spokane is so cold, that there is little or no bathing in the same. The bathtubs should be increased by twice or three times the present number. The laundering is done by Chinese at the bank of the Spokane River, on the reservation. No recommendations.*
>
> *The isolation of this post is almost complete; and the feeling of loneliness, or better perhaps the feeling of stillness is sometimes oppressive; very similar to that experienced on the cessation of hostilities after a prolonged battle between to contending armies.*
>
> *This condition is so painfully evident to persons recently arrived from the busy, bustling East, it has led some to suppose it was here the poet imbibed the inspiration, which found expression in the following brief but pathetic utterance: 'Here desolation keeps eternal Sabbath.' It would be quite natural to suppose that this isolation would induce nostalgia. But it does not.*

Officer's quarters at Fort Spokane. (Courtesy of NWMAC, L86-1024)

For some, life at the fort was too isolated, which caused soldiers and officers alike to turn to other sources of distraction, including drink, drug and desertion. One of the post surgeons was discovered to be addicted to morphine. After an accident left him with blood poisoning, he had to be treated by the hospital steward who found out the doctor had taken his "daily dose" of twenty grains of morphine. Battling his illness as well as recovering from his addiction meant that a doctor from Spokane Falls had to take over his post for a while. This doctor was said to have walked through the snow from Spokane Falls to the fort.

A story in the April 4, 1885 *Spokane Falls Review* documents the all too common desertion by several soldiers. "Four soldiers deserted from the ranks of Uncle Sam's army at Fort Spokane over a week ago. Two sergeants and two corporals were immediately dispatched in hot pursuit without discovering anything as to the whereabouts of the fugitives."

The isolated area where Fort Spokane was built was not only void of excessive amounts of people, but it was also void of much military action. During the nineteen years the fort was in existence, there were no altercations, nor a need to fire a single shot. That doesn't mean that the soldiers did not train regularly, though. With dress parades held up to three times a week, work days ran from 6:15 a.m. to 11:00 p.m. and were packed with drills, roll calls, classes and training practices. Lest anyone feel that they could slide by being stationed out in a rather uneventful fort, the threat of a court martial kept many a soldier in line. Court marshals could be enforced for oversleeping in the morning (for enlisted men), being disrespectful or for drinking too much.

There was also time during the course of a stay at Fort Spokane for education. This came in the form of evening school for enlisted men, the lyceum for officers and day school for the children of enlisted men. The officer's lyceum included lectures on tactics, military law and field engineering. The enlisted men's school was more basic, offering lessons in English and U.S. History to the less educated of the fort.

The pay for civilian employees at the fort was around $80 per month, while infantry privates only made $13 per month. On the other end of the scale, a second lieutenant could make up to $140 per month.

Aside from baseball games against local towns, the early years were bleak as far as amusements; however, in the late 1890s, there was an increase in social activities. Traveling entertainment troupes and theater companies came to the fort, where it was by that time not uncommon to have balls, teas and parties.

Chapel Building at Fort Spokane. (Courtesy of NWMAC, L97-25.3)

The year 1890 brought the arrival of long-distance telephone calls, which could be made from Davenport, Washington, just twenty-five miles south of the fort, to Chicago. It was an amazing advancement. (It did have its problems though. With lines often going down, it was not uncommon to have to rely on carrier pigeons as back up communication.)

As the city of Spokane Falls grew, the location of Fort Spokane became less desirable. A Secretary of War report stated that Fort Spokane was "inconveniently situated, difficult to reach in certain seasons of the year, expensive to maintain and that it served no practical purpose."

In 1895, the Secretary of War said, "In my last annual report I recommended Forts Spokane and Sherman, Idaho, be concentrated in or near the city of Spokane …and the posts be abandoned." That plan came to fruition in April of 1898. Two companies of the soldiers at Fort Spokane were deployed to fight in the Spanish-American War on April 21, 1898; with most of the soldiers gone, the fort was all but abandoned. As a result, in April 1899, the remaining men were moved to the "new fort Spokane" at Fort George Wright.

From Fort Spokane to Fairchild, this region has long been deploying soldiers throughout the world to defend our freedom. While Fort Spokane has long since been forgotten, the role it played in our Army and in shaping our region has not been forgotten. ●

6

Before They Took Their Final Bow

Spokane's Historic Theaters

A woman walks outside of the Empress Theatre in downtown Spokane. (Courtesy of NWMAC, L2003-14.80)

ON SEPTEMBER 3, 1931, THE FOX THEATER IN DOWNTOWN SPOKANE OPENED ITS doors with the fanfare of a star-studded event. It was a joyful celebration for the people of Spokane that was described by the *Spokane Chronicle* as "the city's biggest fanfare celebration outside of The Davenport Hotel opening." The event drew a large portion of the city's residents, causing streetcars to be rerouted while crowds stretched from First Avenue to Riverside, and all along Sprague Avenue from Monroe to Madison. Executives from Fox Studios brought in six stars from the movie *Merely Mary Ann* for the event. The glamour of the day was certainly intoxicating to the residents of Spokane; however, the Fox was neither the first, nor the most elegant of theaters to call Spokane home. Theaters have long been a part of Spokane's history.

The first flicker of theater debuted in Spokane Falls in 1881. Using makeshift costumes, stages and lighting, *East Lynn,* an old English drama, was performed for a small audience by a fledgling group of actors. The play was a hit, and Spokane Falls' love of theatrical entertainment was born. After being staged in tents and improvised theaters, productions were taken indoors to more permanent locations.

In less than a year, Spokane Falls had its first true theaters with the Globe Theater and the Joy Theater both opening in 1882. Soon to follow was the Spokane Falls City Opera House, which was built as a performance hall to house 800. The introduction of legitimate theaters enticed actors to the area, such as Emma Abbott, a well-known actress of the time who came to Spokane Falls in 1883, to perform in *Bohemian Girl.*

Throughout the years, numerous theaters were built, sold, named—and often renamed. By 1910, there were eighteen theaters in Spokane. The Auditorium, Spokane and American /Post theaters had the largest stages of them all. Three theaters—Orpheum, Pantages and Washington—had daily vaudeville performances, while twelve theaters offered motion pictures.

Patrons outside Spokane's Pantages Theater, 1926. (NWMAC, L81-1-31884-26)

The Columbia was a five-story brick theater that had almost as many names as seats during its years of existence. Throughout the years, it was also known as the Orpheum, the Hippodrome, the Music Box and the Avalon. Seating 1,500, it opened in May 1906, at S. 111 Howard. Patrons would come for list-run movies, vaudeville, musicals and shows featuring comedian Frank Finney.

The Pantages, a smaller theater that was built in 1907, lasted to see the likes of Bob Hope and Burns & Allen on its stage. The Granada, which was originally called The Casino when it was built in 1907, showed the 1928 "talkie" *The Jazz Singer*, starring Al Jolsen. This theater lasted for several years, and the 1943 showing of *Phantom of the Opera* brought in the largest single day's attendance in the theater's history. The Liberty, built in 1913, and located at W. 718 Riverside, is remembered for its illuminated marquee, which beckoned patrons in with its bright lights. The Empress was called the "Cinderella of the Spokane Theaters." Built in 1914, at W. 249 Riverside, the five-cent house changed its program four times a week. The Bandbox, also called the Class A, Egyptian and Clemmer, was located at W. 717 Sprague, the current site of the Washington Trust Bank building, and, in 1933, became Spokane's first newsreel house. The Fox, as previously mentioned, opened in 1931, with a star-studded event.

Two of Spokane's most famous theaters stand out from the rest, though. The American and the Auditorium were grand buildings that played an important role in shaping Spokane's history and provided the backdrop for many memorable events.

Interior of the American Theater. (NWMAC, L87-1.41284-30)

The American

In 1909, two businessman known as the Shubert Brothers owned over ninety theaters throughout the United States and wanted to buy one in Spokane. Unfortunately, there just wasn't anything on the market that matched their needs, so they built their own. They commissioned Seattle's E. W. Houghton as the architect to design the building that would sit on the corner of Post and Front Street, which is now known as Trent Avenue. The cost of the theater was $200,000, a pretty penny in the day. In addition to the theater, a fifty-two-room hotel occupied five floors above the main entrance. Outside, six terra cotta columns, with thirty-inch diameters stood twenty-five feet high, supporting the two-story main entrance.

Inside, the theater was an exact replica of the Maxine Elliott Theater in New York City, with the only difference being that at 1,650 seats, Spokane's theater seated 850 people more than the one in New York. This increase in seating was a testament to the popularity of theaters in the life of the residents in Spokane.

Many state of the art features were used in the construction of the theater, including a slanted concrete floor, cantilevered balcony and art gallery, and upholstered seats. Fire escapes were made from ramps, not stairs; however, the hope was to never have to use the fire escape, as there were no combustible materials used in the construction of the building.

Outside of the Clemmer Theater on the night of September 25, 1921, awaiting "The Affairs of Anatol." (Courtesy of NWMAC, L81-1-20326-21)

The thirty-two foot by thirty-five foot lobby was decorated in marble and mahogany, creating an instant cocoon of posh elegance upon entering the theater. Dutch linen paintings decorated the side walls, while chocolate buff draperies, green carpets and light buff walls with ornamental plaster all worked together to create a glamorous look. While patrons enjoyed the elegance of their surroundings, the actors prepared for their entrance onto the stage in one of twenty dressing rooms, which were housed under the thirty-six foot by forty foot stage.

The theater opened on December 15, 1910, as the American. Originally, the name was to be the Shubert; however, by this time, the Shubert brothers had lost interest in the project and put the focus of their attention on their existing theaters throughout the country. They turned over the construction of the new theater to other

Theater patrons line up to get into the Fox Theater in 1945. (Courtesy of NWMAC, L87-1.44834-45)

investors and walked away from the growing Spokane theater scene.

The first performing troupe to grace the stage of the American was the Del Lawrence Dramatic Stock, which performed the three-act play *The Walls of Jericho*, before a packed house. That opening night was the first night of many performances that spanned sixty-two years, and multiple generations of theatergoers and employees.

While many people entered the doors of the theater during those sixty-two years, not all of them went to the American. That is because over the years the name changed several times as new owners, managers and patrons made the theater a part of their life. Some of the American's other names include the Woodward, Maylon, Post and Post Street Theater. The Post or Post Street Theater seem to be the most often remembered names for this establishment.

George L. Lufkin wrote about the theater in the 1973 second quarter issue of *Marquee* journal, remembering his visits to the theater as a young boy. "Accompanied by his grandfather, the seven year old boy was held spellbound as he watched the Bellclair brothers, popular equilibrists of the 1910s and 1920s, go through their athletic routine in front of the traveling curtain. For the dress *piece de resistance*, the curtains parted to show a large metal structure, a narrow-gauge track that resembled a loop-the-loop."

Such dynamic and fascinating performances were a treat for residents of early Spokane. Without the distractions of televisions, computers, telephones and limitless travels, people spent more time attending events like the theater. Vaudeville, motion picture, dramatic stock, musical comedy, operettas, musical and religious events, concert artists, symphony, ballet, lectures and burlesque were all performed in theaters. The installation of a Robert Morton pipe organ in the American in the 1920s created an opportunity for an even greater diversification in the types of performances presented. The organ was removed from the theater in 1928, and reports say it went either to a church or a theater in Wallace, Idaho.

The management of local theaters seemed to change as often as props and equipment came and went in theaters. Twice in the 1920s, the American was traded for wheat and a cattle ranch in Montana.

Several years after his first attendance, Lufkin wrote of another experience at the American. "As a boy of 13, he was seated in the orchestra section, front row, center, watching a single act, a lady aerialist executing her daring balancing stunts on the flying trapeze. The boy was completely hypnotized as he watched her swing back and forth, going farther out over the audience and directly above him each time. Suddenly, the lady dropped from the bar and, with one ankle tied to a long rope, fell and swung out over the heads of the audience, missing by inches in her plunge, the boy who became so frightened that he tumbled off his seat onto the floor. While the adults

The marquee of the Liberty Theater in downtown Spokane. (Courtesy of NWR, SPL)

around him roared with laughter, the boy's heart almost stopped."

Thrilling performances like this one continued throughout the American's years, despite changes that happened along the way. In 1930, the American was renamed The Post, and in 1933, Arthur O'Niel and W.L. Evans took over operations of the theater. They spent $8,000 refurbishing the interior and relocating the entrance to Post Street, which was thought to be a more desirable and profitable location.

The Auditorium Theater was one of the most impressive buildings in downtown Spokane, ca. 1890. (Courtesy of NWR, SPL)

The Auditorium

In 1890, the Auditorium, one of Spokane's most beloved theaters and event facilities opened on Post between Main and Trent with performances of *Manon* staged by the Carlton Opera Company.

Opening night was a grand gala. According to the *Spokane Auditor*, "Tonight, the evening of September 16, 1890, will mark one of the most notable events in the history of Spokane. It is the opening to the public of the Auditorium, built at an enormous expense by Hon. A.M. Cannon and J.J. Browne, two of the city's oldest and most respected citizens. The Auditorium is a theater that any city east or west might well be proud of, for it lacks nothing that goes to make a perfectly appointed, practically safe and artistically beautiful place of amusement."

Not to be outdone by any other theater in the country, the Auditorium boasted the largest stage in the country at the time it was built. There were three tiers of boxes, a balcony and a gallery, which all together could seat 1,400 of the 22,000 members of Spokane Falls' population. Ushers wore evening clothes and helped patrons to their seats each evening, adding to the elegance.

A March 24, 1978 article in the *Spokesman-Review* looked back on Spokane's Auditorium Theater and reflected, "Society fold out-rivaled each other in the splendor of their equipages to the Auditorium, and there, richly garbed, bejeweled and gowned, sat amid the theater's magnificent designs, enthralled by the great dramatic stars."

Making a good first impression is important, and the Auditorium certainly did just that. Patrons' first impression of the theater was gained as they walked through the main entrance, which was tiled with marble. Mexican onyx wainscoting ran up the walls on three sides where it met stained glass windows depicting Shakespeare and Beethoven. A large stained glass window with the words "Spokane Falls" arched over the entrance along with a stained glass design of Melpomene, the muse of tragedy. Steam, heat and electric and gas lights were luxurious modern conveniences in the theater, along with hot and cold running water in the dressing rooms and call buttons.

The *Spokane Auditor*, on Tuesday September 16, 1890, claimed, "The building throughout shows that the owners have spared neither effort nor expense and that the designer labored arduously to perfect every minute detail required for convenience and comfort."

Creating the incredible theater, which was designed by J.B. McElfatrick and Sons of New York, took time and effort. Ground was broken and work on the theater began in April 1889. It took twenty-one teams seven weeks to move 28,000 cubic feet of dirt to make room for the theater's foundation, which was made out of granite from a local quarry. Nineteen thousand panes of plate and window glass were used throughout the building, including a twelve foot by twenty-four foot skylight created from colored stained glass panels. Five tons of white lead paint were needed to cover all of the walls in the theater. A forty foot by ninety foot hall on the third floor was used for events and social gatherings, while on the other floors there were fifty-five rooms (most likely used as apartments and offices). A two-story tower, which started on the seventh floor, rose up in the air to a peak where Thalia, the goddess of music perched, looking out over the city. From the sidewalk out front to the top of Thalia was a 165 foot rise.

"The Auditorium was the largest, most perfectly appointed and most costly theater on the coast outside of San Francisco," claimed the September 17, 1890 edition of the *Spokane Falls Review*, on the morning after opening night.

For nearly twenty-three years, the theater served as the jewel of the city, hosting plays, performances and social events. In the summer of 1913, however, tragedy struck. A fire destroyed much of the theater on August 18, 1913. It was believed to have been started by a "lighted match or cigarette dropped by someone in the gallery as he was leaving the theater after the show," according to a report in the morning paper.

When the fire started, the actors were asleep in their beds at the American Hotel in the upper floors of the American Theater. They were resting after one of their packed house performances of *Passing Show of 1913*. The play, starring Trixie Friganza, was running at the Auditorium Theater at the time of the fire.

The *Spokesman-Review* newspaper told the story of the theater's demise to the people of Spokane in the August 20, 1913 edition. "Yesterday afternoon the lobby, foyer, boxes and orchestra pit were three inches deep in water. A small cascade poured from the balcony into the parquet, having previously seeped through from the gallery

Townsfolk walk past the Auditorium Theater on dirt roads, ca. 1890. (Courtesy of NWR, SPL)

into the balcony. The entire roof is gone, with the exception of a few charred rafters that a breath of wind would have sent flying to the flood below. The galley is a complete wreck and is piled high with twisted, gnarled steel roofing and fallen timbers. Not a vestige of a seat remains....The remains of the ornate chandelier that hung from the center of the dome is part of the ruin on the floor. The floor is inches deep in dead embers and the rugs are ruined. Piles of burned timbers cover most of the seats. ...The orchestra chairs and music stands were floating in a small lake yesterday morning." The losses for the theater were estimated to be $30,000 to $50,000. If there was one bright spot in the tragedy, it was that most of the damage was covered by insurance.

The interior of the Auditorium Theater after the fire in 1913. (Courtesy of NWMAC, L2003-14.45)

As they say though, the show must go on! Jesse Gentry, the manager of the American, and John Hoppe, an owner of the Auditorium, arranged the transfer, and *Passing Show of 1913* was performed at the American Theater across the street.

The loss of the Auditorium dealt a blow to the theatrical community in Spokane. "Upon its spacious stage great names in the art dramatic have portrayed every passion and emotion of the heart, and all the follies and wisdom of mankind," reported the August 21, 1913 issue of the *Spokesman-Review*. The people of Spokane and the owners of the theater all wanted to see more great names upon the Auditorium's stage; therefore, a decision was made to rebuild the damaged parts of the theater and ensure the curtain would rise again.

Rebuilt, the theater reopened on January 9, 1914, with William A. Brady's production of *Bought and Paid For*. Audience members were seated in one of the 521 seats in the lower level, 435 in the balcony and 300 in the gallery. This total number provided less seating than the first Auditorium; however, it was rumored to provide better views.

On that morning, the *Spokesman-Review* reported that "Joseph Hagen...who opened the first carriage door when the Auditorium was opened...in 1890, called at the office of the new theater yesterday and asked to be allowed to perform the same service tonight." Hagen was gladly given the honor, and that night he helped reopen the theater.

"It would have been a calamity if the city had been deprived of its Auditorium when it was burned a few months ago, and at that time there was serious doubt as to whether it would ever be restored to us," said Spokane Mayor W. J. Hindley, on the re-opening night of the Auditorium. "Its opening night is an earnest of the confidence which these gentlemen have in the permanent prosperity of Spokane, whose advent is even now at our doors."

The Auditorium continued to attract a wide variety of performers, including Russian dancers Anna Pavlova and Mikall Mordkin, French actress Sarah Bernhardt and the Maylon Players. In 1925, during seventeen weeks of performances, the Maylon Players drew 750,000 admissions to their performances in the Auditorium.

Like they say, all good things must end, and the Auditorium was no exception. After years of serving the citizens of Spokane, its glory days began to fade. In 1934, after the curtain fell for the last time, it was torn down.

Though both the American and the Auditorium have long since ceased being a part of Spokane, they have not been forgotten. Their beauty, glamour and the tales of their glory days continue to play out in an encore of memories, which have yet to take their final bow. ●

7

Cheney's State Normal School

The Unique and Not-So-Normal History of Eastern Washington University

Benjamin P. Cheney. (Courtesy of Archives & Special Collections Department, Eastern Washington University Library (ASCD, EWUL))

IN 1879, DEPOT SPRINGS—LATER REFERRED TO AS WILLOW SPRINGS, AND EVENTUALLY renamed Cheney—was an up and coming town, experiencing growth thanks to the Northern Pacific Railway. Years later, though few would have believed it at the time, it became home to one of the state's universities.

Benjamin P. Cheney Academy, ca. 1882. (Courtesy of ASCD, EWUL)

"Admittedly, the Cheney's Sate Normal School was conceived in ambition, both personal and civic, and in the inordinate desire to recover prestige lost in the county seat contest with Spokane Falls," wrote Cecil Dryden in her book *Light for an Empire: The Story of Eastern Washington State College.*

Though Cheney lost the county seat to Spokane Falls in 1886, there was still a greater hope that Washington Territory would become a state. In 1889, the Enabling Act was passed, which put forth requirements for becoming a state. One requirement was for the presence of a normal school, and Cheney wanted to house one.

A "normal school" was a school especially for training high school graduates to be teachers. It was meant to establish teaching standards, or norms, which is where the name comes from. The school had to be established with the goal of training teachers. Instruction was mandatory in "the mechanical arts and husbandry and the fundamental laws of the United States."

Benjamin P. Cheney founded the United States and Canada Express Company, a stagecoach and freight company, which in 1879, he merged into the American Express Company. Cheney became the largest shareholder as well as the treasurer and director of American Express. He was also a director and major stockholder in the Northern Pacific Railway.

"Mr. Cheney had all the qualities which made for a successful career," wrote Dryden in *Light for an Empire: The Story of Eastern Washington State College.* "From his youth, he was hard-working and persevering. Since he had to earn every dollar he spent, he early learned the value of money; he developed an acute business sense, and became an almost infallible judge of character and motives of men."

Cheney not only had business sense and success, he also had a town named after him. In 1880, Depot Springs changed its name to Cheney, honoring the man who ran the railroad on which the livelihood of their community existed.

Though he was not a resident, Cheney had an interest in the town and its people. In 1881, when it became apparent the town needed a school to educate its young, he was approached as a potential patron for the school. He eagerly gave a $10,000 donation, which was prompted by his desire for "the children of Cheney to have the educational opportunities, which were denied to him," wrote Dryden. Northern Pacific Railway donated more than eight acres of land on which the school would be built.

Construction on the building began in 1881, and the two-story brick building, named Benjamin P. Cheney Academy, was completed and ready for students on April 3, 1882.

The Academy had formed a partnership with the Cheney School District in 1883, serving the district in exchange for much needed funds to pay for maintenance and teacher's wages that were not covered by the original $10,000. That relationship began to unravel in the late 1880s, at which time the Academy turned its focus to recruiting a State Normal School to Cheney, seeing the increasing population, and knowing there was a huge need for schools and teachers to serve the population.

The people of Cheney believed, "nature endorsed the town by providing beautiful surroundings and health conditions unparalleled by any other community in the state. The place was easily accessible by rail, yet isolated enough to remove the students from the baleful influence of a city," wrote Dryden. It was the perfect place for a school.

Admissions building, 1908. (Courtesy of Archives & Special Collections Department, Eastern Washington University Library)

The trustees of the Benjamin P. Cheney Academy offered the building as well as the surrounding eight acres of land to the state of Washington, "on the condition that an institution for the training of teachers be established in Cheney and maintained in perpetuity." That last clause would come back to haunt the state later.

A bill to create a Normal School in Cheney was introduced in the state House of Representatives, January 16, 1890, and passed on March 18, 1890, with twenty-three in favor, two opposed and ten not voting.

Admission to the Normal School was based on "good moral character" and successfully passing the entrance exam. Students had to be at least 16 years old, and they had to come with a recommendation from a county school superintendent. Teaching certificates were obtained after at least twenty-two weeks of satisfactory work and study, although, students then had to apply to the state for their teaching license.

The school year would be divided into two eighteen-week terms. Students who passed the entrance exam and signed a contract, committing to teaching in the state of Washing for two years after graduation, would receive tuition, textbooks and library access for free. Those who did not pass the entrance exam had to pay $10 for preparatory (high school) classes and $15 for the regular normal school academic program.

Cheney's Sate Normal School opened on October 13, 1890 and welcomed fifty students – twenty-nine women and twenty-one men.

Only $18,300 had been provided by the legislature in 1890 for the cost of the school, but that was not enough, leaving some of the financial responsibility to fall on the townspeople's generosity. The school population continued to grow, so on faith that the legislature would approve more funding, an addition to the building was commissioned. This brought a new library, meeting room, laboratory and housing.

As the building neared completion, tragedy struck when fire erupted on August 27, 1891, destroying not just the addition, but also the original Benjamin P. Cheney Academy building. With the building and all of their

Principal William J Sutton. (Courtesy of Archives & Special Collections Department, Eastern Washington University Library)

equipment destroyed, the Normal School had to start from scratch. They begged and borrowed stray pieces of equipment from different schools throughout the state, and space was rented out as a temporary schoolhouse in the Pomeroy Building, on First Avenue in Cheney, from 1891 to 1893.

During this time, in January 1892, William J. Sutton became principal of Cheney's Normal School. While the building was ill fitting, Sutton's relationship with Normal School proved to be a great fit and one that later would be essential to the success of the school.

In 1893, the school bid adieu to the Pomeroy Building, moving into the Cheney Junior High School building, which had been recently finished. This was just a temporary home, as $60,000 in funding from the state legislature was approved in 1895 and would be used to build a new home for the school. Though the two-and-a-half story brick building with a bell tower was new, it had ties to its predecessors; it was built on the same site the original academy had occupied before it burned down. After this building was completed in 1896, it was another eleven years before the sound of hammers and saws were heard again, this time for the addition of a tin-clad heating plant and a two-story brick building.

The school expected funding from the state legislature would help them rebuild from the fire and cover expenses. In 1891, Representative Louis Walter had presented Cheney's Normal School Bill asking for over $85,000 of much needed financial support. There was great celebration when word came that the bill had passed. Sadly, Governor John H. McGraw decided to veto the bill when it got to him, which, in Dryden's words, left "the school, so recently created, to fend for itself or die."

At the end of 1893 school year, Mr. Sutton, the principal, presented a case to the Emergency Board, pleading for funds for the school. He pointed out that the state of Washington had entered into an agreement with the Benjamin P. Cheney Academy trustees to locate a school on the donated land. "If the state fails to maintain the school at Cheney, she fails to perform her part of the contract," declared Sutton.

Despite the state's promise to maintain the school when they were given the land and building, the board voted no on the funding. In order for Cheney's State Normal School to stay afloat, sacrifices were made. Faculty willingly reduced their salaries to "only enough to meet the bare needs of living," wrote Dryden. "In fact, the faculty received less than one half of their stipulated salary, trusting that a future legislature would reimburse them."

In 1895, the Cheney Normal appropriation was finally passed, providing funds to pay its debts and cover its bills, as well as provide a new building to replace the one that burned, at a cost of $60,000.

Cheney's State Normal School continually had to fight, not only for funding, but also for a secure future. Aiming to keep an eye on spending, there seemed to always be a low-level rumble of threats coming from the west side of the state to close Cheney's State Normal School. The expense as well as the belief that all the state normal schools should be on the west side were given as reasons.

By September 1897, the rumblings were growing louder, while the funding was growing smaller. The school closed for the year. Most of the faculty, convinced the school had no hope of continuing, began looking for jobs elsewhere as students left the school. "The new, towered brick building stood locked and silent, gazing eternally down Normal Avenue as if in expectation of the students that never appeared," wrote Dryden.

"During that long bleak year, when Normal was closed, the townspeople had ample time to look back and consider the consequences of their dissensions. It was the consensus of many people throughout the state that the factional strife in Cheney, broadcast through so many channels, played an important part in the closing of the institution. In Olympia... where an economy-minded governor sat watching for every opportunity to pare the budget, the petty strife over the Cheney Normal sounded loud indeed," wrote Dryden.

Cheney State Normal School during the winter of 1904. (Courtesy of Archives & Special Collections Department, Eastern Washington University Library)

The loss of the school, which with it took a portion of the population, was an economic sucker punch, but most noticeable, it was a blow to the community's civic pride. Nursing their wounds from the loss, the community rallied, coming together with a common goal of seeing the school open again. They selected six faculty members and a principal and decided the school would be funded by a $15 tuition charge.

The 1903 season football opener. (Courtesy of Archives & Special Collections Department, Eastern Washington University Library)

The burned admissions building, after the fire of 1912. (Courtesy of Archives & Special Collections Department, Eastern Washington University Library)

First president of Cheney State Normal School, Noah D. Showalter. (Courtesy of Archives & Special Collections Department, Eastern Washington University Library)

Residents of Cheney contributed their own money to get the school established. Twenty-eight businessmen pledged money to pay for "incidentals," pooling together $875. Other things were contributed as well. According to Dryden, "Mr. Louis Walker, former board member and the town's harness-maker, contributed wood enough to heat the Normal building for some months." A local attorney, J.M. Adams, had a new practice in town, and as he worked to build up his practice, he offered to teach law, history and civics.

The school decided to ease back into existence by offering a summer school session in 1898 to test the waters of operating without state aid to keep the doors opened. The school then reopened for the 1898-1899 school term. That was enough to impress the legislature, which, on February 24, 1899, secured an appropriation of $25,000 for two years' maintenance. The school continued growing until 1912, when the school was dealt another blow.

Women's basketball team, 1907. (Courtesy of Archives & Special Collections Department, Eastern Washington University Library)

Fire struck again on April 24, 1912, in the administration building. "The alarm was sounded about 1:30 (a.m.) by Mr. N.E. Hinch, head of the English department ...His attention being arrested by the cracking of glass, he looked out to see smoke and tongues of fire issuing from the manual training department on the northeast end of the building."

Two faculty members, Max Miranda and J.R. Work, were sleeping in the upper level music room, which left them unable to escape the flames any other way than jumping out of the window. That was a daunting option considering the only thing between them and the ground was a rug stretched between the hands of the volunteer fire crew. Injured in the jump they at least were saved, which was more than could be said of the building. Piano teacher Max Miranda had to take a leave of absence because his injuries were so severe that he could not return to work for quite some time. The other faculty member, Work, was injured but recovered quickly.

The school building had been insured for $5,500, but because the policy was not written in-state, in order to get the money the school had to wait for a special act of the legislature. In addition to the insurance money, the board of trustees requested $25,000 to cover maintenance expenses for the school and $60,000 to cover the cost of a new building.

According to the City of Cheney history site, "The fact that the institution weathered this [second fire] and subsequent hardship was largely due to the efforts of two men: William J. Sutton...and Noah D. Showalter." Showalter was the first president of Cheney's State Normal School, and Sutton, who had been principal of the school, later went on to become a state senator and helped obtain a $300,000 appropriation bill to pay for new construction at the school. Unfortunately, Governor Ernest Lister, who did not see the need to keep Cheney's State Normal School open, vetoed that bill. "Due to the untiring exertion of Senator Sutton, the state legislature was moved to pass the bill over the governor's veto. Once again the local hero had saved the school from extinction."

With funding secured, the school was ready to build a new administration building, with the responsibility for the task falling on the shoulders of architect Julius Zittel. Mr. Zittel, who, in 1897, was named the state architect, became the go-to architect for most of the construction done on campus during the early 1900s. Selecting the

Cheney State Normal School's school photo, December 1902. (Courtesy of Archives & Special Collections Department, Eastern Washington University Library)

same site where the two previous, burned buildings had stood, the trustees must have felt confident that the third time was a charm. The site overlooked the city, standing as a beacon atop a hill, proudly proclaiming to the residents of Cheney that this was a place of great prominence. The building not only showcased the best of the city, but the best of the state; all the materials used in the construction, save for some Alaskan marble, were from Washington state. In 1915, the building, which was later named Showalter Hall, was completed.

The year 1915 also saw the arrival of stone pillars and walls, which lined the campus entrance, drawing the eye to Showalter Hall at the end of the road. Members of the Alumni Association, who raised over $1,200 to pay for the memorial to the original Normal School building, contributed these. Granite from that building was used in the construction of the wall and pillars, tying the old to the new.

Construction didn't stop as student enrollment continued to climb, and 1916 brought with it the opening of the first student dormitory. Within three years, the dorm was overflowing and a second women's dormitory had to be built. It wasn't until 1922 that the male student population was large enough to warrant a men's dormitory. Though the numbers were there, state funding was not. To pay for the dorm, the Cheney Building Company, a group of local businessmen, financed the project.

As the population of Cheney's State Normal School grew, changes continued to be seen on campus with the addition of buildings to meet the growing school's needs. Changes came to the school's name as well. In 1937, the school became known as Eastern Washington College of Education, and after WWII it changed to Eastern Washington State College. Finally, in 1977, the Washington State Legislature changed the name to Eastern Washington University.

Though the name of the school has changed, the pride with which it was established, and the pride of Cheney, the town that fought for its school, remains strong today. ●

The Gift of Books

Spokane Falls' Carnegie Library

SALOONS, HOTELS, THEATERS, A RAILROAD AND CITY HALL - IN 1883, SPOKANE FALLS had nearly all the requirements of a city with growth, population and prosperity, save for one thing: there was no library. Knowing a library meant a community was viable, growing and civilized, many citizens in Spokane Falls felt it was time for the city to have a library.

In order to accomplish this, in 1883, a house-to-house canvas for book donations was initiated by Dr. Thomas G. Watson, the pastor at First Presbyterian Church; Mrs. I.S. Kauffman and Mrs. Eugene Fellows. With the books they collected, a small library was opened to all citizens of Spokane Falls.

Construction workers take a break from construction of the Carnegie Library. (Courtesy of NWR, SPL)

Within several years, another small library began; although, it was only available for the members of the Spokane Labor Union and not accessible to the remaining citizens of Spokane Falls. Their reading room and small library were located in the old Auditorium Building. The two very small libraries operated separately until 1891. Around that time, interest in a larger library was beginning to brew in town, particularly among three groups: Spokane businessmen, the Carpenters Union, and the local branch of the national Sorosis Club, a women's group.

One of the great supporters of a larger library was Dr. Mary Latham, the first woman doctor in Spokane Falls, who was well respected in the community. In one of her frequent letters to the newspaper in which she attempted

Laying of the cornerstone for the Carnegie Library. (Courtesy of NWR, SPL)

to stir the coals and ignite the fire in the interest of a library, she wrote: "I had been talking for a library since I first came to the city, but that the fire had made us all such heavy losers that nothing had been done lately, the struggle for bread and butter having been in many cases the all absorbing subject for consideration. But it seems to me that our hardest times are now over, and I am sure that next to the bread and butter question, that of good literature comes in importance."

In reaction to the growing interest in a library, businessman Mr. Robert Harvey called a meeting for the evening of February 26, 1891. At the same time, the Carpenters Union scheduled a meeting to likewise discuss options for a library, on February 25, 1891. As stated in their minutes, they saw a great need for a library. "The greatest obstacle of organized labor is ignorance on the part of workingmen…the best and surest way of becoming the most helpful to each other as well as the promotion of the best interests of all workingmen is the ready and free access to the current literature of the day." Both groups agreed to come together for the formation of a library, and on April 6, 1891, announced they were working to support a single library for the city.

The third group that was interested in a library, the Spokane Sorosis Club, had already embarked on their own collection of materials. A call for books resulted in seventeen books, one magazine and two monthly magazines – thus a library of twenty items. The Spokane Sorosis Club agreed to donate their books to the businessmen and the Carpenters Union, calling it the Union Library Association, which was later renamed Spokane City Library. It formally opened in the Auditorium Building on May 5, 1891.

"At the inception of our enterprises we had neither books, money nor credit, and yet by the aid of merchant and professional men of laborer and capitalist, we have succeeded almost beyond our fondest expectation in our effort to furnish good and wholesome reading to all," proclaimed the *First Annual Catalogue of the Union Library Association.*

Financial struggles, both locally and nationally, caught up with the fledgling library when many of the unions that had joined the Association, and paid dues to finance the library, could no longer support it and had to pull

A view of the front and of the side of the completed Carnegie Library. (Courtesy of the Washington State Digital Archives)

out, leaving the city to manage it. Financially, the city could not pay to improve the library; however, they did provide a rent-free location, with a room in the new City Hall, which opened in the fall of 1894, near where the Looff Carousel is located today.

For seven years, the meager library existed in City Hall; however, it became apparent the library needed to be improved, expanded and moved to a more accessible location. The location of City Hall, and the library within, forced ladies and children to "run the gauntlet of two blocks of saloons, variety theatres, gambling halls and houses of ill fame," in order to get to the library.

On March 14, 1901, a petition for funding was sent via telegraph to Andrew Carnegie, the Pennsylvania steel magnate who generously funded libraries with his great wealth. Included in the request was a description of Spokane that was sure to win anyone over to our great city. "In the center of fine agricultural and mineral regions larger in area than New York and Pennsylvania combined, is a city of homes, with an unusual proportion of literary and artistic residents."

Unfortunately, Mr. Carnegie had sailed for Europe the day before the telegraph arrived and did not immediately receive the request. When he finally got it, he declined to send funding, believing Spokane already had a complete library and only wanted funds to build a bigger, more attractive building. Two years' worth of disappointment and misunderstanding were cleared in 1903, when the Reverend George Wallace of the Westminster Congregational Church in Spokane, through correspondence, explained that Spokane did not have a current library, rather only a collection of books in a tiny room at City Hall. Once Carnegie learned of the actual condition of the library, he agreed to fund a new building in Spokane. On April 2, 1903, Carnegie agreed upon a donation of $75,000 toward a new library.

With the funding in place, land for the library was donated by Amasa B. Campbell, one of the principal developers of the mining districts of Coeur d'Alene, Idaho, and Slocan, British Columbia.

With the $75,000 and the land secured, building began on Spokane's Carnegie Library. Mrs. Estella

Book Week, 1948, in the Carnegie Library. (Courtesy of NWR, SPL)

Deffenbaugh, sister-in-law of Mrs. I.S. Kauffman, who had worked to collect books door-to-door back in 1883, served as project manager during the construction of the building. Toward the end of construction, when it was discovered that no one had taken the cost of furnishings into account for the building, Deffenbaugh was responsible for soliciting Carnegie for an additional $5,000 in order to furnish the library. Although his reply included a stern rebuke for not having managed their money better, Carnegie did end up giving more funds.

Deffenbaugh's commitment to the library helped it grow into its new home. When she was appointed librarian in 1902, before funding was secured, there were only 8,000 volumes in the library. Her reign at the library ended in 1911, when George Washington Fuller took over as librarian. A well-educated man, Fuller devoted library money to procuring books, including some very rare ones. With the efforts during both of their terms, Deffenbaugh and Fuller were able to build up the library's materials. At the time of her death in 1945, Deffenbaugh saw the number of books grow to over 181,600.

In 1905, the Carnegie Library opened its doors to the public. Sitting on the corner of Cedar and First, the three story brick building was not only an elegant addition to the town, but a representation of Spokane's success and growth, both financially and intellectually. The determination, vision and generosity of local citizens and an East Coast philanthropist, created a much-needed service for Spokane. Over 100 years later, Spokane's library has grown from a single, stand-alone building to a multi-branch organization serving all citizens of Spokane, providing them the gift of books. ●

A beautiful snowy night outside of Carnegie Library. (Courtesy of NWR, SPL)

9

Fourth and Stevens

The Cornerstone of Education in Spokane

EDUCATION HAS REIGNED SUPREME ON THE CORNER OF FOURTH AND STEVENS on the south side of Spokane for over 122 years. The land where Lewis and Clark High School now stands has been home to several different schools, including South Central High School, which was destroyed by fire in 1910. Out of the ashes of that building, with its rich educational and civic history, rose a new school, which became one of Spokane's greatest architectural prizes and sources of pride.

In the late 1800s, Spokane's population was booming due to the discovery of silver in the mines in North Idaho. With increased population came a rise in the number of students who attended Central School, the second schoolhouse in Spokane. The two-story, four-room wooden building opened for classes in October of 1883.

Spokane High School was built in 1891 on the site of the current-day Lewis and Clark High School. (Courtesy of NWR, SPL)

With a continued increase of students, it became obvious that Central School needed to be divided into separate elementary and high schools. Financed by citizen-voted bonds, five new schools were built in 1891. Of these, four were elementary schools and one was a high school, named Spokane High School. Occupying the same corner where Central School had stood, was the new high school, a four-story, beautiful brick building with round towers, pointed rooflines and a massive clock tower.

In 1891, the first high school class in Spokane graduated with seven members. That first class looked forward to holding their graduation as the inaugural event in the auditorium of their new building. Unfortunately, Spokane College, a Methodist institution, had a graduating class of three and requested to use Spokane High School's auditorium for their ceremony. The high school students objected; however, it is said that two of the school board members were Methodist and whole-heartedly gave their approval. The high school graduation, therefore, became the second event in the auditorium, which was filled to capacity.

President Roosevelt laying the cornerstone of Lewis and Clark High School on April 9, 1911. (Courtesy of NWR, SPL)

Girls Basketball Team 1907-1908. (Courtesy of NWR, SPL)

The population of Spokane continued to grow, as did the number of students in the city. In order to accommodate the expansive student body, an additional high school was built on the north side of the river in 1908, housing 2,000 students. Naming this second school North Central High School prompted Spokane High School to change its name to South Central High School.

South Central's glory came to an abrupt and sad end on June 20, 1910, when a fire broke out in the school. An account from the June 21, 1910 *Spokane Daily Chronicle* described the scene. "At 6:30 a.m. on Monday June 20, a fire of unknown origin swept through the old Spokane High School, leaving it a mass of smoldering ruins. By 10 a.m. all that was left of the once grand old building within its schoolyard granite-stone fence was a scattering of flame-scorched office file cases pushed back onto the concrete walkway, clear of the smoldering debris."

Five thousand people, drawn by the horrifying glow of the flames and the commotion, came to watch the building burn. Among the crowd were the school superintendent and some students, who bravely risked the flames to salvage files containing student scholastic records. Aside from these records, the entire building and its contents were lost. The highly visible clock tower, which stood strong and tall above the school, bleated out its final chime at 7 a.m., just before it toppled to the ground. Amazingly, as the charred remains of the building continued to smolder throughout the day, a fountain on the school grounds, which was a gift of the class of 1910, sat unharmed and continued to cheerfully spout water into the air.

According to a report in the June 24-25, 1983, reunion issue of the Lewis and Clark High School newspaper, *The Journal,* "The board decided that since half the city's high school system was destroyed, reconstruction would begin as soon as the ashes cooled."

South Central had been completed in 1891, for $110,000, and was insured against fire by an $86,000 building policy and an $11,000 policy for furnishings. Although these funds would be available, the cost of a new building was more than the Board of Education could afford. Much of the Board's funds had been spent two years earlier, to build North Central High School. Realizing they needed to rebuild the school, the Board decided to borrow $50,000 to begin financing the project and set a deadline of eighteen months in which to design and complete the new building.

It was decided that the South Central students would attend classes at North Central High School, where the schedule would be adjusted to accommodate the crowds of students. Classes were shortened from six, one-hour classes, to five, forty-five-minute classes, and the school day was condensed to four hours. Originally, North Central students were scheduled to attend classes from 8 a.m.-12 p.m., and then South Central students would attend classes from 12:30 p.m.- 4:30 p.m. The two schools had been rivals though, and officials and citizens were worried about "school ground clashes and school building rumpuses." In order to create a spirit of unity, they decided to integrate the two schools. Juniors and seniors from both schools were assigned to morning classes while freshmen and sophomores occupied the building in the afternoons.

The red and black flag of North Central and the orange and black flag of South Central flew together

Shell of burned South Central. (Courtesy of NWR, SPL)

Spokane High School Class of 1899. (Courtesy of NWR, SPL)

Botany classroom at South Central. (Courtesy of NWR, SPL)

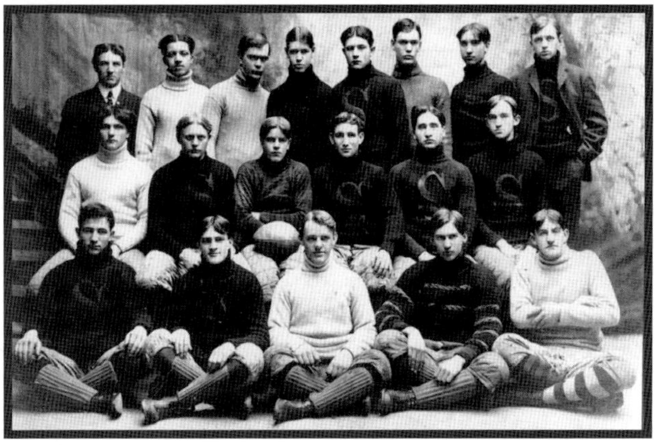

South Central 1903 Football Team. (Courtesy of NWR, SPL)

Lewis and Clark High School, after being rebuilt. The high school still occupies the corner of Fourth and Stevens. (Courtesy of NWR, SPL)

under a large blue and white flag that signified the unity of the schools during the rebuilding.

Requirements for the new school included that it be modern, fireproof and cost between $300,000 and $400,000. Just weeks after the fire, McMurphy Construction Company was awarded the contract to build the new high school for $349,261. In February 1911, they received a permit to construct a building of brick, steel and concrete.

On April 9, 1911, the formal construction began the day after President Theodore Roosevelt laid the cornerstone. "You are engaged not merely in building this material building, but in building the state, for you are building the commonwealth when you train the children of the commonwealth. And the most important task before us today is to try aright the generation that is to come after us and to leave that generation the commonwealth in such shape that it will be a benefit to them," he said.

The people of Spokane got their first glimpse at the inside of Lewis and Clark High School (the name had been selected at the February 6, 1911, Board of Education meeting, in honor of Meriwether Lewis and William Clark, who had explored the west during the Corps of Discovery Expedition, 1804-1806) on April 1, 1912. Like the old South Central, the new building was yet another source of architectural pride for the city. Inside it had wide white Vermont marble staircases, an aquarium in the science laboratory that accommodated 300 brook trout, a conservatory with tropical plants, peanuts, cotton and tobacco, and a gymnasium with an indoor swimming pool. The outside of the building was equally impressive. Massive terra cotta frieze ornaments were placed at the base of the new clock tower. They were the gods of Science (holding a globe), Literature (holding a two foot length of scroll) and Mechanical Arts (holding a cogwheel).

Lewis and Clark students were proud of their school and as each class graduated, they made their mark on the school, while some even brought fame to the city. A January 17, 1925 picture in the *Spokane Daily Chronicle* of graduates in rarely before seen caps and gowns carried the caption, "It is claimed the Lewis and Clark graduates will be the first of any American high school to break into cap and gown wearing."

Since 1883, the corner of Fourth and Stevens has been home to numerous school buildings. From Central School to Spokane High School to South Central High School and finally, Lewis and Clark High School, the one thing that has remained the same is the city's enthusiastic support of education. This was again demonstrated in 1999, when Lewis and Clark High School students were relocated for a two-year renovation of the building. The finished product once again made the building at the corner of Fourth and Stevens a source of pride for the city of Spokane. ●

Burn Baby Burn

The History of Spokane's Fire Department

ON THE NIGHT OF JANUARY 19, 1883, IT WAS A BONE CHILLING 26 DEGREES BELOW zero with snow drifting against buildings and an icy wind whipping through the air. Not ideal conditions to be outside, but that is where a group of Spokane Falls residents found themselves, slopping chilly buckets of water onto the roaring hot flames of one of the city's first significant and destructive fires. Started inside of the F. R. Moore store, the only way to fight the fire was with a bucket brigade and hope.

The Union Warehouse & Machine Co., burns as people watch helplessly, 1904. (Courtesy of NWMAC, L87-1-464-4)

Spokane Firemen Gleason, Brown and Downey, 1898. (Courtesy of NWMAC, L86-365)

Spokane Fire Department, Station No.1. (Courtesy of Washington State Digital Archives)

As the flames licked at and consumed half of a city block and destroyed five businesses, the fledgling group of firefighters quickly learned that flames and fire will outwit an unskilled and unorganized bucket brigade any day of the week. Although the fire was relatively small, destroying only half of a city block, Spokane Falls was a small, new city and the demolition of five businesses took a large chunk of the city's livelihood with it.

While creating fire was one of the first accomplishments of man, finding a way to fight it was one of the first priorities for the people of Spokane Falls. On July 7, 1884, the city council, which included Spokane Falls' founding fathers and society men with names such as Havermale, Deuber, Berg and Turner, as well as Mayor James M. Glover and A.M. Cannon, discussed the city's need for fire protection.

The council decided to take action by purchasing some much-needed equipment with which to start a fire department. On August 8, 1884, the city purchased 1,500 feet of hose and two two-wheeled horse carts. While there was the start of a fleet of equipment, there were no men to operate it. The first ordinance for a fire department was issued on October 1, 1884. Shortly thereafter, the first volunteer fire company had been organized, with twenty men from the community. It was named Rescue Hose Company No.1.

The formation of the volunteer department came one week before two large fires struck the area, wiping out seventeen businesses, including the Sprague House Hotel. Although the first company had been formed, they unfortunately had not yet been trained and, therefore, were unfamiliar with how to operate the equipment, so it was of no use.

The charred spaces where the businesses once stood served to strengthen the community's resolve to create a strong and successful fire department. The city and citizens decided they had to put their money into forming an improved, organized and supplied department. On December 13, 1884, the city appointed Eugene Hyde as temporary fire marshal until a chief engineer could be elected. This election did not happen until June 11, 1885, when Mr. Frank Dallam, founder and editor of the *Spokane Falls Review*, was elected. What made this newspaperman qualified for the job of fire marshal was not given. Whether it was skill or popularity that got Dallam the job, he did strive to better the department.

Old City Hall, home of Central Fire station. Note the burned building in the foreground. (Courtesy of Washington State Digital Archives)

Under Dallam there were two companies: Rescue Hose No.1, and Spokane Hose No.2. Each company was made up of twelve-man teams that pulled 1,345-pound carts. No.1 was housed on Main Street, east of Howard, while No.2 was on the corner of Railroad and Howard. The addition of another company brought not only a more evenly dispersed force with more equipment, but it also brought with it a thirty-foot bell tower with a 1,500-pound fire alarm bell. This was a great improvement because previously it had been church bells and whistles from the Northern Pacific railroad that served as fire alarms, along with the firing of pistols to alert people to the danger. Sometimes citizens didn't know if it was a fire or an incoming train that was being announced.

When the men of the companies weren't fighting fires, they found other ways to amuse themselves, including participating in hose cart races as a way to increase their skill and ability. Other city fire departments enjoyed the races as well, and in October of 1887, they came to Spokane Falls from Seattle, Tacoma and Walla Walla for a festive tournament. Spokane Falls' team, known as "The Comets" did quite well.

It wasn't all fun and games in the department, though. There were plenty of fires and troubles with which to deal. In January 1888, all of the fire hoses were found to be frozen and could not be used. Because of storage problems and heating issues, the exposed hoses froze, making them unusable. Similarly, on January 31, 1889, a hydrant that firemen tried to use was frozen. As a result, a house burned, killing two children, and twenty-four businesses also burned.

Firefighters showcase their axes during a public display. (Courtesy of NWMAC, L92-38)

An all-volunteer department posed another problem. When a fire broke out, an alarm would sound, the volunteers would hear the alarm, stop what they were doing, go to their station, assemble, get the carts and go. This lengthy process made it almost pointless for them to even go to the fire because the flames would often be out of control by the time

Ruins of the Great Fire, 1889. (Courtesy of NWMAC, L86-140)

they arrived. On August 16, 1888, they were called to a fire that, by the time they got there, was burning too fiercely for them to do anything.

According to an article in the September 1950 issue of *The Fire Fighter*, "In those days, speed of arrival at a fire was the standard by which fire departments were judged. In many cases the running team removed their trousers and shoes and ran in their under britches and stocking feet in order to beat the other company or to impress the ladies and sidewalk firemen with their speed. Whether the building burned down or not seemed not of great importance. The main consideration was for the 'injuns' to arrive in a great burst of speed. Firefighting did not enter into the picture."

The fire in August 1888 prompted the city to look into creating an on-call, around-the-clock department, rather than a volunteer one. Along with the few paid positions came a new firehouse on a corner of Broadway, north of the river, named Washington Hose Company.

One month later, in September 1888, a fire burned out of control despite firemen attacking it from every angle and several getting burned in the process. The problem was the weak stream of water from the old, unreliable water truck system. "The time for idle talk is past," declared the *Spokane Daily Chronicle* the next morning. "We must have, at whatever cost, an adequate water supply and adequate facilities for using it at fires. It is only a question of time."

As much as the city council, the citizens and even the newspaper declared the need for a full service fire department with ample and necessary equipment, it would take a devastating event to make it come to fruition: the Great Fire of 1889.

The Great Fire started in the attic of a lodging house near Post Street on the night of

The Spokane and Seattle fire departments participate in a horse cart race, 1884. (Courtesy of NWMAC, L86-1039)

Washington National Bank after a fire, 1889. (Courtesy of NWMAC, L86-1058)

August 4, 1889. In four hours, it destroyed thirty city blocks, and caused $5 million in loss, only fifty percent of which was insured. There were less than thirty men on the department's roster that night. Of the Great Fire of 1889, Stephen Bruce Emerson, author of *A History of the Spokane Fire Department*, wrote, "The fact is, in view of the town's limited resources, it is doubtful the fire could have been stopped even had everything gone right."

During the Great Fire, flames ate two-thirds of the firemen's hoses, and their firehouses were destroyed. Two new hose carts, a new steam engine and a chemical engine had been ordered but did not arrive in the city until December 1889 – four months after the fire that destroyed much of their equipment. Fortunately, there was not much left standing that could burn during the subsequent months.

The catastrophe that was the Great Fire served as a catalyst to get the city to put their money where it needed to go. On December 18, 1889, they officially passed a specific ordinance creating a fire department of twenty-five men with an annual budget of $33,000. Additionally, two hose houses, or fire stations, were built, which in addition to the new carts and engines, would house two horses to pull the carts quickly to a fire. The new station was to be dedicated on January 1, 1890. Unfortunately, on December 31, 1889, a fire broke out, and with the new equipment not yet in service, they had to use the old hand-pulled carts, which did not fare well in deep snow.

There were fires of some size nearly every day during Spokane's boom years, and the city was determined to not be caught in a position where they did not have enough equipment to fight these fires; therefore, the city committed a great deal of funds during 1890 and 1891, dramatically increasing the firefighting resources. These purchases included a second class Silsby engine ($5,150), a double, eighty-gallon chemical engine ($2,500), and another fire alarm for one of the stations ($1,800), a Preston turnable Aerial truck ($3,900), two Lingreen Maha chemical trucks ($3,900) and two third class Silsby engines ($8,300).

On August 22, 1893, the city council passed an ordinance officially naming the department. "A department of the city government is hereby created and established to be known as the Fire Department of the City of Spokane," it read.

In the early days of Spokane, firemen worked twenty-four hours per day, six days per week, with one day a week off for the purpose of spending it with their families. It was a grueling job and one that kept them on their toes. With increased organization, resources and skill, the Fire Department of the City of Spokane quickly became one of the most important parts of the city. Through the fires of yesterday, the fire department became stronger and polished. The dedication and sacrifice of the early firemen laid the groundwork and tradition for a great fire department, which continues to serve us today with sacrifice and honor. ●

The remains of the Great Eastern building. (Courtesy of NWR, SPL)

11

Powering Spokane Falls

How Electricity Kept the City Current

Monroe Street Station construction, 1891. (Courtesy of WWP)

ELECTRICITY FIRST CAME TO SPOKANE ON SEPTEMBER 2, 1885, WHEN GEORGE A. FITCH built the first generator station in the basement of a local flourmill with a Brush dry arc dynamo. The dynamo (generator) had proven itself powerful, as it had been used on the S.S. Columbia, which was the first steam ship with an Edison lighting system, sailing from New York, rounding Cape Horn in South America, and heading for Portland, Oregon. The dynamos eventually made their way to Spokane Falls where they powered ten arc lights in the small downtown.

"That fall many a trapper, prospector and settler coming into the village for supplies, halted his cayuse and gazed in amazement at the strange lights and wondered at the cause of such a celebration of illumination," Ted Crosby wrote in his book *Washington Water Power Company*.

In 1886, Fitch was bought out by a group of local businessmen and entrepreneurs who were ready to use his dynamo by capitalizing on the possibilities that existed with it. This group of men made up the Spokane Falls Electric Light and Power Company.

The Spokane Falls Electric Light and Power Company placed a contract for an Edison electric lighting plant and leased the north side of the river in the bay near the end of the Post Street Bridge. A man named S.Z. Mitchell, an associate of Thomas Edison, made a career of building Edison stations across the country, so it was no surprise he was the one who oversaw the construction of the 30kw dynamo station. The power from this station supplied lighting to a large area in downtown, which left citizens longing for more power. They had seen the light and wanted it to shine everywhere.

The Jeannie Winston Opera Company came to Spokane Falls in 1887, and because of the lack of a permanent theatre in which to perform, the citizens of Spokane built a theatre with a wood floor and a canvas siding and top.

The harnessed power of the Spokane River was a natural resource that helped Spokane thrive. (Courtesy of WWP)

Monroe Street Station construction. (Courtesy of WWP)

Generators at Monroe Street Station, 1900. (Courtesy of NWMAC, L97-69.33)

There was no lighting, though which was needed for the evening performances, so the city council met and agreed to let the show committee temporarily install two arc lights in the canvas-encased structure.

It wasn't just citizens who were drawn to the new lights – so were the bugs. While it might not have been planned, that night in 1887, Spokane Falls may have created the first bug zapper, according to the following account by Crosby.

"Antediluvian monsters vied with the opera stars for the attention of the spectators, for June bugs were plentiful on these summer evenings and when they alighted on the arc lamps, their shadows, magnified many times, were projected on the scenery – distorted shapes that moved jerkily on the scenery – now seeming to swoop upon the actors, now retreating into classic glades emblazoned on taut canvas."

It wasn't just opera patrons who were fascinated with the lights. The young boys of the city were drawn to them as well. "The wires running alongside the bridge were not insulated, and in short time the small boys of the village discovered that if a piece of wire were dropped across them, the resulting short circuit would give a fireworks display – at the same time causing the belt on the machine in the power house to be thrown off, plunging the lighted district into darkness," wrote Crosby.

Another risk to the supply of power was high water in the Spokane River. Water in the river below the power station got so high the water was unable to discharge from the wheel and the dynamos wouldn't work. When the river was high with the spring runoff, which usually lasted for several weeks, it was back to the dark ages for citizens, with illumination requiring kerosene or candles.

More lights meant more power, which also meant repairs and building of additional generators. In order to finance such an undertaking, Spokane Falls Electric Light and Power Company needed some more power themselves – financial power.

Union employees, ca. 1892. (Courtesy of WWP)

Mr. Henry H. Hoyt was sent from Spokane Falls to drum up financial support to expand Spokane Fall's electrical supply capacity. It was 1887, and there were not yet people in Spokane Falls who had financial means to invest in electrical power, which was somewhat of an unknown. Hoyt was effective, though. He went straight to the Edison Electric Light Company—*the* electrical company at that time, based in New York—and he brokered a deal with them, creating a partnership. In exchange for their money and machinery, the name of the company was changed to Edison Electric Illuminating Company of Spokane Falls.

This new partnership provided the financial firepower to build a new station that had four times the capacity as the first one. It started providing power to the people of Spokane Falls in 1888 – one year before Spokane Falls' great fire. This plant was called "No. 1."

Work continued through the winter, which brought temperatures of thirty degrees below zero for a week. The hard work paid off as the new station had four times the capacity of the original station and could service a greater area; additionally, this new station brought around-the-clock power to Spokane Falls for the first time.

Electric service extensions were made to Sixth and Howard, and then to Pacific and Chestnut Street. One person who took advantage of the power was a Spokane resident named Mr. Bailey. Until then, electricity had been used for lights only, but in 1888, Bailey, who owned and operated Windsor House, a local hotel, came up with the idea of using electricity to power a circular saw that would quickly cut wood with which to heat his hotel.

Spokane Falls loved its power, and quickly had over 1,200 electric lamps, which was the second highest number in the Northwest. Where street lamps illuminated the roads, people wanted to be able to use them more often; henceforth, streetcar companies looked at ways they could provide more efficient and frequent service. One option was to electrify their cars, rather than to continue using horsepower. All of that would require an ever-increasing supply of power. In order to generate more power, the local leadership of Edison Electric Illuminating Company of Spokane Falls recognized the need to secure part of the rights to the lower falls of the Spokane River. The investors back east balked at the idea. "Eastern investors, including Edison, who believed that steam power was preferable to water, claimed water power had little or no value," wrote Steve Blewett in *A History of the Washington Water Power Company*. How wrong they were.

The men of Spokane Falls saw with their eyes the power of the Spokane River. In order to power the city, they sought the assistance of those who possessed wealth and had sway within the community.

Washington Water Power, Main Office Personnel, 1908. (NWMAC, L97-69.23)

Natatorium Park, owned by Washington Water Power. (Courtesy of NWMAC, L93-65.133)

A group of ten wealthy and powerful men banded their finances and forces to secure rights to the lower falls. Together, they formed The Washington Water Power Company in Washington Territory on March 13, 1889. This made them the third power company in the area. The other two were the Edison Electric Illuminating Company of Spokane Falls, and the Spokane Falls Water Power Company (which was only two months old and was also targeting the power of the upper falls.) The ten men who began Washington Water Power Company were F. Rockwood Moore (the first president of the company), J. W. Chapman, JPM Richards, J.D. Sherwood, W.S. Norman, D.C. Corbin, Cyrus R. Burnes, Wm. Pettet, H. Bolster and J. Prickett.

According to Blewett, these were "among the wealthiest, most enterprising, successful and reliable businessmen of the city. As a rule, they are young men and are credited with having made much money by successful operations in real estate."

Not only were they successful, but insightful as well. "The men who organized the Washington Water Power Company thought enough of their belief in the value of water power to include the phrase in the corporate name of the new company," wrote Crosby. "By the ingenious use of flumes, ditches, penstocks and water wheels to which were connected dynamos that were duplicates of the queer apparatus Thomas A. Edison had turned out in his Menlo Park laboratory a year or so before, a group of Spokane pioneers were utilizing the fall of the water to generate electricity – an unexplained phenomenon which could furnish illumination and turn motors."

While waterpower was quickly becoming revered, it was firepower that had a more startling impact on Spokane Falls' history. On August 4, 1889, destructive and devastating flames destroyed much of the city.

People acted quickly to save the arc lamps hung downtown, knowing it would be expensive and timely to replace them. "Through all of this confusion, the lineman scurried seeking arc lights – quartering the business district as hounds quarter a field," wrote Crosby. "When an arc lamp was seen dangling from a store ceiling a lineman wasted no time hunting for a ladder. A running jump and a clutch at the lamp – and down could come lineman, lamp and coils of wire – beneath a shower of plaster, or with a ripping of boards."

The day after the fire, employees of Edison Electric Illuminating Company gathered to find any lines that remained. Hooking off of an intact portion of line near Trent Avenue, anything that conducted electricity was strung, including wires that were still hot to the touch from the fire the night before. There were no poles on which to hang the wires, so employees became creative, hanging line from trees, remnants of buildings and bridges.

As the sun set that evening and the burned out town was looking desperately for a bright spot, it found it in the glow of lights that came on in the smoky haze. There may not have been much left of the business district, but there was one thing even the greedy flames could not consume: the spirit of pride and the determination of the employees of Edison Electric Illuminating Company to keep their town illuminated. Crosby wrote that this act set the tone for the town that electric service must always be maintained, regardless of the obstacles that made it seem too great a challenge.

As the people of the city rebuilt they turned to brick buildings rather than wooden ones, and developed an almost insatiable desire for power. The Washington Water Power Company saw there was no stopping it, and they decided to build a station that would more than double the amount of power being produced by all the power companies on the river combined. Building it on the lower falls took advantage of the forty-foot drop on the river that occurred near the end of Monroe Street.

The station was started in 1889, but construction had to be put on hold during the spring runoff, which raised the river's level. Finally, construction was completed and Monroe Street Power Station went online November 12, 1890, at 3:30 p.m. The finished station had six Edison dynamos stored deep within it, churning the power to the hungry businesses and citizens of Spokane.

"The completion of the Monroe Street Power Station sounded the death knell for the group of smaller stations which had been operated previously along the lower falls of the Spokane River," wrote Crosby. Realizing they couldn't compete, most stations closed and their dynamos were incorporated into the Monroe Street Power Station.

F. Rockwood Moore, the first president of Washington Water Power. (Courtesy of NWMAC, L94-9.63)

In 1891, the Northwest Industrial Exposition was held in Spokane in a building at the corner of Hatch and Sprague. Because electric service did not extend that far out from the heart of town, some creative adjustments had to be made. How embarrassing it would have been had the hosts of the Industrial Exposition been unable to provide power. Two dynamos from the Monroe Street station were removed, and transferred to a sawmill engine at the exposition. The dynamos churned out the electricity and provided ample illumination for the event.

For the wealthy stockholders who had invested in The Washington Water Power Company, it was not a get-rich-quick scheme. While many citizens were striking it rich in the Coeur d'Alene Mining District, or watching their fortunes amass thanks to the success of the railroad industry, those who invested in power found it to be a difficult way to make a fortune. The company was incorporated in 1889 and didn't post the first dividend until 1891 (2%); in 1893, the dividend dropped to 1¾%. As low as that was, 1893 was the last time they posted a dividend until 1899, when it was a mere 1%.

In 1892, the first AC generator was placed in the Monroe Street Station. It was a 60kw generator. Only direct current (DC) had been available, but alternating current (AC) was coming onto the scene. Direct current provided a continuous flow of electricity while alternate current delivered electricity in pulses. Direct current could not be transformed to higher or lower voltages, but alternating current could, which made it highly desirable because it made it suitable for transmission, which would allow the company to cover more territory in which they supplied electricity.

When the financial Panic of 1893 arrived, it brought with it the first drop in demand for power. As a result, the Monroe Street Station's maximum production load plummeted from 1,049kw to 898kw. Lower demand, a financial crisis, the buying up nearly all of the shares of Edison Electric Illuminating Company of Spokane Falls, and the high cost of expansion and construction culminated in tough financial times for The Washington Water Power Company. Not only were dividends not pouring in for the ten founders, but they were also behind in their bond interest in 1895, and they hadn't paid their taxes since 1893. They had purchased the majority interest in Edison, and had also purchased Spokane Street Railway Company, and a park known as Twickenham Park.

A "friend" of The Washington Water Power Company, who also happened to be a bondholder in the company, was a financier named William Augustus White of the Franklin Trust Company in New York. White headed a committee to reorganize the company and get it profitable. Not only did he have a professional interest in seeing the company succeed, but he had a personal one as well, knowing he would reap a profit if the company did well.

Reorganizing the company and turning it to a profitable one took some sacrifices on behalf of the stockholders and founders. They were required to surrender forty percent of their stock holdings at a value of only $10 per share.

The Monroe Street Station, tucked beneath the bridge. (NWMACL2007-1.4.8.2)

Because they owned so many streetcars, the management of Washington Water Power needed to utilize that to their advantage. After reviewing different options, they decided to turn Twickenham Park, which they owned, into a destination location that would increase streetcar ridership. The park was renamed Natatorium Park, a gem of Spokane that became a popular recreation and entertainment destination for years. With a pool, rides and picnic grounds as well as spot for dances and entertainment, Nat Park, as it was affectionately called, became one of the hottest spots in town. As owners of Spokane Street Railway Company, The Washington Water Power Company enjoyed the profits from riders.

A consolidation of all of their companies and holdings into one company occurred, and shortly thereafter, things began to look up. "In 1899, therefore, The Washington Water Power Company emerged from its chrysalis as a purely water power developing concern and became a full-fledged electric service company," wrote Crosby. "This was done through the conveyance of the properties of Edison Illuminating Company, the Spokane Street Railway Company, the Spokane Cable Railway Company and other properties."

In 1901, Washington Water Power received a five-year contract to supply light and power to Great Northern Railways shops in Hillyard, which was their first foray outside of city limits. That same year, a transmission line was built from Spokane to Hillyard, which could transmit 6,600 volts. Transmission was a very difficult process, meaning electric power was limited to those within close proximity of power stations.

The next goal was to get power to Coeur d'Alene. It could be profitable because of the booming mining industry and the increasing size of the population. When the line to Post Falls was completed in August 1903, and transmitted 60,000 volts, it was a first. Bay Counties Power Company in California had achieved the next largest transmission in 1899, when 30,000 volts were transmitted over a distance of seventy-three miles.

This was just the beginning of the spread of electrical power in Spokane and the surrounding areas. A power station at Post Falls was also started. Having a plant located there "would enable engineers to store waste in Lake Coeur d'Alene, to regulate the level of the river, assuring ample water for station operation," wrote Crosby.

As power demand grew, the management of Washington Water Power knew the planned Little Falls Power station, to be built thirty-nine miles west of town on the Spokane River, would not be completed in enough time to meet the need, so they decided to build a steam plant as a temporary solution. The steam plant was built and operating by 1907.

In 1910, Washington Water Power acquired the site for the Long Lake Power Station, which would begin operating in 1915. The site included a 170-foot high dam, which was the highest spillway dam in the world at that time. Long Lake was five miles upriver from the Little Falls Station. The dam formed a lake twenty-three miles long.

With their ascent to a successful company, Washington Water Power took an active role in the community. They donated twenty-eight acres of property to the city of Spokane, in 1900, which eventually became part of Manito Park. They also created an Aid Department in 1903 to help employees, and they set up their own ward for employees at St. Luke's Hospital. The president of the company even matched himself with a newly paroled convict as his "friend" and setup a memorial for the assassinated President William McKinley.

These actions were all based on a sense of responsibility to the community, which empowered the company to grow. That sense of community continues today in the many ways this local power provider gives back to the community. Washington Water Power continues to play an active role in our community, though the name was changed to Avista on January 1, 1999. While names and technologies may change, when the sun goes down and the lights come on, it is because of a company that saw potential in our community and still does today. ●

Caring for a City in Need

Sacred Heart Hospital

Above: Sacred Heart Hospital, built in 1887, on Front Avenue. (Courtesy of Washington State Digital Archives)

Right: Mother Joseph, designer of the first Sacred Heart Hospital. (Courtesy of Washington State Digital Archives)

HEALTH CARE ARRIVED IN SPOKANE ON APRIL 13, 1886, IN THE form of two women, Mother Joseph of the Sacred Heart and Sister Joseph Arimathea.

As more people moved to the area, drawn by the railroad and the lure of wealth available in the mines of North Idaho, one thing was clear: an increasing population required an organization to tend to the sick, injured and needy of the growing town. Recognizing this need, the Jesuit Fathers who were already in Spokane Falls made a plea to the Sisters of Providence who were operating out of Vancouver. As described in *Fifty Golden Years: A Short History of Sacred Heart Hospital*, "This was the only order which maintained hospitals and refuges for the afflicted along the Pacific Coast to California. The new project was confided to Mother Joseph of the Sacred Heart, business manager and architect for the community, and Sister Joseph Arimathea, first superior of the foundation. To them fell the duty of securing desirable property and of erecting a suitable building in which to carry on the works peculiar to the Order."

They women arrived in Spokane Falls via the Great Northern Railway and spent their first night lodging at the California House, one of the few hotels in town. More adept at providing hospitality than taking it, they did not bother their hosts for long. They soon built a small wood cabin in which to live while they began their work. Not long after, they found a two-block parcel of land on the corner of Trent and Browne, south of the river, which was ideal for a hospital.

Less than two months after arriving, the land had been purchased, plans drafted and Mother Joseph and Sister Joseph joyfully watched the laying of the hospital cornerstone on July 2, 1886.

Though they had been sent to the area with instructions to start a hospital, the name for that hospital had not

Student Nurses, 1907. (Courtesy of NWMAC, L87-1.1.5)

been given to them, and communication with their superiors was slow in arriving. During the dedication, there was an awkward pause when the Jesuit Priest conducting the ceremony asked for the name of the hospital that was to be built on that spot. Rev. Aloysius Ragaru, S.J. saw the look of uncertainty in Mother Joseph and Sister Joseph's eyes, and made an on the spot decision, declaring the name would be "Sacred Heart Hospital."

Mother Joseph had more than a title behind her name; she had construction skills. As a young girl, her father had taught her the art of drafting and construction. It was under her watchful eye and direction that the hospital's first buildings were established. She could often be found climbing ladders to test the strength of the beams and prying under the flooring to check on the foundation.

The town's people took a sense of pride in the hospital, knowing Spokane Falls could not only claim the status of being a town with a hospital, but also one with a brick building, which symbolized stability and longevity.

Sacred Heart Hospital accepted its first patient on January 15, 1887. The hospital was not yet completed, and workers were still putting finishing touches on the brick building, but illness and need have no comprehension of a contractor's timeframe, and care must be administered when it is needed, so they accepted the patient. His name was John Cox. A transient with little to nothing to his name, he had been found in a shed, battling pneumonia. Mr. Cox was so ill, he was beyond hope of being saved and indeed did not survive. He did, however, receive love and care in his final days in the hands of the sisters. Though the first case was not a success story, there was soon a steady stream of patients flowing through the doors of Sacred Heart Hospital. Six years later, on November 21, 1893, the first baby born at Sacred Heart Hospital was delivered.

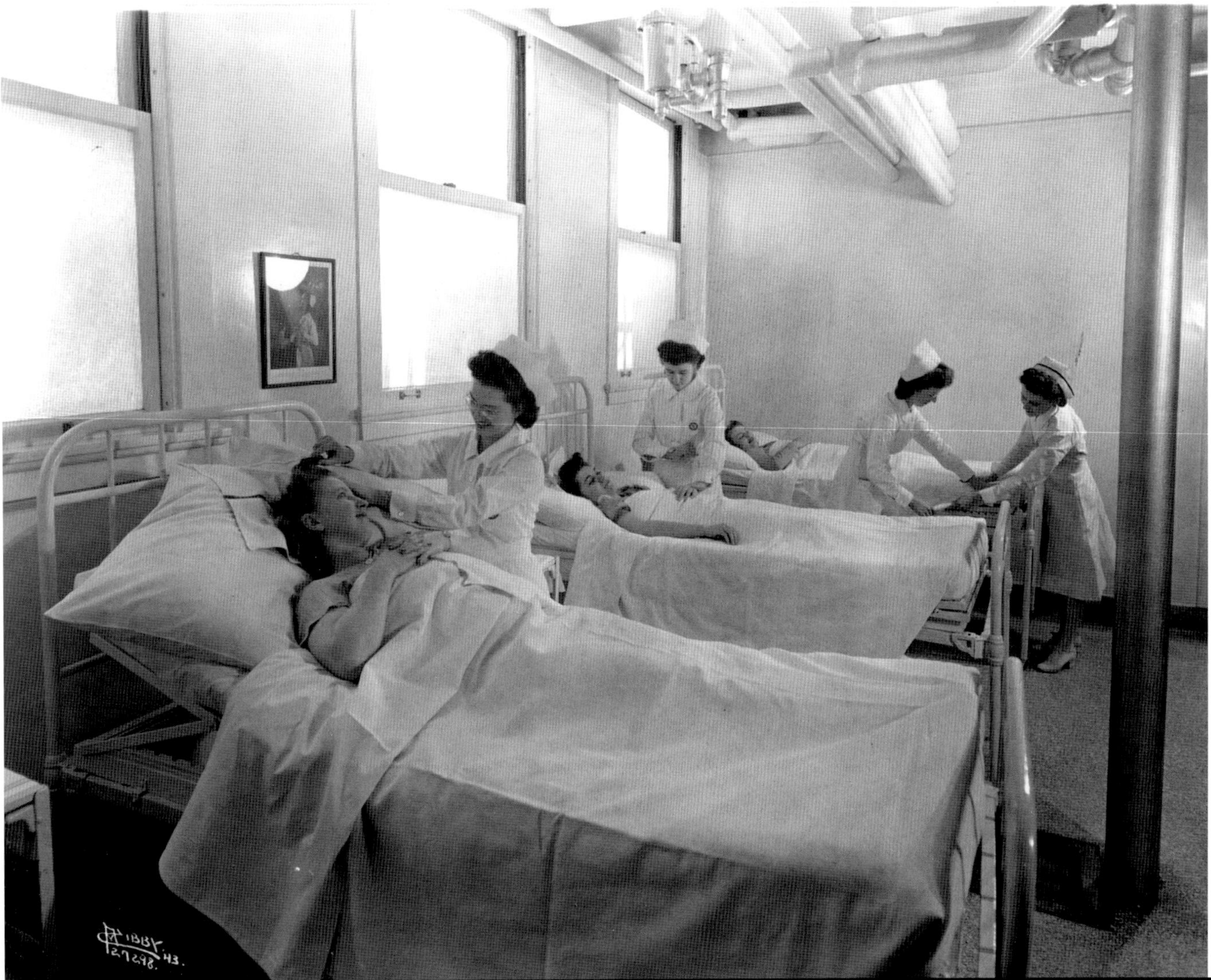

Sacred Heart Hospital ward, 1943. (Courtesy of NWMAC, L87-1.27298-43)

In a time before insurance reimbursements or endowments, the cost of maintaining and funding the hospital fell on the shoulders of the sisters. Knowing they needed to raise money, they headed to the mountains of North Idaho in the Coeur d'Alene mining district. Two sisters were sent to collect money from the miners, and they were quite successful, according to this entry from *Fifty Golden Years*. "Everywhere the miners greeted the sisters with generous response and a cordial invitation to return the following year. This gracious welcome more than repaid them for the hardships endured at times in their journeys through the mountains."

Lovingly referred to as "the Angel of Mercy" by the citizens of Spokane Falls for her extreme generosity and care toward everyone, regardless of any religious affiliation, Sister Joseph also possessed an ability to convince people to part with their money in the name of supporting the hospital. On one trip to the mines to collect funds, she convinced the first man she spoke to, Phil O'Rourke, to part with $100. Not a bad start. Another story in *Fifty Golden Years* shows that this was not a one-time case. "Sister Joseph's favorite story was about her meeting with Dennis Clark. He had just received his first day's wages, and he debated whether he should split the day's pay with Sister Joseph or give to charity the entire amount. His generosity was equal to her errand of mercy. He subscribed the day's pay. In after years he often related how he struggled to do this, and ascribed all of his later prosperity to this particular act of generosity."

That money came in just in time, as there were an ever-increasing number of patients seeking care at Sacred Heart. By 1888, just a year after opening, an addition needed to be built onto the hospital. A western wing was added, bringing with it two surgical rooms and a doubling of the hospital's bed capacity.

An exterior view of Sacred Heart Hospital, 1952. (Courtesy of NWMAC, L96-2.164)

Under the leadership of Mother Mary Antoinette, in 1898, the hospital started the Sacred Heart Hospital Training School, which was the second nursing school in the state. It started with two students, Annie Arnold and Ella Sullivan. According to *Living the Legacy: A History of Sacred Heart School of Nursing*, "A considerable part of the instruction in the 'good ol' days' had to do with the making of poultices and application of fomentation cups and leeches and bandaging; the dressing of wounds and blisters and sores of all kinds." The instruction was broken into a two-year program, but after the first class graduated in 1900, the program was extended to a three-year program.

By 1901, the enrollment had increased greatly. While the increased number of nursing students, and eventually graduates, was a welcome relief for the overworked staff, it was a double-edged sword because it brought with it a housing shortage for the nurses, who lived on-site. An addition built in 1901 solved the problem, providing rooms for nurses, as well as additional space for patients. With the newest addition, 130 patients could now be cared for at the hospital.

According to *Living the Legacy: A History of Sacred Heart School of Nursing*, "Nurses in training had living accommodations at the hospital, were provided laundry services and a stipend of $5 a month. If they became ill, they received free care, but had to make up the lost time. Time off was limited to one afternoon a week, unless an emergency arose."

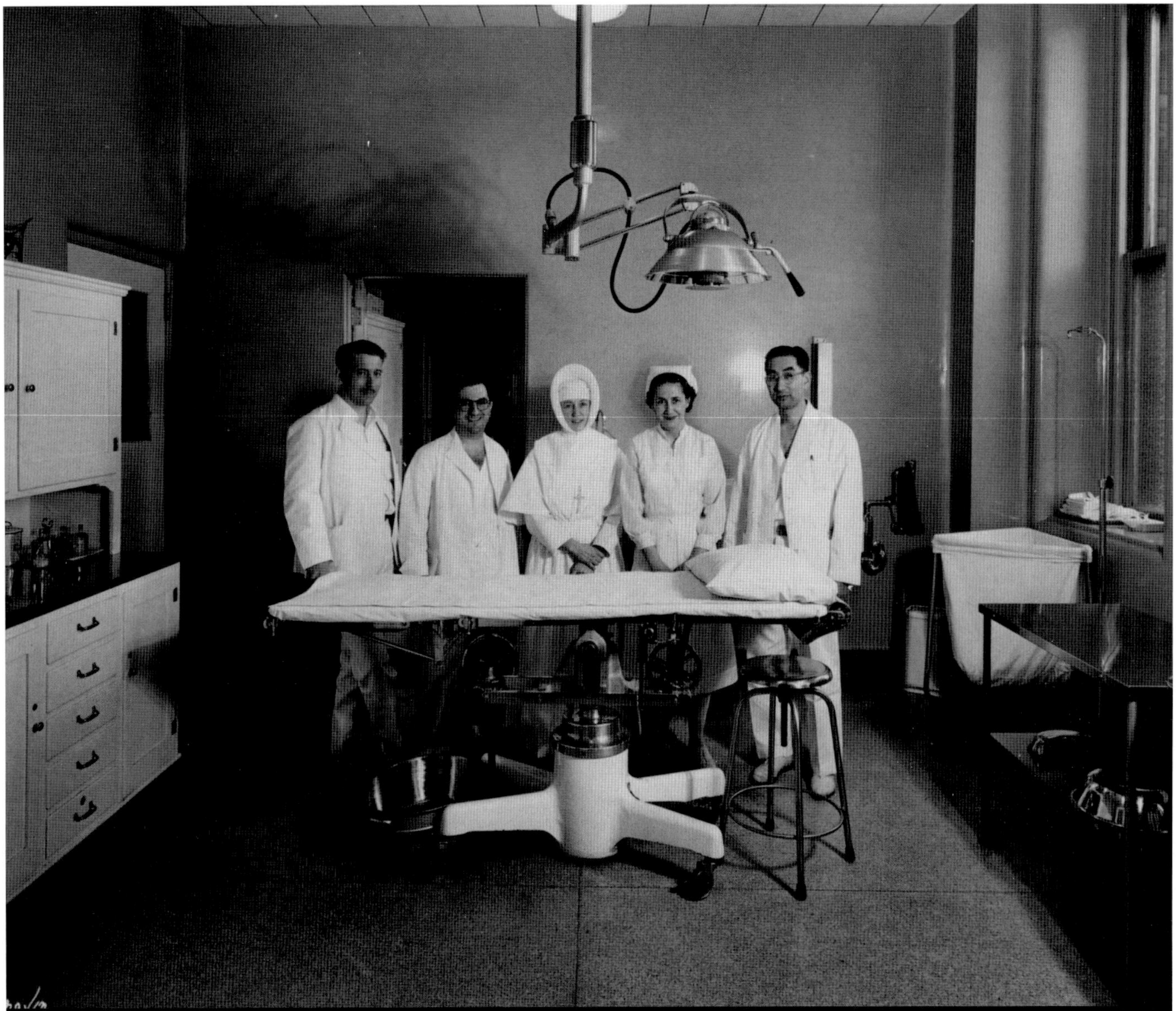

One of Sacred Heart's "modern" operating rooms, 1953. (Courtesy of NWMAC, L87-1.73408-53)

The mission of the sisters continued to be to care for the sick and needy. Sometimes the needy weren't just the ones lying sick in a hospital bed, but were also those in the town who were facing tough financial times. The hospital kitchen prepared meals for patients, but it also drew lines of poor and needy each day. Under the direction of Sister Mederic, no one was turned away, and they were all fed even though they were not patients and could not pay.

No elevator existed in the four-story building, so everything from equipment and supplies to patients themselves had to be carried up and down the stairs. Two welcomed amenities which arrived with the newest addition, and helped make up for the lack of an elevator, were electric lights and electric bells, which did a better job of lighting the hallways and altering nurses to a patient in need.

Lack of an elevator was not the greatest concern for the sisters. Given both their location near the established rail lines, and the expansion plans of the railroad, it seemed inevitable that the hospital would be boxed in. As the railroads expanded, they were encroaching on the hospital's land, limiting any further expansion.

Scouting land south of the hospital, Sister Vincent Ferrier selected two city blocks on the corner of Eighth and Browne, which she thought would be ideal for a new location. The sisters agreed to sell their property to the railroad and build a new hospital on this spot. It wouldn't be a fast build though. While construction of the original hospital building had been completed in six months, this was a grander undertaking; therefore, construction took five years, from 1905 to 1910.

Sacred Heart Hospital, 1952. (Courtesy of NWMAC, L87-1.69797-52)

Student Nurses, 1952. (Courtesy of NWMAC, L87-1.69796-52)

It wasn't until August 6, 1909, that the sisters sold the final portion of their property. They received $310,000 from the railroad, with the agreement that they would be completely off of the property by May 1, 1910. This was a great incentive to get the new hospital completed. The motivation worked, as the new building was completed more than a month ahead of time, at the end of March 1910. Another motivation came from Mother Mary Melanie, who set the goal for all patients to be transferred to the new hospital in time to celebrate Easter Sunday there. On March 24, 1910, during holy week, all women were moved to the new hospital, and the next day, the remaining patients were transferred. The official blessing of the new hospital was on June 3, 1910.

The exquisite new brick hospital had six floors, with 500 beds. Of those, 300 were for patients, while the remaining 200 were for doctors, nurses and student nurses. The School of Nursing was housed on the sixth floor of the new hospital, but it soon was too small. The nursing school enrollment continued to grow, so to accommodate the need, a seven-story wing off of the west side of the hospital was built in 1922. In addition to housing the nursing school and dormitory on four floors, this wing housed a new maternity department and the first pediatric wing.

Even the landscaping was beautiful, and thanks to one sister, it was completed at no charge. As told in *Fifty Golden Years*, "An estimate from Olmstead Brothers of Boston asked $11,000 for the job. Sister Mary Magdalene only smiled, knowing that no money was available, and set about to do the work herself. Many of the men who had been fed and nursed by the hospital were pressed into service to dig the soil and prepare the ground for seed. Sister canvassed her friends for trees and shrubs and seeds. Two of the most beautiful trees in front of the hospital were the gift of Mary Awkwright Hutton, champion of women's rights, given in recognition of the achievement of the sisters as women."

The hospital was committed to staying true to the mission of the Sisters of Providence: to care for the needy. By 1936, Sacred Heart Hospital had cared for 21,543 charity cases, provided 321,561 free days of hospital care for these cases, served 290,769 meals to the poor, and distributed $47,105 in alms and clothing to the needy.

As the years passed, the size of the buildings and the expertise of care available at Sacred Heart grew. The name was changed to Sacred Heart Medical Center, and the nursing school graduated its last class in 1973, when it was felt the hospital should focus on medical care while the education of nurses should be placed on the local universities. Despite the changes that have occurred, one thing has stayed the same. Sacred Heart continues to shine as a beacon in the community, as a place of refuge in a time of need; a place that opens its doors and cares for the community it serves. ●

13

Going the Distance

Spokane's Streetcars Go Down in History

WALKING, RIDING A HORSE OR HITCHING UP A WAGON.

Those were the options when it came to traveling around town in Spokane Falls' earliest days. In the late 1880s, the lack of available public transportation was beginning to take a toll. As the city grew, both in population and geographical boundaries, there was an undeniable need for some form of mass transit.

A young city with hopes of successful growth, Spokane Falls took cues from larger cities on the West Coast, mimicking their successes and avoiding their failures. One success that Spokane Falls wanted to duplicate was the use of a streetcar system, able to transport people throughout the city, boosting the economy and adding to the desirability of the city as a place to live and bring business.

Cannon Hill Streetcar. (Courtesy of NWMAC, L2003-28.48)

Real estate promoters were especially interested in developing a street railway system in Spokane Falls because it allowed for the development of subdivisions, such as Browne's Addition and the Manito neighborhood, and it encouraged sales of lots in these neighborhoods, which, without a streetcar system, would be too far away from downtown businesses to be attractive to buyers.

Horse-drawn cars had been introduced in 1832, but they came with concerns. There were many problems with using horses as part of the transportation process. One was the fear of the spread of diseases among the animals. There had been an outbreak of equine influenza in 1872, called the Great Epizootic, which sickened and killed so many horses on the East Coast that it effectively shut down the developed streetcar industry in America for a time.

There was one other aspect of horse-drawn cars that stunk – literally. The abundant piles of steaming horse droppings that would fill the streets, emitting a strong odor once the hot sun got to them, created roadway obstacles for those crossing the street by foot or driving a wagon. Despite these concerns, horse-drawn cars were the available option, when Spokane Falls' streetcar system was first built.

A sreetcar that traveled to Natatorium Park. (Courtesy of Washington State Digital Archives)

In 1873, cable cars were first used in San Francisco, and seemed like a desirable alternative to horse-drawn cars in Spokane Falls. The cost of building cable cars was a massive and expensive undertaking, though, as it required laying cables under the streets and building a cable plant.

In 1888, the search for a clean, efficient, affordable streetcar system was answered with the invention of the electric streetcar by Frank J. Sprague. Power to move the car was delivered from an overhead trolley pole. The construction and operating costs of electric cars were below that of steam or cable cars, and there were no messy side effects. Now, the only mess would come from the battles between the many streetcar companies.

Spokane Street Railway Company filed articles of incorporation on December 17, 1886, in Spokane County, Washington Territory. The goal for the company was to connect Browne's Addition with downtown Spokane Falls with a horse-drawn line, helping to make downtown a more thriving center of commerce. Both J. J. Browne and A.M. Cannon, two of Spokane Falls' founding fathers, and both entrepreneurial businessmen who would benefit from increased commerce, were on the board of directors for Spokane Street Railway Company.

In 1887, construction began on the line's track, with work taking place from June through December, and then breaking until the next spring. On April 15, 1888, Spokane Street Railway Company's first line opened to riders.

The track was a wooden roadbed, with wooden stringers tying together iron rods that supported the rails. Their horse-drawn cars ushered in the streetcar system, delivering people to and from downtown Spokane.

By the fall of 1888, more lines had been built around Coeur d'Alene Park, looping through downtown, across the river and up around the courthouse. The entire route could be ridden for a fare of five cents. Residents responded favorably, and according to *Spokane's Street Railways: An Illustrated History*, "The *Spokane Morning Review* of October 21, 1888, claimed that receipts were expected to average about $30 per day, and that in the eight months it had been operating, the Spokane Street Railway Company had paid for itself."

Encouraged by the popularity and financial success of Spokane Street Railway Company, many competitors burst onto the scene, hoping for a piece of the action. Competitors included Spokane & Montrose Motor Railroad, Ross Park Street Railway and Spokane Cable Railway, among others.

Sixteen and a half miles of street railway were in use by the end of 1889, and five new bridges were built across the Spokane River within the year. Two were built by Spokane Cable Railway, two by Ross Park Street Railway and one by the city.

Personnel of Spokane Street Railway Co., 1895. (Courtesy of NWMAC, L2003-14.3)

Spokane Street Railway Company operated horse-drawn cars over three and a half miles, from Division on Riverside, through Browne's and Cannon's additions. Spokane & Montrose Motor Railroad ran for two miles, and Spokane Cable Railway Company ran three miles of track. Ross Park Street Railway Company had four miles of double track, and transported 4,980 passengers on its first day of service, November 17, 1889.

"My but that car was crowded," declared Mr. J.A. Meyers, of being one of the first passengers on the Ross Park Street Railway line, the first fully electric line in Spokane Falls. "It was so slow getting under way, most of us thought we would have to get off and push."

Spokane Street Railway Company was originally built by A.J. Ross, who left to start his own line, Ross Park Street Railway. A battle occurred in the fall of 1889, when Ross Park Street Railway began laying track on Sprague Avenue, between Lincoln and Howard. Fast and furiously, with its former superintendent now leading its competition, Spokane Street Railway Company began laying its own track on the same block. The scene was disastrous, as described in *Spokane's Street Railways: An Illustrated History*. "Both sides sent reinforcements, and there were about 150 men on the scene. The city sent police, who arrested both foremen, and left the two companies to settle their differences in court or between themselves, rather than on the city streets. It was the first of many conflicts between the street railways themselves and the city."

That would not be the last of skirmishes between streetcar companies. A fight over laying track on the Division Street Bridge broke out when, on the night of April 15, 1890, the City Park Transit Company tore up tracks that had been laid a month earlier by Spokane Street Railway Company. For legal reasons, the City Park Transit had a deadline of midnight April 15, 1890, to complete its track, and it believed that Spokane Street Railway Company was dragging its feet on their construction, therefore, keeping City Park Transit from finishing on time. So City Park Transit took action, pulling up Spokane Street Railway Company's tracks so they could lay their own track and finish their line by the deadline. It took until August 1890 to come to an agreement. The two companies called a truce, agreeing to share the Division Street track, both operating their cars on the one line across the bridge. The truce didn't last long, as one week later the two companies were again warring, this time over tracks on Sprague Avenue.

Spokane United Railway Car No. 255. (Courtesy of NWMAC, L2003-14.140)

The Spokane Street Railway Company did not enjoy a good working relationship with the city of Spokane Falls, especially with the city council. There were disagreements over where their tracks were laid, how much room the tracks took up and that they limited the space on the road for wagons. There was also anger over disruptions to the streets while repairs were made to the lines. While many other streetcar companies had similar problems, Spokane Street Railway Company was the first, and seemed to have a special tension with the city council.

Despite the bureaucratic tape, the popularity of the line continued. In 1891, the company announced its plans to extend its service east to Liberty Park. In order to complete the line, $30,000 would need to be raised. The company hoped to have it up and running by November of 1891.

Eighteen new cars were ordered for the extended lines. Designed by B.C. Riblet of Spokane, who designed them for the J. G. Brill Company of Philadelphia, the new cars boasted Burton electric heaters under the seats. This was especially welcomed on cold Spokane mornings.

While real estate was the catalyst to get everyone on board with a streetcar system, it was the utility companies that truly became intrigued. Real estate developers couldn't maintain and operate the rail lines; however, the utility companies could, and they could do so in a manner that was quite lucrative. The utility companies could easily use the streetcar poles as a way to distribute electricity, knowing that a streetcar line was a built-in customer, as it gobbled up power.

According to *Spokane's Street Railways: An Illustrated History*, "The ownership of street railways benefited a utility company in several ways, including the ability of the power company to use the street's railway pole line for its electrical distribution lines. A street railway was also a large power customer, but utility-owned electric railways often got very favorable rates from the parent firms."

The Washington Water Power Company, which had been incorporated in March 1889, "began purchasing the stocks and bonds of several street railways in Spokane in 1891." One of those companies was Spokane Street Railway Company. In 1892, Spokane Street Railway Company, which was by then a subsidiary of The Washington

Passengers waiting for a streetcar at the depot. (Courtesy of NWMAC, L88-408.587)

Water Power Company, purchased fifty-one acres of forested land along the river and developed Twickenham Park (later known as Natatorium Park, or the Nat) with the purpose "to stimulate street car patronage."

Despite the great success of the Nat for the streetcar companies, there were still trials to be had. In 1894, the flooding Spokane River wreaked havoc on many of the lines, and several bridges, including the Greenacres, Mission Street, Olive and Ross Park Railway Bridge.

As described in *Flat Wheels and Five Cent Fares*, "The falls looked like a steady cascade of planking, timbers and tresses. The flood finished its work by taking out the cable railway Twickenham Bridge. Public works authorities debated whether to cut their wrists or head for Dutch Jake's bar."

It wasn't just washed out bridges that caused chaos for streetcars over the years. There were accidents with the cars, just as with any other vehicle sharing the road. In 1898, 13-year old Eddie Roberts was struck by one of the cars while out for a bike ride. He lost a leg, but survived.

A horse-drawn car collided with a power pole, resulting in the electrocution and death of the horse. Though that was sad, it was not nearly as tragic as times when an accident led to the death of passengers.

One such fatal accident on a streetcar is described in *Spokane's Street Railways: An Illustrated History*. "The north

A streetcar passes over the Monroe Street Bridge. (Courtesy of NWR, SPL)

span of the steel bridge gave way shortly at 6:00 a.m. on December 18, 1915, with an outbound Hillyard car almost clear of the bridge, and an inbound Astor line car nearer to the center of the span. The Hillyard car slid back into the Spokane River but fortunately no one aboard was seriously injured. On the Astor car, five were killed and twelve injured as a falling girder crushed one side."

Sometimes accidents were averted, despite the danger the cars were put in thanks to the antics of young boys. On Halloween night, 1898, a group of mischievous young boys slathered the tracks along the Perry Street curve with axle grease. This prank was popular because it made the wheels of the cars spin and spin, but they got no traction and couldn't move.

Although a reliable means of transportation, the streetcars did have a few glitches along the way, making them seem one part streetcar, one part rollercoaster. Sometimes, riding a streetcar was a terrifying adventure that, when riders lived to tell about it, became legend around town.

"One winter, ice built up on the Grand Hill streetcar rails to where the wheel faces weren't touching and there was no traction," recalled Mr. Harold C. Stevens, a fifteen-year veteran streetcar conductor, in *Spokane's Street Railways: An Illustrated History*. "The streetcar rolled down the hill faster and faster, out of control." It wasn't until the car reached to bottom of the hill, at the curve in front of Sacred Heart Hospital, that Stevens was able to regain control.

Another runaway car slid from 25th and Howard down to 18th and Lincoln, crashing into the front yard of Dr. Charles E. Butt after jumping the tracks. The car, on the Cannon Hill–North Monroe line, had mechanical

Old Monroe Street Bridge and streetcar, from an elevated view. (Courtesy of NWR, SPL)

The collapsed Division Street Bridge, with a Washington Water Power streetcar in the Spokane River. (Courtesy of WSDA).

Spokane United Railways, Car No. 202, is ceremonially burned, at Natatorium Park. (Courtesy of NWMAC, L94-24.207)

difficulties, and Conductor John Connor needed assistance. Because the car was empty at the time, he left it parked on the corner, and went to a nearby residence to use their phone to call for help. After placing his call, he returned to his car, only to find it was not there. He followed the tracks down the hill until he found the car, and quite a crowd gathered around it!

Accidents, antics and adventures alike, there was always something new happening with Spokane's streetcar system. In 1905, The Washington Water Power Company's first interurban line, which offered service between Spokane and outlying communities, offered service to Medical Lake for sixty cents. The inaugural run was on September 3, 1905, and a brass band helped greet the car upon arrival in Medical Lake. This became a very popular line, with people leaving from Spokane for overnights at resorts on the shores of Medical Lake. On July 4, 1906, there were twenty-two round trips to accommodate all of the vacationers and picnickers.

If there were any doubts as to the popularity of the streetcar service in Spokane, one number would clear that up: 27,730,145. That was the total number of rides passengers took in 1910.

By 1910, competition and acquisitions had whittled the number of streetcar companies in Spokane down to two: The Washington Water Power Company and Spokane Traction Company. They merged in 1922 into Spokane United Railway, which was controlled by Washington Water Power. The cars were dark green with yellow lettering that read "S.U.R."

In the early 1930s, busses began to replace streetcars. Realizing motorized busses were more economical, Spokane United Railway began converting all of their streetcars to busses. The last day of streetcar service in Spokane was on August 31, 1936.

Though the mode of transportation was ending, such a memorable and important part of the city's history could not simply be transitioned away; instead, a deserving farewell to the streetcars took place. A crowd gathered downtown to see the last of the streetcars owned by Spokane United Railways. Car No. 202 had traveled a total of 1,625,789 miles in twenty years of service. That summer day, it led a parade to Natatorium Park where it was burned in a massive bonfire, bringing Spokane's streetcar system to a poignant end. ●

14

Spokane's Architectural Artist

Kirtland K. Cutter

Kirtland K.Cutter. (Courtesy of NWMAC,, L94-9.4)

CITIES ARE MUCH LIKE GREAT PAINTINGS. WHEN AN ARTIST FIRST DIPS HIS BRUSH into the rich colors of paint and holds it above the barren, unblemished canvas, there is a brief moment when he pauses, brush hovering, knowing that with his next stroke, he will be making the marks that will serve as the foundation for the painting. With each stroke of the brush, application of paint and bit of imagination transferred from artist to canvas, a beautiful scene begins to unfold. Where once there was only blank space and unlimited possibility, now the beginning of something more beautiful exists.

Exterior shot of D.C. Corbin's home, built by Kirtland K. Cutter. Corbin was also Cutter's former father-in-law. (Courtesy of NWR, SPL)

In the early days of Spokane Falls, the town was little more than a blank canvas. A few drops of color were splattered here and there indicating there was potential for something beautiful to take shape, but for the most part, it was an untouched area. Over the years, a multitude of people left their mark on the city, bringing everything from business, religion, railroads and entertainment into the town. It was the arrival, however, of Kirtland K. Cutter that had perhaps the greatest impact on the beauty of the city. Helping to transform it from the blank canvas to a beautiful town with impressive and magnificent homes and stately buildings, Cutter proved to be one of Spokane's most influential citizens. A society architect who lived in Spokane from 1886 to 1923, it was with Cutter's skill and talent that Spokane, like a painting, went from a blank canvas to a rich and beautiful scene.

A drive around town reveals some of his well-known works that still stand today. These include the JP Graves home at Waikiki, the TJ Humbird home on Sumner, the two Corbin houses, the Patsy Clark mansion and the Campbell house (at the Northwest Museum of Arts and Culture), the Washington Water Power Post Street substation, the Spokane Club and the Davenport Hotel, which was considered his "greatest achievement in Spokane."

Cutter grew up in Cleveland, Ohio, where his family was well connected and a part of the wealthy upper class society. With his school focusing on military training rather than art classes, which was Cutter's true passion, it was his years spent traveling in Europe that opened his eyes to the world of architecture. In 1886, having returned from Europe and not wanting to settle into a life in Cleveland, Cutter was intrigued by the mystique of the "wild west" and soon found himself on his way to Spokane Falls where his uncle, Horace Cutter, had helped found the First National Bank in 1882.

After having spent months within the grandest buildings in Europe and among the high society of Cleveland, it must have been a shock for Cutter when he stepped off the train and onto the platform in the dusty town of Spokane Falls. Rather than recoiling from the bleak surroundings though, Cutter viewed the town as an area of untapped possibilities.

The first house Cutter designed was built for his Uncle Horace and Aunt Emily. It was located at the "head of Seventh Street," which at that time, was on the outskirts of town. After the success of this first house, he purchased a lot for himself in the same area, and built a small house, before he built his main home, Chalet Hohenstein, a Swiss-style chalet.

In 1887, Cutter's widowed mother and his two sisters came to live with him. In order to accommodate the increase in occupants, and to help transform it from a "man cave" into an acceptable society home, Cutter added onto his home, the first of several additions and remodels throughout the years.

On August 4, 1889, what was a devastating blow to the city turned into an opportunity for Cutter to flex his architectural muscles. Spokane Falls' Great Fire of 1889 swept through town that night and burned thirty-two city blocks. Mythology says that out of the ashes shall rise the phoenix, and Cutter was just that for Spokane. As the smoke cleared and the citizens brushed aside the ashes and debris from the fire and looked to the future, it was Cutter's chance to step forth and make his mark on the city. On the blank canvas of Spokane's skyline and architectural front, Cutter was about to make his first marks as an artist.

By 1889, after three years in Spokane Falls, Cutter had established himself as a talented architect and was gaining a steady following. The grand houses of the time boasted "tall mansard roofs" and an emphasis on vertical greatness. Cutter, however, preferred a house that sprawled along the property and filled out, not up. He liked his houses to look like they were comfortably settled into, rather than standing out from the landscape as massive structures, which were added to the setting.

The entryway of Patsy Clark's mansion, built by Cutter. (Courtesy of NWMAC, L88-343)

The exterior of Patsy Clark's home was "stunning and eye-catching," per Clark's request. (Courtesy of NWR, SPL)

"I always built to achieve the effect of age, at least to make the building fit into the surrounding to look as if it had grown there and had not been superimposed," Cutter said in a newspaper interview years later.

The year 1892 brought with it the arrival of Cutter's former traveling companion, a gentleman named Austin Corbin. The Corbin family moved to Spokane from back east where they had been a wealthy and socially elite family. The father, D.C. Corbin, was a railroad magnate, and when he headed for the Northwest, his family followed. Having spent time traveling together in Europe, it was a joyful reunion for Cutter and Austin Corbin to meet up again in another corner of the world. It was not just their renewed friendship that brought Cutter joy; it was his introduction to Mary Corbin, Austin's sister.

Being an educated man from a well-to-do family, and one who was schooled in the ways of social graces and charm, it did not take long for Cutter's charm and sophistication to win over Mary. On October 5, 1892, less than a year after having come to Spokane, Mary Corbin and Kirtland Cutter were married. As a testament to the Corbin family's wealth and prestige, the dress that Mary wore to her wedding was the same one that she had worn when she was presented to Queen Victoria the year before, during her extended European travels.

Construction was slowing down on a national level as the country dealt with the Depression of 1893; however, the depression did not have as strong an impact on Spokane as it did the rest of the country. Natural resources like lumber and mining, as well as the harnessed power of the Spokane Falls and Spokane River helped Spokane stay financially secure and somewhat of a desirable place to live and do business. As a result, many wealthy business owners and entrepreneurs come to Spokane and created a new client base for Cutter.

The Davenport Hotel and Davenport's Restaurant, 1914. The Davenport is one of Cutter's most noteable projects. (Courtesyof NWMAC, L87-1.10592X-14)

While at the World's Columbian Exposition in Chicago in 1893, Cutter saw many different styles of architecture, reflecting a smattering of cultures. This, paired with his international travels, sparked a creative flair that could not be contained or overcome by one style in his designs. As a result, Cutter designed in a variety of different styles, and he included several unique cultural themes in his architecture, such as Turkish, Moorish and Japanese. Cutter was also known for including artistic glass in the houses that he built. An example of this is the Tiffany stained glass he included in Patsy Clark's house.

Though business was going well, the home fires did not burn so brightly for Cutter. In fact, while he was building warm, cozy homes for the families of Charles Conrad and Henry M. Richards (president of Washington Water Power), the homes fires on his own domestic bliss had cooled to nothing but charred embers and the ash of what was once a strong flame of love. Mary Corbin Cutter came from a very privileged and wealthy family, and had spent many years in Europe mingling with royalty and nobles. The move to Spokane was difficult for her, and the meager frivolities of life available in a town Spokane's size left Mary more interested in increasing her social network than in helping her husband's business grow. In an attempt to satisfy her, Cutter took his family back to Cleveland where there was a larger society of who's who.

From Cleveland, Cutter, Mary and their son Corbin went on a trip to Europe. In 1896, when the family arrived in Paris, Mary informed her husband that he was no longer wanted or needed, and he should go home to Spokane. A divorce ensued, during which time Cutter fought for and was denied any custody of Corbin. Their son stayed with Mary, who remained in Europe and soon remarried.

Living room of D.C. Corbin's home, designed by Cutter. (Courtesy of NWR, SPL)

A passage in Henry C. Matthews' book, *Kirtland Cutter Architect in the Land of Promise*, states, "Margaret Bean, then a neighbor on Seventh Avenue, describes a poignant moment a few years later, when she saw Corbin playing in a nearby garden while visiting his grandparents. Kirtland Cutter, passing by gazed wistfully at the boy, and walked on, knowing that there was little he could do to establish a relationship."

Later on, when Corbin was older and had his own child, he was reunited with his father. He would meet Cutter in public places for visits and would bring along his own son. The young boy thought they were only visiting and having tea with a nice older gentleman, though; he was never told Cutter was his grandfather.

Despite failures in his personal life, Cutter was about to embark on one of the most successful periods of his career. From 1897 to 1900, eight Cutter mansions were built in the Spokane area. According to Matthews, these eight houses "represented both the transformation of Spokane from brash frontier town to sophisticated metropolis, and Cutter's progress from novice to mature professional."

Browne's Addition and the South Hill were the locations for houses of Cutter's magnitude. One of the most famous houses from Browne's Addition was that of Amasa B. Campbell, on First Avenue. Built in 1897 with an "Old English" theme, the house was a stunning declaration of the wealth and power of Campbell, a mining and railroad magnate.

The Campbell house still stands today and looks much the same on the inside thanks to the Northwest Museum of Arts and Culture (NWMAC). Open to the public as one of their permanent displays, the house offers one of the few opportunities people have to transport themselves back to the turn of the century 1900s and see firsthand what it was like to live in the elegance and luxury of a Cutter home.

Cutter's lack of formal training as an architect may actually have given him more creative freedom because he was not held to a certain style. Because of this freedom, he created a varied collection of houses. On First Avenue was the stately white, column-infused house of John A. Finch, which was built in 1897, and slightly resembled a Southern plantation. This was just a few houses down from the "Old English" style of the brick and timber home of Amasa B. Campbell. A few blocks away, also in Browne's Addition was the Patrick Clark mansion, also built in 1897, which was built with Moorish influences. The JWC Wakefield house, also built in1897, was situated between the Finch and Campbell homes and was unlike either of its neighbors. With a "Mission Revival" feel, which was influenced by Spanish and Mexican architecture, it proved that Cutter could dabble in a multitude of styles.

Patrick (Patsy) Clark, a self-made man who came from humble beginnings in Ireland, was looking to put his poor and meager days behind him with his new house. Gone were the days of keeping scrupulous track of his pennies; when Clark commissioned the house, he gave Cutter an unlimited budget with which to work. Nothing was too good or too expensive. In fact, Clark's only requirement for the house was that it be the most stunning and eye catching house west of the Mississippi. Cutter delivered. With a red roof and caramel sandstone exterior, it stood out from every other home in the city. Two towers, arches, columns and balconies, all were delicious architectural treats upon which the eyes feasted. Inside, dark wood with intricate carvings was accented by ornate stained glass windows.

Even though Cutter was divorced from Mary Corbin, in 1897, one year after their divorce, her father, DC Corbin, selected Cutter as the architect of his home. Cutter was also selected to design a house for his old friend and ex-brother-in-law, Austin Corbin, which was built in 1897. The prices for the houses were hefty at the time, but they seem like pocket change compared to today's housing prices. DC Corbin's house cost $17,000 and Austin Corbin's house cost $30,000.

In 1906, Cutter's personal success caught up with his business success. At the age of 45, he married Katharine Philips Williams who was divorced from a Spokane businessman named Jack Williams. Although the marriage was a joyful event for the two of them, it also was the cause for much gossip. The interest in the gossip is evident in this September 4, 1907, front page story from the *Spokesman-Review* discussing an attack against Cutter by Katharine's ex-husband:

"According to the chronicles of those who saw the melee, it occurred on a Manito park-bound car at 5:40 o'clock last Thursday afternoon. The car was crowded with home-going residents of the hillside and Manito Park neighborhoods. Because of the crowded condition of the car, and the fact that Mr. Cutter kept going after the kick had been administered, most of those on the car were not aware of what had happened.

'The first that I knew that trouble had broken out between the erstwhile friends, Cutter and Williams, was when I heard Mr. Williams say, 'You [expletive], get off the car,' said a wealthy resident of the hill who was just in the rear of Mr. Williams.'"

Cutter received the kick as he descended the steps to get off the bus. The rumor was that Mr. Williams had been waiting for an opportunity to attack Cutter for quite some time due to the fact that his wife divorced him and quickly married Cutter.

Not long after the attack, Cutter was back in the news, but this time as part of a project for which his career may best be remembered. When Louis Davenport decided to build a 550-room, eleven-story hotel, it was no surprise that by his side in the project was Kirtland K. Cutter. His work on the Pennington Hotel had earned his place on Davenport's team, and together they were prepared to create a most glorious and grand hotel. In order to successfully do this, Cutter and Davenport visited many elegant and opulent hotels in the Midwest and on the East Coast during 1908. They noted popular styles and features, the way rooms were decorated, the level of service and the design of the interior and exterior.

With the opening of the hotel in 1914, Cutter's work was showcased for all of the city and the world to see. As one of Spokane's most socially prominent citizens and the successful architect of Spokane's grandest homes and most important buildings, Kirtland K. Cutter should have had a comfortable and carefree life. Unfortunately though, he struggled greatly with managing his money and often found himself in debt.

According to Matthews, "Cutter enjoyed expensive tastes. He liked to dress well, to entertain generously and to dine in style; he traveled widely and preferred to do so in luxury. Although he received many prestigious commissions, he was usually short of money....In 1911, he borrowed $7,000 and in 1913, even after receiving the fees for the Davenport Hotel, he was deep in debt and chose to mortgage his beloved chalet to his client, Charles Corbet for $16,000."

The Capital Commission and Jury of Architects. Kirtland K. Cutter is on the far left. (Courtesy of NWMAC, L84-207-4-41)

By the 1920s, the grand homes of Spokane had all been built, and projects like the Davenport Hotel were no longer common. With his heavy debt, Cutter needed to find a way to earn a living, so he turned his sights to California, where James Dawson, an old associate of his was working on a large development. Cutter's old client, Harry Wraight, hearing of his financial situation had written to Dawson on his behalf.

Cutter and his wife moved to California in 1923, and they stayed there for the remainder of their days. His death in 1939 prompted the following obituary in the *Spokesman-Review*. "To him perhaps goes the distinction of having contributed more freely than any other man to the architectural beauty of Spokane, in the artistic homes he designed, and for the metropolitan appearance of the buildings for which he was also the architect."

When he had left town in 1923, Cutter was rumored to be at a financial rock bottom point in his life, yet he left behind a rich legacy of architecture. The marks he made on the canvas of Spokane have remained throughout the years, a reminder of the artist who helped shape Spokane into the city it now is. ●

15

A Spokane Treasure

Amasa B. Campbell

WELL BEFORE PIONEERS SETTLED in the rugged mountains of North Idaho, long-in-the-making riches were buried deep beneath the earth. Silver and lead, first discovered in the area in the 1880s, were used to aid the expansion and industry of our country. They also created some of the richest men in local history – not just rich financially, but rich in personality and character – who shaped our region's destiny.

Amas B. Campbell and his daughter. (Courtesy of NWMAC, L86-287-1)

Amasa B. Campbell was one such man, though his simple beginnings betrayed the life he would one day lead. Born in Salem, Ohio, on April 6, 1845, Campbell was the youngest of ten children. His father died before he was born, stripping him of the chance to get to know the man who headed the family. Without his father to provide, Campbell quickly learned the need for hard work to secure financial stability in what could be a tough world. Shouldering that responsibility at the age of 15, he took a job in the grain and wool commission.

In 1887, Campbell accepted a job as an agent for a group of wealthy spectators from Youngstown, Ohio. He and a fellow agent, named John A. Finch, were sent to the Coeur d'Alene area to find mines and businesses in which their employers could invest.

The Campbell's carriage and driver, ready to depart from the Campbell House, 1900. (Courtesy of NWMAC, L88-454)

Both men were bachelors who were willing to live a rough and tough life in exchange for the adventure and potential for wealth that came with the job. Neither Campbell, forty-two at the time and working at the freight terminal, nor Finch, an unemployed salesman for a bankrupt iron mill, could have guessed they would become two of the wealthiest, most successful and socially respectable men in young Spokane Falls' society.

Truth be told, neither Campbell nor Finch knew much about mining, but they developed a smart system for navigating the industry. When a mine in the area struck a vein, they would quickly invest in nearby mines for their employers, assuming the fortune spreading deep beneath the earth would be found in their mines as well. It was a well-planned system, and as they made money they became more respected in the mining industry.

After buying into the successful Gem mine in Coeur d'Alene, they helped organize the Milwaukee Mining Company. This was followed by their investment in the Standard and Hecla mines in 1891, which would prove to be brilliant moves. By 1893, they had expanded their mining enterprises to British Columbia with the knowledge that they were two of the most successful businessmen in the mining industry. The book *Spokane and the Inland Empire* described their success: "There was hardly a successful mining enterprise in the whole district in which they were not interested financially and otherwise, and no firm did more to develop the mining industry in the Inland Empire. The firm name of Finch & Campbell became synonymous with the important mining activities

Mrs. Grace Campbell with daughter, Helen Campbell, 1908. (Courtesy of NWMAC, L91-119.3)

The Campbell House, shortly after Kirtland. K. Cutter completed building it. (Courtesy of NWMAC, L85-128.2)

The impressive main staircase of the home. (Courtesy of NWR, SPL)

of the Northwest."

With a solid business reputation and an equally solid income, Campbell was ready to marry. His career was spent hunting for great mines and investment opportunities, but when it came to women, he was hunting for a fox – specifically for Grace M. Fox, a schoolteacher back in Youngstown, Ohio, who had captivated Campbell's heart while he was living there.

When they married in Youngstown on March 26, 1890, Amasa Campbell was 45 and Grace was 31. Being a single woman at the age of 31 was strange for the day, but it bode well for Grace, who married an established and successful man. After marrying, Mr. and Mrs. Amasa Campbell boarded a train together and headed west toward their new home of Wallace, Idaho. Campbell owned a fine house in town – it was large with two stories, a porch and a lovely fence – but it was nothing compared to the house they would later build in Spokane.

Many parties and celebrations were held in the Campbell House dining room. (Courtesy of NWR, SPL)

When the local Mammoth mine hit a vein, Campbell and Finch knew that where there was smoke there must be fire, and so they heavily invested in two nearby mines, the Standard and the Banner, assuming they, too, would be successful. Campbell and Finch had struck gold, so to speak (actually, they had struck silver and lead). During the

The Campbell's 1904 trip to Egypt. (Courtesy of NWMAC, L86-479A)

Postcard from the Campbells. (Courtesy of NWMAC, L95-57.44)

years they held Standard's stock, it paid out more than $2.5 million in dividends.

Campbell and Finch also helped to organize the Mine Owners Association, which helped "to unite managers against arbitrary smelter and railroad rates." In 1892, the Mine Owners Association closed their mines in response to the increasing railroad rates. The railroads, serving as the veins through which the blood of the economy pulsed, carried ore to the smelters and the finished product to people and industries that needed the materials. The mines and the railroads were dependent on one another to coexist, but with the mine closures, a storm was brewing. The unions and the workers were soon embroiled in a nasty war, which saw the arrival of strikebreakers from Michigan, accompanied by armed guards.

Realizing they were in the middle of a firestorm, Campbell decided to move Grace away from the dangers of Wallace and to the safety of Spokane. Angry miners had already blown up the Frisco mill in 1892, and Campbell didn't want to wait to see what their next act of violent outrage would be, nor did he want to put his wife at risk. Not only did Campbell have himself and Grace for which to be concerned; Grace was pregnant with what would be their only child, Helen, who was born in Spokane on May 14, 1892.

His financial success in the mining industry allowed Campbell his pick of any Spokane neighborhood in which

The English Tudor Revival style of the Campbell House was an impressive addition to the neighborhood. (Courtesy of NWR, SPL)

to live. He bought six lots in Browne's Addition, the up-and-coming neighborhood of Spokane's society members. The cost for the lots totaled $9,000, but it was well worth the price tag for Campbell, who wanted to live in this prominent area of town where well-to-do citizens enjoyed the finest luxuries money could buy, including electric lights and horse trolleys, which ran near a neighborhood park. Here he commissioned the famous Spokane architect, Kirtland K. Cutter, to design and build a massive English Tudor Revival house with a handsome exterior of stucco, sandstone, brick and heavy timbers.

From this location in Spokane, Campbell could conduct his business, while the proximity to Wallace meant he could occasionally visit the mines and oversee business dealings. As workers mined for riches from the earth, Campbell was reaping money with his interest in the mines, while able to extract himself from the day-to-day business. The hard work was done; he could watch the money roll in while living in Spokane and enjoying the people of his social circles.

One family with whom he and Grace were close were their neighbors and fellow mining businessman, Patrick "Patsy" Clark. The Campbells toured the Mediterranean and the Middle East with the Clarks in the early 1900s. On this trip, Campbell (whom Grace lovingly called "Mace") broke both of his arms in an automobile accident.

Grace Campbell wrote home to her dear friend, Mrs. John A. Finch in this postcard message dated March 10, 1904. "My dear Mrs. Finch: Did you do this when you were in Cairo? It's good fun for once. We have thought of you so many times and now I can appreciate your feeling about it all. Never knew what dirt was until we drove through Old Cairo. It has all been most interesting, but we were glad to get away. Mr. Moore has no doubt told you of our automobile accident. Mace is getting on very well. He has one hand out of the cast now. The other will be out in about ten days. It is a mystery how any of us escaped being killed. Hope you are very well. All send love. Sincerely, Grace M. Campbell"

Grace was a woman of society, spending her days visiting other ladies as well as entertaining callers in her parlor. Dressed always in the latest styles from the fashion houses in Paris and New York, she was a staple of society. Despite her society standing and extreme wealth, Grace treated all with love and kindness. While some in her circle looked upon the "hired help" with disdain, Grace was extremely kind to the staff members who lived with the Campbell family, even visiting with them on their time off and filling the parental role for some of the younger staff members who came to live with them.

As a woman of the times, Grace was also involved with and supported the temperance movement and didn't like

Mrs. Campbell's parlor was where she welcomed the society ladies who called on her. (Courtesy of NWR, SPL)

alcohol in her home. One must wonder if her husband respected that wish when he entertained fellow gentlemen in his basement game room. Out of sight and off limits to the women, it is not hard to believe that this room was surely the sight of many card games made complete with cigars and brandy.

In addition to being a frequent dinner host, Amasa Campbell was an avid writer, penning letters and journal

Horses and carriages, trolleys and bikes, often passed by the Campbell House in Browne's Addition. (Courtesy of NWR, SPL)

entries nearly every day. In one of Amasa's letters to a friend, dated July 7, 1909, he wrote, "...my health is not of the best, still, I am in pretty fair shape, but I realize I am getting old, in fact both of us are, and I have to take pretty good care of myself. I have taken up golf and rather enjoy it."

The poor health he referenced did not improve; rather, this was the beginning of a downhill slide for Campbell. In 1910, he developed serious swelling in his throat. In search of the best medical treatment, he traveled to Paris where doctors inserted a tube into his throat to help him breath. After returning from Paris and not seeing any improvement, Campbell traveled with Dr. N. Fred Essig to Rochester, Minnesota, to consult with the famed Mayo brothers, Drs. William James Mayo and Charles Horace Mayo. They diagnosed him with a malignant tumor in his throat. Fearing that if they operated it would lead to his death, the Mayos refused to do surgery. Campbell turned to a cancer specialist in New York, named Dr. Colby, who prescribed serum injections. He took these until a month or so before his death, though they offered little help.

In February 1912, with his wife and daughter by his side, Amasa Campbell passed away in his sleep at his beloved home. The following day in the newspaper it was reported, "...Mr. Campbell's life had been despaired of for many weeks. For the last six months he was unable to speak, and for a month, unable eat nourishment, being injected through a silver tube in his throat."

Campbell's death was mourned by citizens in both Spokane and the Coeur d'Alene region, as evident in this February 20, 1912 *Spokesman-Review* article. "During the funeral hour, from 2 to 3 o'clock, the doors of the Traders National Bank, in which Mr. Campbell was interested, were closed, as were the doors at the First National Bank of Wallace, the Coeur d'Alene Hardware Company and the store of White & Bender at Wallace."

Another article noted, "The death of Amasa B. Campbell of Spokane brings grief to the heart of every man that knew him. Mr. Campbell was big in every sense of the term – big of body, big of brain and big of heart and faith."

Perhaps Campbell's impact on the community can best be summed up by a quote that ran in the newspaper after his death: "The Northwest needs more men like Amasa B. Campbell. An investor not a spectator, a builder not a barnacle, the fortune he gained was not wrestled from others, but was drawn from the deep treasure vaults of old earth and added to the working wealth of the world." ●

16

Moving Spokane Forward

How D.C. Corbin Moved Spokane from a Small Town to a Thriving Metropolis

DANIEL CHASE CORBIN – KNOWN TO HISTORY AS D.C. CORBIN – WAS A MAN IN motion. His life was about moving, whether he was moving to a new town, moving products, moving people or moving ahead in business. His constant movement defined not only his life and personal history, but also the history and future of both Spokane and the Coeur d'Alene mining district.

Born October 1, 1832, in Newport, New Hampshire, Corbin didn't arrive in what was then Spokane Falls until 1888, at the age of 57. By that time, he had years of experience in building up western towns, and he was about to do exactly that for Spokane Falls, helping build it into the Inland Empire. The impact of Corbin cannot be denied.

Daniel Chase Corbin. (Courtesy of NWMAC, L93-18.128)

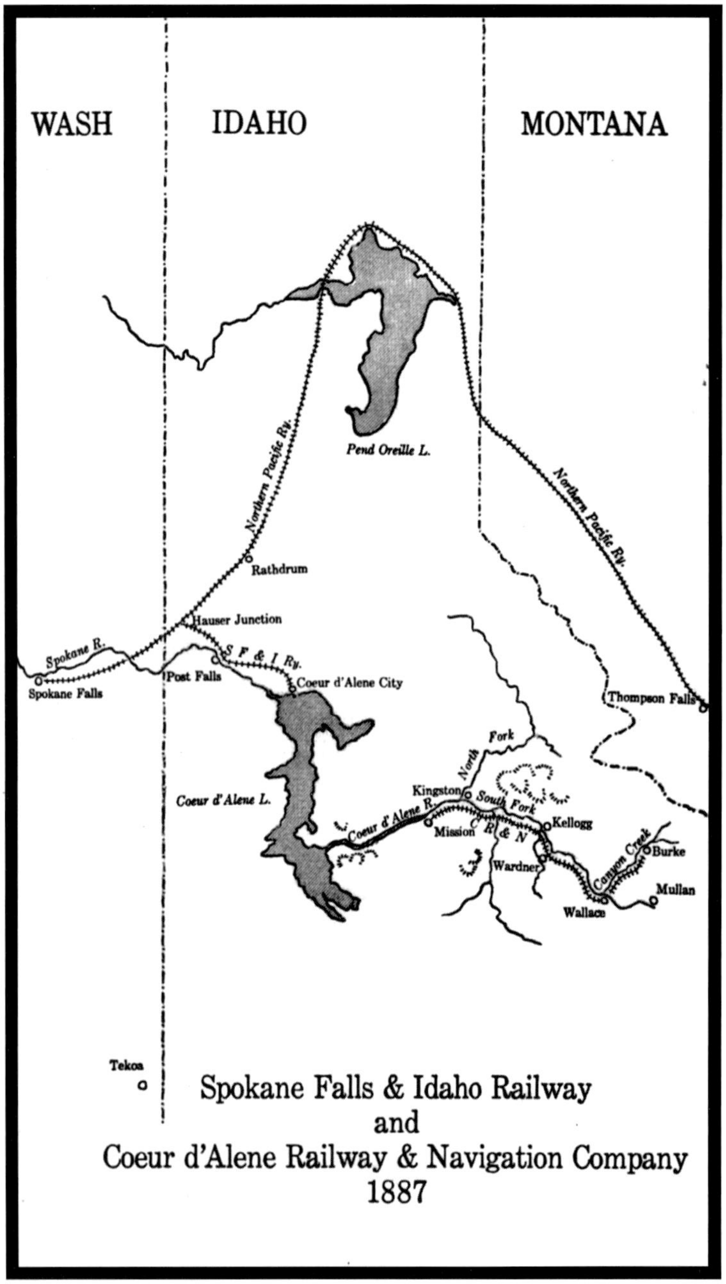

Spokane Falls & Idaho Railway
and
Coeur d'Alene Railway & Navigation Company
1887

Local historian, John Fahey, wrote in his book *Inland Empire: D.C. Corbin and Spokane*, "Without the Northern Pacific [which arrived in Spokane Falls in 1881] and Corbin, Spokane might have evolved in quite a different manner. The town commanded no navigable waterway; it enjoyed less natural attraction than several of its neighbors. Spokane's gravel soil was considered inferior for farming, its water power was useful, but beyond conceivable requirements, and early military trails between Walla Walla and Colville bypassed the falls because the river was easier to cross at other places." Fahey also wrote that Corbin should be held responsible "for delivering Spokane as a thriving metropolis to its present citizens."

In 1865, Corbin moved his wife, Louisa M. Jackson Corbin, and young son, Austin Corbin II (named for Corbin's father) to Helena, Montana, where stories of gold and fortunes ran rampant. This land of great wealth piqued Corbin's interest and created dreams within his heart of finding wealth and success.

Another child, a daughter named Louise, was born in Helena in 1866, as was their third child, Mary, who was born there in 1872. It was after the birth of Mary that Corbin's wife fell ill and never truly recovered. Doctors recommended she be somewhere with more hospitable weather. He sent his wife and children to Europe, while he stayed behind, working in New York. From there, he could fit in trips to visit them in Europe, while also keeping an eye on, and interest in, what was happening out west. In 1886, he was lured back to Montana along with his son, Austin Corbin II, by a former business partner. His wife and daughters stayed in Europe.

The financial success of the Coeur d'Alene area mines was drawing national attention, and caught the interest of Corbin and his business partner, Samuel T. Hauser. They decided the time had come to build a railway to the Coeur d'Alene mines, knowing a railway would move people as well as product to the smelters. They wrote to Northern Pacific, which had lines in the area, for support and received the go-ahead to build a new line that would connect to the Northern Pacific line.

In May of 1886, after a scouting mission to Coeur d'Alene, Corbin returned to New York and outlined a proposed route for the Northern Pacific directors. He wanted his line to begin in Montana and head west toward the Coeur d'Alene mining district, passing the Bunker Hill and Sullivan mines, then head up the south fork of the Coeur d'Alene River, toward Lake Coeur d'Alene. At Mission, the line would end and the freight would be transferred from train to steamer for a trip across the lake. Once on the other side, another line would pick up the freight and travel north toward Rathdrum.

One of Corbin's requests was for Northern Pacific to pay for the portion of the line from Coeur d'Alene to Rathdrum, and for a rebate on shipments that were delivered to the Northern Pacific line that connected in

D.C. Corbin and one of his daughters, Louise, in 1894. (Courtesy of NWMAC, L96-24.3b)

D.C. Corbin's wife, Louisa Corbin. (Courtesy of JF, IE)

Rathdrum.

Corbin set up his company with a Montana charter, naming it the Coeur d'Alene Railway and Navigation Company. Before it could get off the ground though, there was a glitch; one that made a big difference in the future of Spokane Falls. With his company based out of Montana, and built on a Montana charter, Corbin could not lcgally build his linc in Idaho due to commercial laws. He went to Washington D.C. to meet with Idaho's representative to see if any leeway could be granted, but he came back frustrated and unsatisfied. One option that would still let him build his railway in Idaho was to base it out of Washington. Rather than having the line start in Montana and move west, he would start in Washington, near Spokane Falls, and move east toward the Coeur d'Alene mining district. Were it not for this "glitch," Corbin most likely never would have ventured west of Coeur d'Alene, and the future of Spokane Falls would not have been the same.

The Coeur d'Alene mines were thriving, and a recently built concentrator in the area was concentrating ore twenty-four hours a day for months at a time. According to Fahey's book, close to 8,000 prospectors were in the mountains, and "the district was ripe for a railway, and every man asked when it would come."

In July 1886, two months after Corbin sent his proposal to

People welcoming a train that came from Missoula, Montana, to Wallace, Idaho, 1888. (Courtesy of NWMAC, L2003-14.477)

Passengers board the train from the platform at Northern Pacific Depot in Spokane. (Courtesy of NWMAC, L95-12.17)

Northern Pacific, the company agreed to pay to build the line from Coeur d'Alene to Rathdrum, and the name would be the Spokane and Idaho Railroad. It was agreed that Corbin would be allowed to pick where on the lake the line would terminate, which was also where it would meet up with the steamers. He and his business partner would be responsible for building the lines on the other side of the lake, which ran from the mines, along the south end of the lake and to the steamers.

After much consideration by Corbin, the terminus spot was selected, with tracks and steamers meeting on a dock located between Tubbs Hill and the Lakeside Hotel. A special iron-reinforced dock stretching out over the water the length of fourteen freight cars had to be built to accommodate the heavy trains.

In August 1886, the formal contract from Northern Pacific came through, and Corbin was eager to see the railroad built. With two months left of good weather in which to build, Corbin wanted to have construction of the line completed by his birthday – October 1, 1886 – which was a lofty goal.

The Northern Pacific already ran from Spokane Falls to Rathdrum, so grading and track laying for Spokane and Idaho Railroad Company began twenty-one miles east of Spokane Falls, across the Idaho border at Hauser Junction. The contract for the grading and track laying went to John Burns of Spokane Falls. Along with the contract came the dubious task of dealing with property owners who had settled on Northern Pacific land between Rathdrum and Coeur d'Alene and were faced with

D.C. Corbin's home, on the South Hill. (Courtesy of NWR, SPL)

Northern Pacific Locomotive No. 711, in 1903. (Courtesy of NWMAC, L84-368.7)

tracks being laid across what they thought was their land.

On October 24, 1886, the first trains arrived at the Coeur d'Alene waterfront, after traveling from Rathdrum through Hauser Junction, but it wasn't until the beginning of December that the trains were able to venture all the way over the water onto the dock. The total cost for the iron reinforced dock was $7,402.49, while the entire cost of building the railroad from Rathdrum to the Coeur d'Alene dock was $52,496.59, all of which Corbin was able to convince Northern Pacific to pay.

Although the railroad from Coeur d'Alene to Rathdrum was built, it was brought to Corbin's attention that there was no official paperwork designating the railroad as a business entity, nor was there a board of officers. So, in October 1886, Corbin, representatives from Northern Pacific and attorneys gathered in an office in Spokane Falls to officially create the company. The name was modified from the original Spokane and Idaho Railroad Company to Spokane Falls and Idaho Railroad Company, and it was incorporated as a Spokane County entity. Anthony M. Cannon, another famous Spokanite, was named an officer of the company.

While the Spokane Falls and Idaho Railroad Company chugged between Coeur d'Alene and Rathdrum, Corbin was responsible for funding and building the line for Coeur d'Alene Railway and Navigation Company, which provided transport from the Old Mission Landing, up the south fork of the Coeur d'Alene River. Corbin encouraged a robust construction schedule, but the entire tracks could not be completed before the winter weather hit.

Once the spring thaw came in 1887, Corbin set his sights on extending the Coeur d'Alene Railways and Navigation Company line east from Wardner Junction to Wallace, Idaho. The city of Spokane Falls was excited about the possible economic impact of having its railway connected to one that went directly to the very profitable mines. A twenty-four by eighty foot train depot was built on the corner of Sixth Street in Wallace, with Corbin

Northern Pacific Railway Station, Spokane, 1926. (Courtesy of NWMAC, L87-1.30764-26)

providing the materials, and the citizens of Wallace providing the manual labor.

Lines from nearby mines, including Bunker Hill, Sullivan and Tiger, could meet at the Wallace depot, providing a way for cash to flow into the area, securing its reputation as a land of wealth and riches.

On October 1, 1888, Corbin was ready to move on, and he leased the barely two years-old Coeur d'Alene Railway and Navigation Company to Northern Pacific Railroad for 999 years. After that first railroad venture, Corbin, who had been nomadic, traveling for work in North Idaho, Montana and back and forth to New York, stopped in Spokane Falls to visit a friend. His plan was to visit for a few days before leaving to permanently move back east. According to Fahey, "He found the town grown to seven thousand citizens, thriving with its capture of the Spokane County seat in 1886 and the flow of wealth from the Coeur d'Alene mines over the railroads he had built."

Corbin was quite impressed with the growth and potential he saw in the city, and was swayed to move there. He and his son, Austin Corbin II, both settled in Spokane Falls, making it their permanent home. They both built grand estates, funded by their railway successes. The homes were designed and built in 1897, by famed Spokane architect, Kirtland K. Cutter. Corbin was connected to Cutter in another way. One of Corbin's daughters, Mary, who had spent much of her life living in Europe with her mother, came to Spokane and married Cutter.

Corbin's first successful forage into railroads was but the tip of the iceberg for him. He later sold the leased Coeur d'Alene Railway and Navigation Company to Northern Pacific and set out to build, northward from Spokane, a line that would eventually connect with the Canadian Pacific Railway. The impact of Corbin and other railroad giants cannot be denied. By 1898, Spokane was considered the largest northern railroad center between Minneapolis and the Pacific Coast.

One of the last ventures Corbin made into the railroad industry was the creation of Spokane International

Long after D.C. Corbin died, trains continued to be an essential part of moving our economy forward. (Courtesy of NWMAC, L87-1.1602-60)

Railway on January 18, 1905. The railway ran from Spokane to Post Falls, and then curved north, heading almost straight up the Idaho panhandle to the Canadian border. The route went through the North Idaho panhandle, which was becoming an increasingly prosperous area. The line was built mainly for freight, with very little passenger use. One passenger coach was pulled to accommodate the "eight to ten" people who needed to move throughout the region.

The terminal grounds for Spokane International Railroad were located along the north side of the Spokane River, and from this spot hooked into many other rail lines. According to Fahey, it met with "the Northern Pacific and other transcontinental railroads, with the Spokane, Portland and Seattle, and with the Oregon-Washington Railroad and Navigation Company." Once the line had traveled the 139.8 miles north, it met up with the Great Northern line at Bonners Ferry, and crossed over into Canada, where it met with the Canadian Pacific at Eastport, along the Idaho-Canada border.

"Although it did not deliver the desired terminal rates, the Spokane International solidified Spokane's position as hub of the Inland Empire by linking it with the burgeoning farm and lumber industries of northern Idaho." In November 1916, Spokane International Railroad was sold to Canada Pacific Railroad.

Corbin was still a hardworking man on the move when he was cut down in his prime. According to Fahey, "Death came before Daniel Corbin showed any inclination toward retirement. In the spring of 1918, he slipped, fell and fractured his right leg on the polished terrazzo of his tenth-floor suite in the Old National Bank Building… Pneumonia set in and shortly after noon on June 29, 1918, D.C. Corbin died in Sacred Heart Hospital."

When Corbin passed away that day in June, his life ended, but his legacy did not. Thanks to him, the city of Spokane and the neighboring Coeur d'Alene mining district were firmly established on the map as major players in the west. The city of Spokane grew and prospered with Corbin's association. His name lingers on as one of the architects of Spokane; a man who kept moving forward and took Spokane with him. ●

17

A Chorus of Footsteps

Mrs. Franklin O'Neill's Vision for Deaconess Hospital

Maria "Minnie" Beard. (Courtesy of The Deaconess Story)

GREAT SUCCESS OFTEN FINDS ITS BEGINNINGS IN THE SMALL, GENEROUS DEEDS OF one person who is willing to take their vision and act on it, taking the first step to reach their goal. True success is when those few first steps of one are joined by two, and then three and so on, until a whole chorus of footsteps can be heard, pounding the ground as they race toward a goal which is eventually met.

It was Mrs. Franklin O'Neill (formerly Miss Maria "Minnie" Beard) who, in 1892, took the first step toward reaching her goal of providing a hospital to the people of Spokane. It was through the generous efforts of her and her husband, and the many people who were inspired by them and who followed in their footsteps, that Deaconess Hospital came into existence in Spokane.

In 1892, when the city of Spokane recovering from the devastating effects of the Great Fire of 1889, two Deaconesses arrived from the Chicago Training School of the Methodist Episcopal Church to work in Spokane. Deaconesses were women sent out by the church to cities where they would tend to the sick and needy as part of the mission of the church, with their chief interest being social and religious welfare. Believing the Deaconesses needed a permanent location from which to serve and in which to live, Mr. and Mrs. O'Neill donated a home to them, located at 1209 West 5th Avenue.

The home at 1209 W. 5th Avenue, donated by Mrs. Franklin O'Neill. (Courtesy of The Deaconess Story)

The two Deaconesses sent to Spokane, Miss Emma L. Kenyon and Miss May L. Raymond, served for almost a year before both returned to their homes in April 1893. The burden was then picked up by Miss Emily Armstrong, who worked alone until October 1895, when a lack of support workers forced her to quit, bringing to an end the Deaconesses' presence in Spokane.

Seventeen months later, Miss Alice Strong and Miss Stella Miles arrived in town and resurrected the cause. The need for care overwhelmed them and they were soon unable to maintain their practice within the home. As a result, they expanded their location to rented rooms in a building located at Howard and Third.

Wanting to see the Deaconesses' work with the sick and needy expand, the O'Neills committed to tithing if Mr. O'Neill's mining ventures panned out. While he left to seek his fortune in British Columbia, Mrs. O'Neill stayed in Spokane, praying that her husband would be successful, so that they could provide funding for a hospital.

Her prayers were answered. Mr. O'Neill discovered a mine in Sandon, B.C. in 1896, and sold it for $50,000. True to their word, the O'Neills tithed ten percent, donating $5,000 to construct a hospital for the Deaconesses. This paid for the construction of a two-and-a-half story house with twenty rooms, which was built on Fourth Avenue, between Howard and Mill streets, and completed by the fall of 1897.

Mrs. O'Neill selected the name – Maria Beard Deaconess Home and Hospital – in honor of her mother. One half of the building was used to care for sick patients, and the other half was a rest home for the aged. According to April 25, 1896 incorporation papers of the Maria Beard Deaconess Home of Spokane, "The objects and purpose for which this Corporation is formed are to provide, through instruction in the Bible and all that pertains to Home and Foreign Mission Work, to give practical training to City Mission Work to give such aid to Missionaries as may be practicable, to employ Deaconesses, Instructors and Nurses, and, as incidental to such objects and purposes, to establish and maintain a suitable Christian home or homes and such other auxiliary institutions as may be deemed necessary for the proper accommodations and instructions of such persons as may be under the supervision of this society."

Before the new home and hospital was completed, a patient arrived in desperate need of help. According to *The Deaconess Story: Part One* by Priscilla Gilkey, "The Deaconesses were preparing breakfast one morning in the spring of 1896, when a stranger from British Columbia arrived in need of medical care. They sent for Dr. George Libby... the kitchen table was turned into an operating table and the wash boiler and kitchen stove became the sterilization department. Dr. Libby performed an appendectomy and provided the patient with nightshirts from his personal wardrobe...This first surgery at Howard and Third launched the hospitalization work of the Deaconesses."

The construction of of the hospital drew crowds. (Courtesy of The Deaconess Story)

Maria Beard Deaconess Home and Hospital, 1897. (Courtesy of The Deaconess Story)

Mr. and Mrs. Franklin O'Neill
(Courtesy of The Deaconess Story)

On November 18, 1896, Miss Parks, the first nurse Deaconess arrived in Spokane, which was a great help to the other Deaconesses who were not trained as nurses. "It is important to remember that the early Deaconesses weren't nurses and really preferred their charity work to running a hospital," wrote Gilkey.

Finally, on October 4, 1897, the Maria Beard Home and Hospital, located at 715 Fourth Avenue was dedicated. With medical services available, it was not long until the hospital was overwhelmed with patients. Sacred Heart Hospital had been founded in 1896, and St. Luke's opened in 1897, yet even with all of these hospitals there was not enough room for all of the patients in Spokane who needed medical care. By 1898, there was a push for an additional building in which the Deaconesses could serve. Twenty-seven patients per month were treated in the hospital and a place where patients with contagious diseases could be housed was needed.

In August 1899, the board voted to add an "Old People's Home" onto the building, which cost $10,000 to build and was completed in December 1899.

The many expansions meant more patients; therefore, more nurses were needed to care for them. A school of nursing to train nurses for work in the hospital opened in 1899 and the first class graduated in 1901 with six students. Student nurses started on-the-job training, working twelve-hour days with two hours off, six days in a row. They wore striped uniforms with aprons and small round muslin caps. Their classes were taken at night when they went to local doctors' offices for lectures. To the lectures they wore long black coats and mortarboards. Student nurses were recruited to work and be trained at the hospital's nursing school.

They were housed in the home until crowding forced them out and many took up lodging in a nearby house.

Nurses were responsible for daily dusting and cleaning of the hospital, and were responsible for locking the five entrances to the new building each night. According to the hospital rules, "A nurse is required to attend public worship in her own church at least once on a Sunday and to attend daily worship service in the hospital." Nurses also sang hymns as they went on duty each morning and read scripture to each patient every evening.

As the size of the hospital was growing so too was the level of medical care offered to patients. In 1899, one of the local surgeons, Dr. Thomas, performed a hernia operation using injections in the patients' spinal column, which was a new procedure. The first use of medical gloves in Spokane took place in December 1902; an idea instigated by Dr. George Libby after a trip back east in 1901, where he saw the practice

Lunch during a day of working on the hospital. (Courtesy of The Deaconess Story)

was common. In 1911, the hospital purchased its first x-ray machine, thanks to a Dr. W.W. Potter, who served as secretary of the Deaconess medical staff. He donated his fees from every patient on whom he used the machine. The promise of that income spurred on the hospital to purchase the then state of the art machine for $1,000.

Modern medicine had not fully arrived, though. Leeches were still commonly used, most often for head conditions and infections, and it was the nurses' responsibility to handle them. According to the writings of then-student nurse Clara Reedman, the leeches "were allowed to get really hungry" before being placed on the skin. She noted, "The treatment caused nurses much nauseous anguish." Additionally, only ether or chloroform was used for anesthesia, although patients were also given castor oil before surgery.

By 1899, patient numbers were up to 176 patients treated per year, and by 1903, there

Exteriors of Deaconess throughout the years. (Courtesy of NWMAC, L2004-32.703 a-f)

Exteriors of Deaconess throughout the years. (Courtesy of NWMAC, L2004-32.703 a-f)

were 183 medical patients, nineteen obstetrical patients and 188 surgical cases. According to a report by Superintendent Mary Comstock, by 1907, a variety of surgeries were performed, including "103 appendectomies, a two year-old boy had plastic surgery resulting in a new ear, a four year-old girl received new hip sockets. A child burned in a bonfire received nine weeks of care after having gone nearly three months without his burns being tended to."

Exteriors of Deaconess throughout the years. (Courtesy of NWMAC, L2004-32.703 a-f)

The continual increase in demand for services and space meant the hospital continually needed to expand their physical location. In March 1902, Deaconess Esther Finley left a house at 733 Fourth Avenue to the hospital. Originally it was intended as a home for retired Deaconesses, but was used for nurse quarters and exam rooms. It was called the Annex.

Exteriors of Deaconess throughout the years. (Courtesy of NWMAC, L2004-32.703 a-f)

In 1906 or 1907, Mr. and Mrs. B.J. Koontz of Echo, Oregon, donated $10,000 to the Deaconesses, which was used to construct a new building. The money was used to fund a three-story brick building that was built and opened by October 31, 1907. It had fifty beds and a

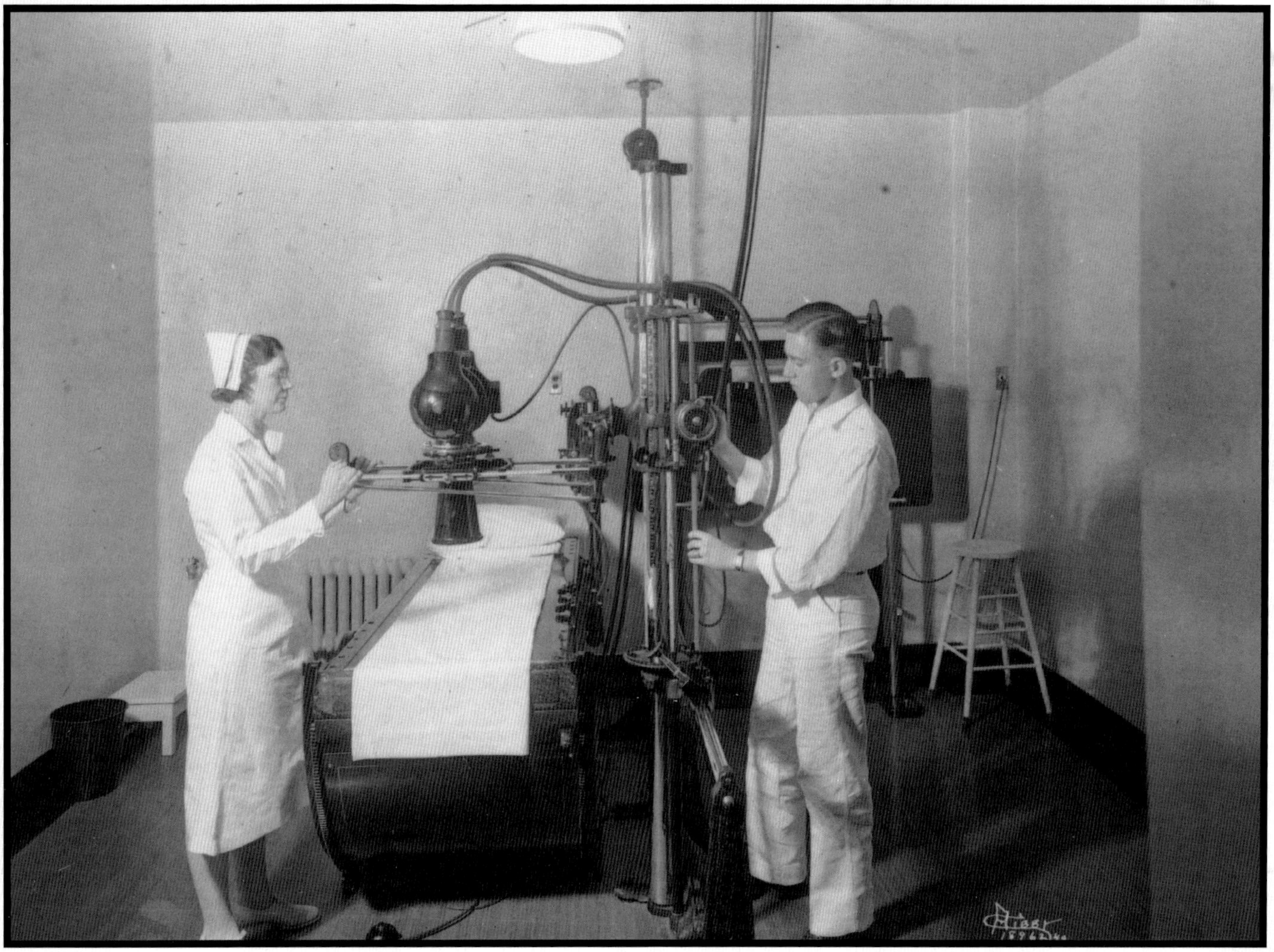

Fumigating the operating room at Deasoness with formaldehyde, 1914. (Courtesy of NWMAC, L93-18.200)

hydraulic elevator, as well as two surgery rooms, a sterilization room and a dumbwaiter in the kitchen.

By 1910, the Annex was entirely dedicated to housing for nurses, with an overflow of nurses lodging in a tent adjacent to the building. Some nurses would set up cots and stay in the rooms of patients who were very ill, allowing them to not only care for the patient, but also to avoid sleeping in the overflow tent.

In 1914, the space between the hospital and the house where the nurses lived was enclosed, creating a two-story building. The lower level was a ward for patients with measles, mumps and contagious diseases, and the second floor was an ironing room where the nurses had to iron "everything but the flatware." Extra tasks like ironing were not uncommon for nurses. "At that time there was more emphasis put on personal service than the art of nursing. Nurses were the cooks and counted the laundry as well," notes Gilkey in *The Deaconess Story: Part One*.

When the Spanish Flu hit in 1918, every bed in the hospital was needed as Spokane was overwhelmed by the deadly flu. The hospital quit accepting any maternity or surgical cases because there was limited room to care for them, and they were safer staying away from the hospital, which became an island of illness and despair behind the shuttered doors. Five nurses became infected while providing care, and died, as did Deaconess Field Secretary Mr. Asa V. Braderick and his wife.

Due to the cost of caring for so many patients, coupled with the loss of income from turned away patients because of the Spanish Flu, the hospital found itself in a tough financial spot. Despite the financial hardship, more space was needed to continue operating, so on September 6, 1919, the cornerstone for the third hospital location was laid at Fourth and Post. It was to increase the hospital capacity by 150 beds; however, it was four years until it was open for use.

Construction, which had begun with the laying of the cornerstone in 1919, was adding up, reaching over $300,000 by 1920. According to *The Deaconess Story: Part One*, "Estimates of the cost had been based on pre-war prices, but much of the construction had been needed [resulting in] paying war prices."

Nurses from classes of 1912 and 1916 . (Courtesy of The Deaconess Story)

It was not until May 12, 1923, that the new hospital officially opened, three and a half years after the cornerstone was laid. Patient rooms were considered state of the art, thanks to the in-room call buttons that alerted nurses at their station. Patients with contagious diseases were sent to a city-county operated isolation hospital, though, called "the pest house."

Dr. Robert Warner, a Methodist minister who became the hospital superintendent in 1923, declared the hospital "not merely a philanthropic institution, but one where souls as well as bodies could be healed."

While all was well with the new building, some of the nurses were getting restless with the rules they had to follow. In 1924, student nurses protested. "Student nurses were required to wear their hair long in those days. A number of them though made arrangements with a barber in the Victoria Hotel to stay open late one evening and they all went down and had their hair bobbed in the latest style. There were deprived of their caps for several weeks and ordered to wear switches and what-nots, their punishment, comparatively slight, since bands and other businesses regularly dismissed employees for social offense."

Hospitals were changing. "Once a place where people went to have surgery or to die, a hospital was more and more the center of medical care." Reflecting this idea, on June 12, 1928, the name changed from Maria Beard Deaconess Association of the Methodist Episcopal Church, to Deaconess Hospital.

In response to the stock market's collapse on October 29, 1929, not as many people were seeking medical care in early 1930s and it was having an effect on the hospital's revenue. As a result, rooms and rates were reduced, taking the cost of patient care down to $4.55 per day, and because "money was becoming shorter, Deaconess was accepting livestock for payment."

Despite the discomfort of the economy, a newly completed thirty-two-bed wing was a place of comfort, providing something new: soft mattresses. It was previously thought a hard mattress was best for someone who was ill. As advances in medicine were made, more thought and compassion went into patient care. All of this came

Nurses from classes of 1912 and 1916. (Courtesy of The Deaconess Story)

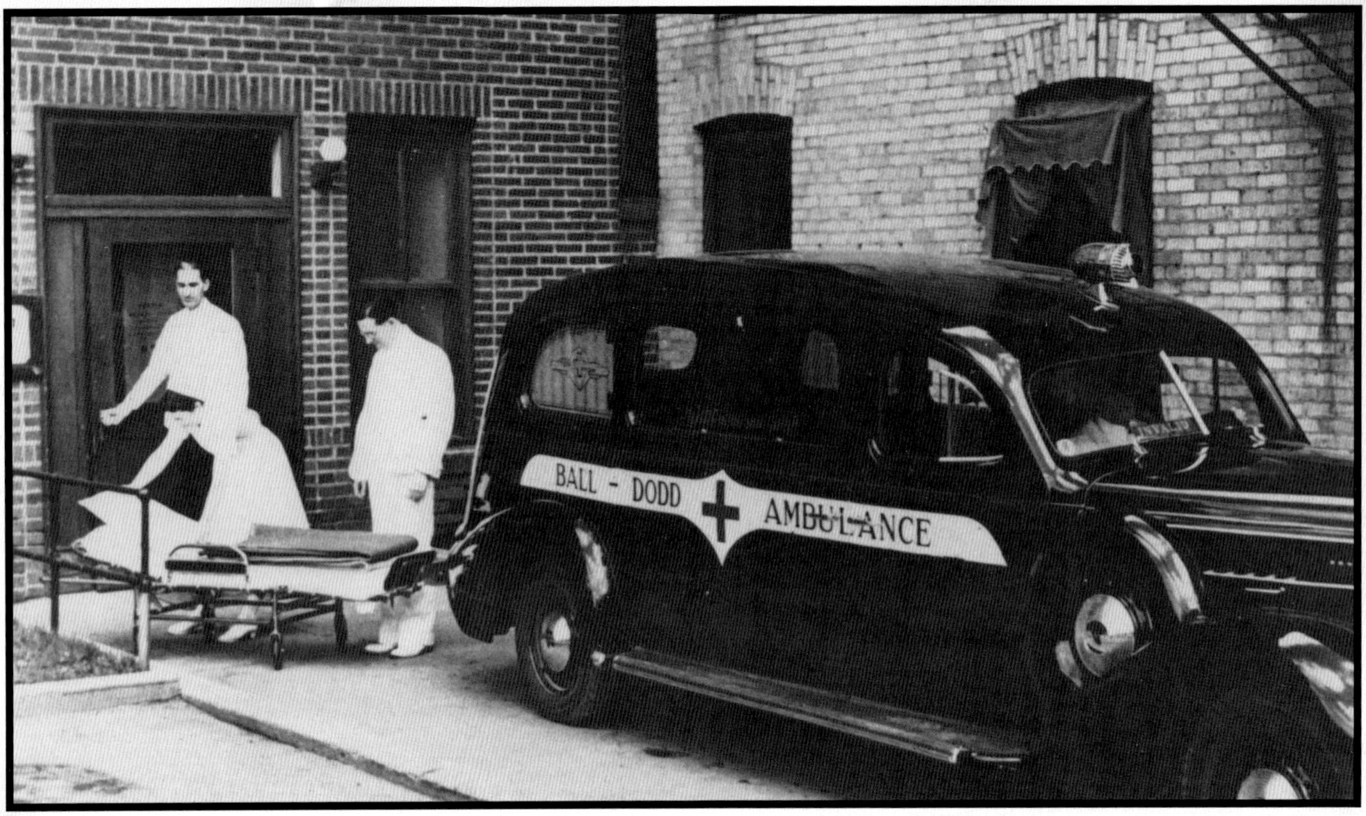

A nurse prepares a gurney to load a patient into the Ball and Dodd ambulance. (Courtesy of NWMAC,86-57.12)

at a price, though. The cost of expensive medical advances and needed expansions to the hospital, combined with the inability of many patients to pay, left Deaconess shouldering a financial strain.

"It is evident that the old days of medical saddle bags and horse and buggy, with kit of pills, powders, calomel and salts have all passed…while the less efficient medical and hospital methods have passed, inexpensive service has passed with it," wrote Dr. Warner in a June 1931 report to the trustees in which he expressed concern about the hospital's financial situation.

According to Gilkey, "But when finances appeared they couldn't get any worse, Dr. Warner decide to turn to God for assistance." In 1933, the Woman's Hotel building, next door to the hospital and which the hospital had earlier tried to purchase, was given to Deaconess with the understanding they would take on the deficit. "As a result of this and other providences, our hospital actually came out of the depression better financially than when it began and very much richer in faith," said Dr. Warner.

A Mrs. Ella M. Letterman Lanning had given her farmland to the hospital on a seven percent annuity basis in 1927. In 1930, she suggested rather than receiving her monthly annuity, the money should go to the deficit on the Woman's Hotel. In 1939, the former hotel was renamed Letterman Lanning Hall, which was home to nursing students.

Financial blessings occurred again in 1939, when former patient, Dr. Theodore Chamberlain of Concord, Massachusetts, gave a permanent endowment of property in memorial to his brother, Frederick Dean Chamberlain. The value of the property was $233,362.

Financial blessings, paired with the hard work and dedication of the staff of Deaconess helped the hospital weather the economic storms of the depression years. When WWII came there was a shortage of trained staff, as many of the doctors and nurses joined the war effort. Just as the first Deaconesses in Spokane worked hard despite the overwhelming load of patients and their understaffed team, the staff of Deaconess would not be deterred from continuing their mission of caring for the people of our community and being a strong presence in the local medical community. That mission has continued over the years and remains firm today.

What started as one woman's goal to provide a hospital and quality care for the people of Spokane has been fortified by well over a century's worth of hard work and the dedication of people who joined her on that path; a chorus of footsteps marching toward their goal. ●

18

Refiner's Fire

How the Great Fire of 1889 Shaped Spokane Falls

Men survey the damage of the burned remains of the Arlington Hotel after the Great Fire of 1889. (Courtesy of NWMAC, L86-1056)

THE FUTURE LOOKED BRIGHT IN THE SUMMER OF 1889. WASHINGTON HAD JUST become a state, with Elisha P. Ferry assuming the role of the first governor, ready to guide the state toward prosperity and success. One of the biggest cities in Washington was Spokane Falls, where the population had exploded to almost 20,000, thanks to the nearby mining and railroad endeavors. As more and more people arrived, eager to make Spokane Falls their home, it was a city on the cusp on greatness that drew them in. The future seemed a guaranteed success, and it was inconceivable to consider anything could cause the city to derail from the route it was on. Those thoughts soon went up in flames, along with nearly the entire city.

It had been a dry, hot summer, with major fires in Seattle in June, and Ellensburg in July; additionally, there had been numerous forest fires in the Coeur d'Alene mining district. On the morning of August 4, 1889, Spokane Falls resident Adelaide Sutton Gilbert wrote to her parents about the thick smoke and the oppressive heat. "The stage lines in every direction are practically abandoned from fires and fallen trees…Now a stiff breeze is prevailing and blowing the smoke away, but it must increase the fires, and I do not know, but before we are through we shall all be burned up."

As Gilbert went to sleep that night, the words of her letter became a reality.

Church bells regularly rang on Sunday mornings, but not in the evenings. On the hot, dry night of August 4, 1899, bells throughout Spokane Falls suddenly rang out, joined by a chorus of alarming shouts and the firing of pistols. As fear was driven into the hearts of the citizens, one toll at a time, word spread that there was a fire blazing in the city. No one could imagine that by morning their beloved city would lie in ruins, smoldering piles of ashes where buildings once stood.

Looking north from Railroad Avenue, at the ruins of the Great Fire of 1889. (Courtesy of NWMAC, L86-140)

There are varying accounts, but the fire is believed to have started from the explosion of an oil-stove in the attic of a lodging house on Railroad Avenue, across from the Northern Pacific depot. Perhaps if it had been extinguished immediately, the fire never would have existed in memory, save for a small mention tucked on the bottom page of newspaper; instead, the fire's flames both destroyed and shaped the future of Spokane Falls.

The fire was not immediately extinguished, and citizens watched in horror as it spread throughout the city. As documented in *Spokane Falls Illustrated*, "After half an hour, it was apparent that the flames had passed beyond the control of the men who so industriously sought to stay their onward march. From a dead stillness the intense heat created a strong current and the fire was carried into the very heart of the business part of the city almost in a twinkling."

In that twinkling, the fire turned from a small burning ember to a violent monster of flames with an insatiable appetite to consume all that was within its path. The sheer terror of the event was sinking in for citizens.

Spokane Falls resident G.W. Roche wrote in his diary, "The scene to those who witnessed the terrible conflagration will long be remembered. The hoarse shouts of the men running in all directions, the shouts of women and children, the rattle of the wagons, the tolling of church bells, the shrill whistles of locomotives as they hurried to and from trying to save the cars lined on the Northern Pacific tracks, the angry roar of the flames, the embers and shingles flying through the air, the explosion of giant powder, all combined to make the night hideous in the extreme."

As horrendous as the fire was, people were not giving up without a fight. Thirteen members of the volunteer fire department reported for duty when the bell atop the fire station at First and Washington initially rang. As they began their assault on the flames, they came to the horrible realization that there was not enough water pouring out of their hoses, and the fire continued to spread.

Without enough water, yet hoping to contain the flames that were hungrily gobbling up the city, men on the volunteer fire department took a bold and proactive step. They decided to blow up buildings in the blocks surrounding the core of the fire. Igniting dynamite within these buildings seemed like the best way to establish a perimeter around the fire, and prevent flames from leaping to other buildings. Spokane Falls Mayor Fred Furth issued the official order to blow up the buildings.

An eyewitness was quoted as saying, "But these grand buildings went down like children's playhouses," referring to the brick buildings, which were thought to be nearly fireproof.

When people saw the hopelessness of the situation, they stopped trying to defend their buildings, instead turning their efforts to emptying their stores, offices and homes of all that they could manage to move. Imagine the pandemonium as everyone screamed, cried and stumbled over one another to escape, only to find the streets overflowing with a snarled mess of horse-drawn wagons brimming with towers of goods, teetering over-head, and a thick smoke in the air.

Daniel H. Dwight, a real estate investor who had a major holding with his mother-in-law in the Falls City block, later wrote to her about his and his friends' attempts to save their office in the Opera House. As Dwight abandoned an oak desk he was trying to salvage and "ran for his life," his friend, a Mr. Galbraith, lingered to gather some personal items. "When he came to the stairs they were a street of flames and his exit was cut off. His only escape was to jump, which he did from Dr. Hawrer's window at the corner, fully twenty feet above the sidewalk. He is here at our house, and hasn't stepped on his feet for two days, but no bones are broken."

It wasn't just the buildings that the firemen were desperate to save. In an effort to save the town's booze, streams of whiskey and wine barrels were rolled down Post Street toward the cool, wet safety of the river.

According to *The Great Fire: 75th Anniversary*, "Burning shingles were wafted on cushions of heat. Flying over the city, they fell on other buildings, starting new fires. With dramatic suddenness, the horrible realization seized onlookers that Spokane Falls was doomed."

When the wind shifted, it turned the flames momentarily south, jumping over Railroad Avenue, just long enough to ignite the Northern Pacific Railway passenger and freight depots.

According to a history article in the August 4, 1964 issue of *The Spokane Chronicle*, "In this manner, the appalling monster held high carnival until about 10 p.m., when, with a mighty crash, the Howard Street bridge went down. A boom of logs took fire and shimmered for hours on the crystal surface of the river."

Within three hours of the fire starting, twenty-eight square blocks of the city had burned and the future of Spokane Falls was forever changed. It is estimated that 800 businesses and private residences scattered

Washington National Bank, after the fire. (Courtesy of NWMAC, L86-1058)

Howard Street, looking north after the fire. (Courtesy of NWR, SPL)

Riverside Avenue, looking west after the fire. (Courtesy of NWR, SPL)

Remains of the Glover / Pioneer Block after the fire. (Courtesy of NWR, SPL)

The first electric line being strung along Main Avenue after the Great Fire of 1889. (Courtesy of NWR, SPL)

among 300 buildings were destroyed, displacing 2,000 residents. The Second Regiment of the Washington National Guard patrolled the streets at night to maintain order.

The next morning, as the darkness faded away and the sun's light forced its way through the thick haze of smoke, a complete inventory of the destruction was taken. The Crescent Block was the only brick building left standing in town, while everything from the railroad to the river, and from Lincoln to Washington streets was destroyed, leaving a charred graveyard in the footprint of the city. The damages were estimated at $6 million.

The Northern Pacific Railway passenger and freight depots were completely burned, as were the rail tracks. A history story in the August 4, 1964 edition of *The Spokane Chronicle*, quoted a citizen as saying, "Well, the midnight train came in and found the city gone and hundreds of the homeless waiting to climb aboard, waiting to get anywhere away from the smell, the sound and the sight of the terror that uncontrolled flames light up in the souls of men."

While the city was in ruins, initially there were great claims there was no loss of life, which was seen as a joyful note in an otherwise tragic event. Sadly, this was incorrect, as there was one life taken by the fire.

George I. Davis, a civil engineer whose office was in the Canon Block, went back in to the building to grab some personal effects. He was driven from the building by flames and tripped in front of Lowenburg's store. A group of men picked him up and took him to the hospital, where he died less than twelve hours later. According to the August 5, 1889, *Spokane Falls Chronicle*, "His body was burned to a crisp from his feet to his hips, and he was also burnt considerable around his head."

In the midst of tragedy, it is essential to hold onto the bright spots of hope. One bright spot was that, luckily, some freight cars at the Northern Pacific Railway station, filled with produce and other goods, had been saved, which provided food for the people of Spokane Falls in the days after the fire.

Other bright spots soon emerged in the form of good news, and of good people stepping up to help one another.

The Western Union Telegraph office was back up and partially returned to service the morning after the fire. Only three pieces of equipment were salvaged from the office, and many were burned, but despite the obstacles 1,600 messages were handled in the temporary office on the day after the fire.

Insurance claims adjusters from numerous companies swept into town and were at work in improvised quarters after the fire. (Courtesy of NWR, SPL)

Mr. Frank Middaugh, owner of the *Medical Lake Ledger* loaned a Washington brand hand press, as well as type and printing accessories, to the publisher of the then-named *Chronicle* so he could print the paper until a new printing press could be ordered. The *Chronicle* foreman, Frank McCarter, had left for Medical Lake as the fire raged and returned as quickly as possible. The paper was set up in a tent and production began. There was no disruption in service, and the Monday afternoon issue of the paper came out as planned.

Amidst the bright spots, there were an increasing number of questions as to why the fire department's efforts to fight the fire were so futile. According to *The Great Fire: 75th Anniversary*, water came out of the firemen's hoses, but the supply soon dwindled down to nothing. With no water to put out the fire, the flames leapt from the wood building to the ones on either side, and soon every building between Post and Lincoln on Railroad Avenue was engulfed in flames. The Pacific Hotel was the first large commercial establishment to be consumed by the flames once the fire leapt across Post Street.

Soon rumors swirled that the Superintendent of Water Works had the key to the pump room but was away at the time of the fire, meaning no one could get into the room to increase the water pressure to fight the flames.

On August 6, 1889, an article appeared in the *Spokane Falls Review* questioning the absence of Rolla A. Jones, Superintendent of Water Works. "When the fire first broke out, the water supply was so inadequate that the firemen could not get an effective stream on the flames, the water not having force enough to break the windows."

The *Spokane Falls Review* said Jones had vacated the pump house, leaving a subordinate in charge who didn't know how to operate the machinery, as opposed to other reports that he had left no key to the pump house. The city council commenced an investigation, which was presented to the mayor and the council on August 14, 1889.

It was discovered that Superintendent Jones left the pumping station from 6:30 p.m. to 9:15 p.m. on Sunday, August 4th. "The man left in charge of pumping station during the absence of Superintendent Jones is competent and reliable and of twenty years of practical experience in machinery and pumps and that said man was in

The John W. Graham store set up business in a tent the morning after the Great Fire of 1889, as did many businesses. (Courtesy of NWR, SPL)

charge of his respective duty assigned him by Superintendent Jones at the hour of 6:30 p.m.," stated the report. "Information received from reliable sources causes an opinion in the mind of your Committee that the main cause of such poor stream from No. 2 hose was the fact that the said hose became bursted only a few minutes after the fire commenced, which necessitated several minutes delay before repair could be made."

With the water pump blame game coming to an end, the people of Spokane Falls were ready to dry their tears, accept their fate and look to the future. No time was lost in rebuilding. By the morning after the fire, tents had begun lining the streets as temporary retail establishments. Additional tents were ordered from Forts Sherman and Walla Walla.

Daniel H. Dwight described the mood in the city in a letter dated Thursday, August 15, 1889. "Every day brings something new," he wrote. "The city is spreading out, and new buildings are going up in every direction. Teams of every description are in great demand, and mechanics of every kind. Nobody seems discouraged or blue. Everybody is hopeful and we will build Spokane up bigger than she ever was before."

For months, the Northern Industrial Exposition had been slated to take place in Spokane Falls in 1890, but the fire seemed to be destroying any hope of that plan becoming a reality. Facing the threat of losing such a prestigious and revenue-generating event, the citizens of Spokane Falls used this event as an incentive to build faster.

With the new construction, wood buildings were out and brick and stone dominated the landscape of the new skyline. In less than one year, 200 new buildings stood proudly along the streets of Spokane Falls, and nearly $5 million was spent on construction within the first year after the fire.

Though the fire had done its worst and left the city reeling, the spirit of the citizens of Spokane Falls blazed even brighter. The attitude of J. H. Boyde, a hardware store owner, seems to have captured the attitude of the citizens. "This is a heavy storm," he said, "but we will weather it through all right and have plenty of happy days which will come along bye and bye."

Happy days were indeed in store for Spokane Falls in the years to come; it was a city that could not be conquered by flames of fury. ●

19

An Age of Elegance

The Crescent Department Store

Interior of the main floor at The Crescent, ca. 1908. (Courtesy of NWMAC, L85-79-32)

FOR MUCH OF SPOKANE FALLS, THE MORNING OF AUGUST 5, 1889, BROKE FORTH from the overnight hours in a haze of smoke and despair, brought on by the devastating fire started the night before, known as the Great Fire of 1889. Smoke and embers were all that remained of much of the downtown, and for many citizens the fire took more than their physical buildings; it also took with it their livelihoods. From a personal and business standpoint, it was one of Spokane Falls' deepest hours of despair; yet, amongst the clouds of smoke, dusty air and dashed dreams sprang a new business destined to be part of Spokane Falls' life for nearly a century.

The Crescent Department Store (other sources list it as Comstock and Patterson's Crescent Store, named for two of its founders) had long been slated to open its doors on August 5, 1889. Taking its name from the crescent shaped front of its brick building, the store planned to offer every day and "fancy" goods, all in one spot. The building in which it was housed was one of the few brick buildings in town, and was spared from the doom that met most of downtown's structures during the fire. On August 5th, its first day open, The Crescent was one of the only dry goods stores still standing in Spokane Falls, and it sold out of its entire inventory in that one day.

Construction of The Crescent store addition, 1918. (Courtesy of NWMAC, L87-1.1494X18)

The manner in which The Crescent conducted business on that first day did not go unnoticed. According to *The Crescent, Romance of Business*, "The store opened. Its stock melted away like snow in the sunshine and every article was sold at exactly the price at which it was marked for business under normal conditions, though the proprietors could easily have gotten anything they might have asked, had they cared to take advantage of this opportunity to 'profiteer'." This fair treatment of customers helped seal The Crescent's reputation as a good company and one that deserved the support of Spokane Falls' citizens.

The store grew so much in its first ten years, it moved three times before construction began on a permanent building. Looking for a new location because of a rent increase, Mr. Comstock and Mr. Patterson were walking in downtown Spokane one day and saw a hole in the ground next to Marble Bank, on the corner of Riverside and Wall. Mr. Comstock was confident it could be purchased quite inexpensively. In 1898, the hole, which was actually sixty-eight feet of property running on Riverside Avenue back to the alley, and thirty-five feet of frontage on Wall Street, was purchased by The Crescent for the bargain price of $42,000.

As the business continued to grow and become an integral part of Spokane's economy and life, the store physically needed to expand as well. In May of 1917, the adjacent property on the corner of Main and Wall was purchased for $125,000, and it was here that the large, seven-story building which still stands tall in downtown Spokane was constructed.

The building officially opened in 1919, and was instantly the place to be in Spokane. Constructing a building of that size was considered quite an undertaking, especially during a time of war. The architect, L.L. Rand, designed not only a store but also a community gathering spot and a temple of elegance. The seven-story building had a basement and sub-basement, as well as a superstructure above the seventh floor. The total floor area was over five acres, all of which were in one of the strongest and most substantial buildings in the city.

The ventilation system in The Crescent was one of the most advanced around. Air in the store was changed

Santa Claus arrives to meet with children outside of The Crescent. (Courtesy of NWMAC, L87-1.27854-24)

every six minutes thanks to the four large ventilation plants in the building which brought in outside air, cleaned it, adjusted the temperature as needed and forced it into the building.

Despite the exterior beauty of the cream terra cotta building, it was the inside that captivated everyone's attention. When it came to its copious amounts of elegance, glamour and beauty, The Crescent was the department store equivalent of the Titanic. Grandeur surrounded customers everywhere they looked, employees were there to meet their every need, and there was no greater goal than to treat customers like royalty.

One of the store's most popular spots was the Arcade. A long gallery running the length of the building, the Arcade stretched inside from the Riverside entrance to the Main Street entrance and was filled with displays. From this center area, individual shops opened off of each side, with beautifully dressed windows separating the Arcade from the stores. The Crescent became well known for these windows, as well as its incredible exterior window displays.

The store's interior was decorated beautifully and "harmonized" with the goods in each department. English brown mahogany fixtures and closed cabinets with glass doors were found throughout the first floor, while the Arcade was decorated in luxurious white and gold colors.

The second floor was painted French gray with a touch of gold. Garments were found on this floor, with ready-to-wear pieces kept in closed cabinets. According to a booklet put out at the opening of The Crescent's new building in 1919, there was a special dressing room for "the fitting of surgical cases. This service is highly appreciated by the physicians of the city." The Baby Shop, which was also on the second floor, had a layette room where selections could be made in quiet, away from the eyes of others. The Millinery (women's hats) was displayed in attractive alcoves, as were the corsets in the lingerie department, to provide "pleasing backgrounds" in displays. The Boy's Shop and The Fur Salon were also on this floor, and each boasted deep mahogany wood as part of their elegant décor.

A Crescent employee shows a customer a rug in the Oriental Rug Bazaar. (Courtesy of NWMAC, L87-1.14359X-17)

The third floor was painted a beautiful ivory enamel and housed a medley of departments: the gift shop, bedding, cotton goods, phonographs, art needlework, rugs, drapes and pictures, an Oriental Rug Bazaar, traveling equipment (luggage) and furniture. A women's restroom on this floor included "hair dressing, complexion treatments and other personal services for women, and the silence room where one may enjoy the complete rest and silence necessary to restore fatigued and disturbed nerves to their normal condition."

The fourth floor offered everything needed for a household, including china, glassware, crystal, pottery and kitchen goods. This floor was decorated with elegant black enamel walls to make the displays appear more striking.

The fifth floor had piano display rooms, a mail order department and the Museum of the Eastern Washington Historical Society, which was housed in space donated by the store until the state could secure a permanent location. The donation of this space demonstrated the deep connection and commitment The Crescent had with the city of Spokane. An indoor golf range open to all players without charge during unseasonable weather was also found on this floor.

Elegant dining and entertainment was the name of the game for the sixth floor, which housed the Tea Room, Men's Grill, employee dining room and an auditorium. The auditorium had a stage, dressing rooms, lighting equipment and a seating area available to the public for "entertainments held during the day." Fashion shows, highlighting the most glamorous and beautiful fashions were often hosted in the formal restaurants as well as in the auditorium.

A fur storage-service was provided by The Crescent for customers. Furs were cleaned, repaired and stored throughout the spring and summer months before being returned to customers in September. The furs were secured in a fireproof vault that was kept at twenty degrees and was housed in the basement of the store.

Mechanical conveyers connected different departments within the store so items could be delivered from stock rooms or other departments to customers. The store also offered services like made-to-order buttons, buttonholes, engraving of society stationery; shoe repair, cleaning and polishing; picture framing; needlework, knitting and crochet lessons, and piano tuning.

The Crescent was known for its incredible customer service. There were few things a customer could request that the store would not do. The service was enough to win over Louis Davenport who selected The Crescent to outfit the interior of The Davenport Hotel. In a special ten-page section of the August 30, 1914, issue of the *Spokesman-Review*, dedicated to The Davenport Hotel, several articles and advertisements spoke of The Crescent. "When the new hotel was to be furnished Mr. Davenport selected The Crescent to do it!" blared one headline. The Crescent received a contract to supply The Davenport Hotel's furnishings, including the carpets, rugs, window shades, draperies, furniture, art and pictures, china and glasses, lamps, bathroom hardware, beds, mattresses and pillows, blankets, slumber robes and bedspreads, linens and the fountain in the lobby. The ad went on to say, "The Davenport Hotel furnishing is offered as evidence of the strength and resources of The Crescent store and its ability to meet any demand made upon it."

A well-known figure-turned-customer was President John F. Kennedy. On November 15, 1961, President Kennedy desired a specific rocking chair for his stay in Seattle. His staff scoured the state and found it only at The Crescent. When the request came in, the staff immediately prepared the special chair and shipped it by Greyhound bus in order to get it to Kennedy's hotel suite in Seattle.

The Crescent Clock. (Courtesy of NWMAC, L87-1.90519-58)

Shopping at The Crescent was a treat, but working there was considered an honor. You were hard pressed to find an employee that didn't love his or her job. Given the way The Crescent treated its employees though, it was no wonder.

Employee rest rooms–not bathrooms, but literally rooms for rest–were filled with books, magazines, table games, phonographs and records for employees to use. There was also an emergency hospital on site with a nurse whose services were free to all employees. A playground was built on the roof for employees to get fresh air and relax during their shifts.

An employees' association hired a physician and a Christian Science practitioner for use for free by members. The association also furnished medicine when necessary and paid sick benefits to employees as well as sending a committee member to look after sick employees.

Employees of The Crescent were treated as family. In Donald Johnson's book, *Under the Clock*, Mable Stingley, a twenty-two-year employee of the store, recalled how she was treated during her illness with cancer. "The Crescent management was very understanding during my times of illness. During the time I was having my chemotherapy, I had to be away from my job for six months. During that time, a week never went by when my supervisor didn't call or come by the house to see how I was getting along. That gives you an idea of the kind of people they were then. They had a real concern for the wellbeing of their employees. It was a wonderful place to work."

The employee cafeteria on the sixth floor was tucked away from the public, but it had the same food that was served in the Apple Tree, one of The Crescent's, and Spokane's, most glamorous restaurants.

In 1948, it got easier for customers to get from floor to floor, thanks to the newly installed escalators. The crowds that came to see these (they were the only escalators between Seattle and Minneapolis) were so large police needed to be there for crowd control. An estimated 8,000 people an hour could ride the new escalators.

Even more popular than the escalators were The Crescent's window displays, especially at Christmas. The world was transformed when small children walked up and pressed their noses against the windows and saw an intricate North Pole scene with elves busy at work, or a winter wonderland with dancing snow fairies. *Under the Clock* recalls the memories of Jean Sullivan, who had a special spot in her heart for the famed Crescent windows. "What fun to see again the wonderful animated windows The Crescent had every year! There were small elves working at making gifts for Santa's sleigh that stood to the side. One window was full of lovely dolls, dressed in suits and dresses of the 1800s. There were many Christmas display windows, each one filled with magic." Those corner window displays cost between $10,000 and $30,000 each year to produce.

When it came to making purchases, whether it was at Christmas or any other time during the year, customers knew they were getting a fair price at The Crescent. In 1939, purchasing items got easier when The Crescent was one of the first stores to offer an equivalent of a charge card. The metal plate cards allowed customers to make purchases and pay later.

The Crescent was famous for treating its employees well, as demonstrated by this annual Crescent employee dinner, ca. 1952. (Courtesy of NWMAC, L85-79-12)

Customer service was the lifeblood of the store with employee manuals heavily emphasizing the importance of satisfying customers. "The Crescent lives for the pleasure and satisfaction of our customers," read the manual. The book *Under the Clock* recounts the following story: "All through the life of the store, the legendary return policy continued to be in force. Salesperson Mortimer Sullivan recalled allowing a full refund on four shirts which were purchased twenty-three years earlier for the customer's deceased husband."

Perhaps the most recognized part of The Crescent was the large four-faced clock that hung from the ceiling, alerting all to the precise time. If you were meeting friends or family downtown, there was a good chance "under the clock" would be your meeting place. Just up the ramp from the clock was Under the Clock, a lunch counter and soda fountain. Swivel chairs at the counter and quiet booths hosted many a lunchtime diner. Whether it was an egg salad sandwich or chocolate malt at the counter, it wasn't just a meal being served; it was a memory being made when it was at Under the Clock.

While "the fountain", which Under the Clock was endearingly called, was a great place to meet up for a fun treat, the upstairs dining rooms were a special setting that offered more elegance and class. The Apple Tree, formerly called the Tea Room, had linen cloths on the tables, and the meals were some of the finest in the city. As you ate your meal, elegant models dressed in the latest fashions would walk through the dining room, allowing you to glimpse the fashionable new looks and work up an appetite for shopping as you satisfied your appetite for food.

"The ladies were always dressed in their finest at the Apple Tree. They all had on their hats and gloves and looked so nice," Margaret Conklin, who grew up shopping at The Crescent, said in *Under the Clock.*

While there were fashion shows for the women, the store also catered to younger shoppers who came with their mothers. When the store opened, a nursery with a uniformed nurse was there to watch customer's children for as long as they needed to shop. Additionally, the store offered several youth-programs, which taught classes, such as modeling, social graces, crocheting, knitting and art.

In 1988, after nearly 100 years of service, The Crescent was sold to F&N Acquisition Corporation of Seattle, due to financial issues and a change in customer's shopping habits. The name of the store was then changed to Frederick & Nelson. Although it was the same building, it was no longer the same store. The charm, history and connection to Spokane were no longer there, and in 1995, the store closed for good.

Though the doors may have closed, inside the building, and inside the hearts of The Crescent's shoppers, remain countless memories of a store that was the heart of the city during an age of elegance. ●

If You Build It, They Will Come

How Natatorium Park Became the Heartbeat of Spokane

An ariel view of Washington Water Power's Natatorium Park. (Courtesy of NWMAC, L93-65-133)

IN THE LATE 1880S, SPOKANE FALLS WAS A DUST-FILLED INFANT OF A TOWN, WITH FEW opportunities for excursions far from home. Needing to increase their ridership, and, therefore, their revenue, Spokane Cable Railways knew that if their line ended at Twickenham Park, which was a popular spot to watch baseball, people would come — and they would ride their trolleys to get there.

Washington Water Power supplied the electricity for the trolleys, and managed the park as well. The cable car traveled at the pace of ten miles per hour and reached Twickenham Park in twenty minutes from its downtown departure. This form of transportation was a delightful change of pace for riders who were used to the labor-intensive task of caring for their horse-drawn wagons. The arrival of the trolley was a big event in Spokane.

"This city is approaching one of the most complete systems of rapid transit to be found in any place of double or three times its size in the country," proclaimed the July 11, 1889 edition of the *Spokane Falls Review*. "It enables a population to accomplish much more than it otherwise could, not only in the strict lines of business, but in the pursuit of pleasure and social duties as well."

This rapid transit was used to connect downtown Spokane Falls with Twickenham Park, which was located west of town on the bend of the river. With forty acres of land, which rolled down slopping hills and made its way gradually to the riverbanks below, the park was located on one of the finest pieces of land in Spokane Falls. Twickenham included a dining hall, shooting gallery, bowling alley and lawn tennis courts. The plan was to make Twickenham Park an oasis from the busy city life and a place to which people would want to travel often. Visitors rushed to Twickenham for baseball when Spokane Falls' first professional team took the mound in 1890. Cable cars, packed with people, arrived from downtown every five minutes.

The popular trolley to Natatorium Park. (Courtesy of Washington State Digital Archives)

An additional draw was the Twickenham Park Casino and Hotel, which had a first class restaurant inside. Heated water and electric lighting drew large crowds, as did the Vaudeville performers who brought their acts to the park. People packed their picnics to enjoy on the manicured lawns, and spent the day reveling in the sights of the park.

For the 1893 season, park management wanted to draw even more people through the gates, and they knew just how to do it. On May 31, 1893, work began on a huge outdoor swimming pool — the first heated pool in the state of Washington. Seventy-degree river water circulated through the pool, which was 100 feet by 200 feet. Additionally, a gymnasium was built, which was described as offering "all the modern appliances, such as dumbbells, clubs, foils, broad swords, gloves…swinging trapeze bars, horizontal bars, rings, spring boards, etc."

Both of these attractions opened on July 15, 1893. Park visitors could buy membership cards that allowed them access to the park anytime, free use of the bath/exercise hall, instruction and training in boxing, fencing, wrestling, club swinging and swimming. They could also enjoy spots for Caledonian games, a bicycle track and a running/race track, and a trip to the park zoo.

The number of visitors increased due to the popularity of the new pool, so in 1895, the name of the park was changed from Twickenham Park to Natatorium Park, as Natatorium is the Latin word for swimming pool. To the locals it was simply "Nat Park" or "the Nat."

Originally, the park had been called a trolley park because it was built to encourage citizens to ride the trolley. According to *Dear Old Nat...Spokane's Playground*, "…the park wasn't intended to make a profit at all. It was intended to generate profits for the trolleys whose coffers clinked with the coins of eager picnickers. In this way, Nat Park was a true trolley park."

Entertainment was an integral part of Natatorium Park's attraction to visitors. The Lendor Brothers Acrobats, "America's Greatest Acrobats"; Mademoiselle Gertrude Pianka and her performing Den of Lions; "The Great Matthews on his Spiral Tower," from San Francisco; and Buffalo Bill's Wild West Show were among the

The Midway at Natatorium Park, 1918. (Courtesy of NWMAC, L89-141)

The Jack Rabbit rollercoaster, 1938. (Courtesy of NWMAC, L87-1.16680-39)

performers that would come to the park in those first years. Evenings were usually capped off with fireworks that would thrill the crowds. Entertainment took on a new twist, however, when the first moving picture show came to Natatorium Park in June of 1899. It was Ed M. Bayliss' "electrical production of *The Battle of Manila*."

The entertainment and interesting shows were not welcomed by all, however. An article in the *Saturday Spectator* said the park "is rapidly degenerating into a resort for the ragtag and bobtail class. The better class, which frequented the place last summer and during previous seasons, being conspicuous by their absence. Not only will it be run by a free and easy place in the future, where the women of the town will have the same welcome and be given the same privileges as the first ladies of the city, but it was the intention of the Washington Water Power Company to permit a shady show to have full swing in the park during the summer. A man by the name of Shields, a general fakir and dirty show manager…is coming as the manager of this part of the park attraction."

Despite the outcries of a few, the park continued to be an endless source of recreation and delight. Rides became the newest demand by park patrons. On May 30, 1905, the first roller coaster, the Figure 8, also called the Scenic Railway, made its debut. Traveling at the same ten miles-per-hour speed as the trolley that brought people to the park, the ride was a huge thrill for visitors.

In 1907, Washington Water Power leased the park to Mr. Audley Ingersoll, whose father managed several large amusement parks in Pittsburgh, Des Moines and other large cities on the East Coast. The opening day of the 1907 season was a big event, as Ingersoll unveiled a park that focused less on athletic adventures and more on amusement park thrills. One of the publicized events was a hot air balloon ascension followed by a parachute drop from the balloon. The daredevil performing the stunt was a gentleman named Professor S. A Cokley. Unfortunately, during the spectacle, Cokley got tangled up in his parachute and landed rather ungracefully in the Spokane River, where the current swept him over a mile downstream. Luckily, he was rescued from the water and was no worse for wear. The new park certainly made an impression on the visitors.

In addition to the balloon spectacle, there were several new rides that captivated people's attention: The Circle Swing (aka Flying Airship), Shoot the Chutes, House of Trouble, Darkness and Dawn, Ye Old Mill, Foolish House, the Ferris Wheel and many more.

Interior of Natatorium Park swimming pool, ca. 1920. (Courtesy of NWMAC, L89-282)

A $20,000 dance pavilion with 1,000 incandescent lights had been added to the facilities, accommodating 1,500 couples and an orchestra of twelve musicians. Ice cream soda stands and a candy store provided plenty of delicious treats. The swimming pool had new springboards, swings, Roman Rings, a high dive and pedestals. The changes were fascinating, but some people found them too garish for the park, leading them to nickname it "Ingersoll's Coney Island" after the New York amusement park.

Behind the scenes, problems plagued the park. In June of 1907, a bear cub and a coyote escaped from the zoo; Ingersoll hired non-union workers, which caused Spokane's Central Labor Union to get involved in the situation; William Wardell, an "aeronaut," nearly died when he plummeted from the sky during a balloon stunt; a man shot his estranged wife in the neck with a .38 caliber pistol after he found her dancing with another man in the park's dance pavilion. He then shot himself. Amazingly, both of them survived. (The marriage, however, did not!). Despite the problems, the park continued to draw large crowds, which were anxious to see all it had to offer.

All that it had to offer came at a high price though, which caused financial problems for Ingersoll. In 1909, after two years of leasing the park from Washington Water Power, his lease was terminated and the power company again managed the park.

Just as Ingersoll had made changes at the park, Washington Water Power thought the best way to spark an interest and, therefore, ensure the highest number of visitors possible, was to give the park a new image. Gone was the carnival feel. "It is understood that the hurdy-gurdy, bally-ho, circus methods of conducting the summer resort are to be done away with," said park manager John W. Pace, in the February 25, 1909 *Spokane Daily Chronicle*. The smaller fairground-like buildings that Ingersoll had erected were torn down to make room for more flower-bed displays, a sewer system was installed and the grounds were refurbished. In order to pay for the pricey changes, 1909 was the first year there was a daily admission fee to the park (previously, weekday admission

A group of Kinman University students at Natatorium Park Plunge, 1938. (Courtesy of NWMAC, L87-1.14154-38)

had been free). For ten cents, visitors were granted entrance through a new admission gate.

With less emphasis on the amusement park, swimming once again became the popular draw for the park. In 1909 "the plunge," as the swimming pool was called, was rebuilt and boasted a 500,000-gallon capacity tank in which people swam. (In 1905, the pool had been enclosed in a dome-shaped wooden superstructure three to four stories tall, for year-round use). To heat the large pool, 319 tons of coal were used in one season. Swimmers changed into park-issued swimsuits in one of the 226 dressing rooms. Men wore wool and cotton one piece suits "with a short skirt," while women wore the "conventional style" suits. After each use, suits were sanitized in mercury bichloride. One strict rule of the pool was that "forcing attention on women bathers" was forbidden. No children were able to enjoy the new pool the summer of 1909 because all children were banned from the park due to an outbreak of Scarlet Fever.

By 1913, more people began driving to the park, which meant less money was made by the trolleys. They had been the original reason the park was opened — to increase trolley revenue. In 1913, there was talk by Washington Water Power of closing the park because they no longer needed to increase revenue on the trolley lines. There was an outcry from the public, however, and the park was kept open by Washington Water Power for an additional sixteen years, during which time the attendance stayed very high.

Due to fewer trolley riders, two rail companies, Jay P. Graves' Spokane Traction Company and Washington Water Power rails, merged into Spokane United Railway (SUR) to survive financially. They were still losing thousands of dollars per month though, so, in March of 1929, they had to sell the park. In April 1929, Louis Vogel (son-in-law of Charles Looff, who built the Looff Carousel, which is now in Riverfront Park) bought the park for $137,500.

Despite the financial strain of the Depression, Vogel was able to keep the park a popular destination. People

1921 Laundrymen's Picnic at Natatorium Park, outside of the Plunge. (Courtesy of NWMAC, L87-1-20129-21)

were footloose and fancy-free inside the park, checking their worries at the entrance gate. During this time, Vogel continued to make changes in order to keep the people interested. A geyser that shot forty feet into the air was brought back in 1935, and there were tropical trees planted, including lemon, orange, grapefruit, fig, date and palm trees. This all came at a cost though, and the admission price for the park went up from ten cents to twenty-five cents for ladies, and fifty cents for "gents."

Spokane's love for Natatorium was not dampened by the increased cost. Dances would draw 3,000 to 5,000 people. In 1941, under the weight of 5,000 people who came to dance to the Kay Kayser Band, the floor collapsed. (No one was injured, and the floor was quickly repaired.) These dances were a form of escape during the war years, during which time crowds remained large. According to *Dear Old Nat...Spokane's Playground,* "Though regrettable, war was good for business at Nat where a spirit of celebration and camaraderie persisted."

Natatorium Park was well-loved not just by the citizens of Spokane, but by the well-known names it drew from nationwide: the Grand Ol' Opry and Fats Domino performed there, as did Glenn Miller and Phil Harris, and Babe Ruth hit one out of the Natatorium ballpark.

With an increase in the number of city parks and public swimming pools, Natatorium's pool began to dwindle in popularity. In the 1950s, Vogel decided to turn the pool into a seal display. Children from around the city would buy fish to feed to the seals during their performances.

The park once again changed ownership when the El Katif Shrine Temple purchased the land in 1962 and closed the park, with the intent of refurbishing the grounds and reopening it. In 1964, they signed a six-year lease to operate a public amusement park, and Natatorium Park was open once again.

Fewer crowds then had been expected came back to the park, as it was easier to travel farther away from the city by then, and people were choosing to go out of town for their recreation. As a result, 1967 was the last season for the park. When the gate was closed for the final time, items were sold for souvenirs and The Jack Rabbit, the most popular roller coaster, was burned to the ground. The Shrine kept the land, and developers turned part of it into a mobile home park called "Sans Souci West."

Although the gates to Natatorium Park have long since closed for the final time, in the hearts of those that lived, laughed and loved there, it will forever be alive in their memories as one of the best parts of life in Spokane. ●

All That Can Be Obtained

Louis Davenport's Magnificent Hotel

THERE WAS NO GRAND HOTEL WITH CRISP LINENS, FINE CHINA, ELEGANT surroundings and top-of-the-line customer service to which Louis Davenport could check in when he arrived in Spokane Falls in the spring of 1889. Such a luxury would not entice and delight visitors for another twenty-five years. In the years in between, though, Davenport would be hard at work learning about hospitality, customer service and how to create *the* place in town in which to see and be seen.

When he first arrived in Spokane Falls, Davenport took a job with his uncle, Elijah Davenport, who had been living in Spokane Falls for a while, running restaurants and rudimentary hotels. Louis took a job at his uncle's restaurant, Pride of Spokane, and he eventually took over the restaurant, just days before the Great Fire of 1889. When the flames of the fire swept through downtown Spokane Falls, there were few buildings, businesses or lives not affected by the fire. While despair may have made some think, "It's over, this is the end," this was not the case for Davenport. Not one to be kept down, he bounced back to work on August 6, 1889, just two days after the fire, and began the process of rebuilding his business and getting a restaurant up and running again. The surroundings

1922 portrait of Louis Davenport. (Courtesy of NWMAC, L87-1.21145-22)

The Davenport Hotel and Davenport's Restaurant, 1914. (Courtesy of NWMAC, L87-1-10592x-14)

may not have been as nice as the Pride of Spokane had been, and there may have been a smoky and sooty stench in the air, but Davenport knew people still had to eat, so they might as well eat at his restaurant. He put an ad in the August 6, 1889 *Spokane Falls Review*, stating, "L.M. Davenport. Formerly proprietor of the Pride of Spokane Restaurant is now ready for business at 318½ Sprague Street. Back of the Review Office."

Though legend has it that Davenport's restaurant, opened after the great fire, became the cornerstone restaurant of The Davenport Hotel, it appears that it and the restaurant he opened immediately after the fire may not be one in the same; rather, there was likely another short-lived restaurant there first. This theory is supported by an entry in *Spokane's Legendary Davenport Hotel,* by Tony Bamonte and Suzanne Schaeffer Bamonte. "According to an interview with Davenport, which appeared in the December 8, 1895 edition of the *Spokesman-Review*, that very day was the sixth anniversary of the opening of his restaurant in its temporary 'tent' location. This, no doubt, was referring to his Waffle Foundry. Because of the emphasis given to that date as his well-known restaurant's point of inception, it appears the restaurant he opened immediately after the fire did not continue for a long period of time."

Though his interim restaurant may have folded, or simply changed names, Davenport's restaurant was a huge success, drawing hungry patrons from all over the area. They were hungry not just for the food that was served, but also hungry for the excellent service and the air of excitement that surrounded the restaurant. It became a hub of social activity, the place to see and be seen. The tented restaurant could only last so long, not just because of growing popularity and crowd size, but also because of the rough weather doled out in Spokane Falls' winters. A more substantial structure was needed.

As the city rebuilt from the fire, businesses found new homes tucked into big brick buildings in the heart of downtown Spokane. One of those buildings, located on West Sprague, had the words "Davenport's Restaurant" painted across the top. The restaurant opened in its new, "permanent" location on July 10, 1890.

Immediately, it was a beloved and revered restaurant. The *Spokane Falls Review* gave its endorsement of the restaurant in its July 13, 1890 edition. "One of the requisites to life's contentment, and which affords the general happiness, is to enjoy our daily repasts amid pleasant surroundings, together with an inviting cleanliness and a good service…An establishment possessing these features has been a long felt want in this city, the supplying of

The Davenport Hotel Restaurant, Sprague Avenue entrance, ca. 1914,. (Courtesy of Washington State Digital Archives)

The Davenport Restaurant interior, ca. 1914. (Courtesy of Washington State Digital Archives)

which many futile attempts have been made by various caterers, but only until Thursday last was it shown that the proper idea had finally been grasped, and that by L.M. Davenport, who opened to the public for the first time a restaurant managed in accordance to fill this popular demand."

Though it was considered a "permanent" location, permanent is a funny word when it comes to buildings in a frontier city. Permanence faded in 1893, when a fire hit the restaurant, destroying most of it. Davenport had proven once that flames could not keep him down, and he was about to prove so again. Rebuilding and remodeling his restaurant, making it larger and grander than before, Davenport displayed a spirit of persistence and entrepreneurial determination that inspired the community and earned their respect and support.

The financial strength that allowed Davenport to continue to expand was a result of his steady and healthy business. People flocked to Davenport's Restaurant for many reasons, and once they experienced it, the unique offerings on the menu kept people coming back for more. "Ox Tongue with Cream Sauce, Antelope Chops with Jelly Sauce, Lobster Cutlets ala Hollandaise and Frog Legs Any Style" were just some of the exotic offerings on the menu.

In 1900, when another remodel and expansion of the restaurant was slated, Davenport hired a young architect named Kirtland K.Cutter to take on the task. Cutter fashioned the exterior of the restaurant in a Mission style, which made the restaurant even more of a source of interest both to those in the city and visiting from afar. According to *Spokane's Legendary Davenport Hotel,* "The exterior Mission style design was unique and somewhat

Musicians up in the restaurant balcony performed for diners in The Davenport Restaurant. (Courtesy of Washington State Digital Archives)

of a novelty amidst the business sections' more conservative architecture; the white stucco provided an eye-catching contrast to the surrounding brick and granite structures."

Three years after the 1900 remodel, Davenport again expanded, this time purchasing the building in which his restaurant was located, as well as the two connecting buildings. This purchase, which greatly expanded his territory, was not an inexpensive one. It cost more than $120,000, which equates to roughly $3.3 million in today's economy. Part of the new building was slated to hold apartments, which was Davenport's first foray into the world of lodging. He was looking for long-term renters rather than hospitality or short-term renters as explained in the November 9, 1903, *Spokesman-Review*, where it was noted that the apartments were to be "leased unfurnished for stated intervals…and not rented month to month."

While not yet officially in the hotel business, Davenport had plans for every inch of his new property, including an envisioned greenhouse built atop the restaurant, and a modern wine cellar built below it.

Where there is food and drinking, dancing naturally

Women outside of The Davenport. (Courtesy of NWR, SPL)

The Davenport Hotel Lobby, on a postcard. (Courtesy of NWMAC, L83-126-55)

follows, so it was natural that Davenport's next improvement to his property was to build a ballroom fit for dancing and celebrating in opulent elegance. What was unusual was the incredible beauty and design of the ballroom, which came to be known as the Hall of Doges. The domed-ceiling room cost $30,000 and was a lavish masterpiece with hand-painted relief work found throughout. Thirty-six stunning pillars held up the domed ceiling, and walking through the arched pillars led to a twenty-foot-wide promenade that surrounded it on all sides.

Wanting to ensure his patrons in the restaurant below were not bothered by the raucous sounds of stomping feet and riotous noises, Davenport had the floor built on steel pillars, which absorbed any sounds, betraying the fact that there was a wild celebration taking place above the heads of the patrons as they dined on their fine foods.

With the restaurant and ballroom rapidly becoming the social center of Spokane Falls, Davenport wanted to spend more and more time at his establishment. This became easier to do when, not long after the ballroom was built, Davenport requested Cutter design an apartment for him in the building. "It had large, arched leaded-glass windows facing on Sprague and Post, oak paneling and a hammered copper fireplace as the center of focus of the living room," is the description in *Spokane's Legendary Davenport Hotel.* The apartment, as well as a small dining room within the main restaurant, called The Peacock Room, was done in the Art Nouveau style, which was a change from architectural styles found in Spokane at that time.

Additions to the building included The Orange Bower, which was a men's bar that opened in 1904. When prohibition came to Spokane, it was converted into a soda fountain, presumably no longer just for men.

Changes weren't just happening in Davenport's business, but in his personal life as well. On August 6, 1906, Louis Davenport married Miss Verus E. Smith, sister of Mrs. M.C. Pennington of Spokane. Smith had lived with her sister for five years after moving to Spokane from Portland, before marrying. It was in the Art Nouveau apartment above Louis Davenport's restaurant and property that the newlyweds lived. In June 1907, the

A banquet in The Davenport Hotel's Hall of Doges, ca., 1914. (Courtesy of Washington State Digital Archives)

Davenport's first child, a son, was born.

With Davenport's restaurant inarguably the most elegant and popular spot in town, investors saw an opportunity to cash in on it. Knowing the city needed a fine hotel - not just a lodging hotel; rather, a grand and elegant hotel where people would gather and which would draw in visitors from out of town – the investors determined Davenport's Restaurant, and Louis Davenport's business knack were an essential part of the plan.

When approached by these businessmen about the idea of building a hotel on his property, Davenport didn't just nibble, he bit. According to *Spokane's Legendary Davenport Hotel,* "The exact agreement Davenport made with

Hotel patrons in the Davenport lobby. (Courtesy of NWMAC, L87-1.15827X-19)

Loading a car onto the second floor during the1915 Spokane Auto Show, held at The Davenport Hotel. (Courtesy of NWMAC, L87-1-11587x-15)

his backers is unknown, but as history indicates, he quickly became the controlling partner with an apparent complete buy-out option. Upon his immediate assumption of the role as key man, he personally directed all aspects of the hotel's construction, development and management."

One of the directions Davenport issued was to insist there be a rooftop garden. In order to accommodate that, the roof needed to be flat. Towers on the corners gave a more stylish look to the roof from the exterior, hiding the flat roof from view. Plans for the hotel indicated it would be twelve stories tall and built in a U-shape, guaranteeing every room had a window and outside view.

To purchase all of the property necessary for the hotel was $600,000, while the cost of construction was expected to be between $1.75 million and $2.2 million ($46 to $59 million in today's economy). That money would be divided amongst the many expenses. Marble was $50,000, interior paint cost $15,000, and tile used throughout the hotel totaled $25,000, while the plastering came in at a whopping $85,000. One of the most technologically advanced aspects of the hotel was an ice water system – unheard of in hotels at that time – that cost $25,000.

Throughout the city, excitement was building for completion of the hotel, and the newspaper followed the planning and construction phases closely. The October 11, 1908 edition of the *Spokesman-Review* reported, "The building will have a lobby of forty-six by ninety feet with fine mosaic floors and huge terra cotta pillars forming arches set at the outer end. These arches will support a balcony thirty feet wide, extending all the way around the lobby and over this will be a huge dome of art glass, thirty-five feet above the lobby floor. All of the rooms in the

The Davenport Hotel's Sprague Avenue entrance, 1927. (Courtesy of NWMAC, L87-1.33052-27)

building will have outside light and a private bath."

The people of Spokane were eager for the hotel to open. They viewed it not just as a lodging house, nor just a place to bunk for the night. The Davenport Hotel was going to bring Spokane on par with other cities in the west, making it known to one and all that this was a city of sophistication, class and elegance, and that it was on the rise and a hub of business and culture.

In September 1914, the wait was over, and the hotel was ready for business. Floors were shined, linens pressed, ties straightened, aprons smoothed down, and with a fling of the door, the hotel was open, ready to serve the guests, as well as the people of Spokane.

The September 18, 1914, edition of the *Spokesman-Review* noted of the opening, "The spirit of the occasion, however, did not lie in the formal part of the observances, but in the open admiration with which Spokane at large regarded its latest acquisition."

When it first opened, there were 405 rooms in the hotel. The hotel, as with Davenport's restaurant, would undergo many additions and expansions over the years. In 1917, fifty-three more rooms were added, and then another eighty rooms were added when an eleven-story addition was built onto a portion of the hotel that was originally only three stories high.

Atop of the hotel was a rooftop garden, which was an expansion of Davenport's original dream to have a rooftop greenhouse above his restaurant. The rooftop garden had an "indoor/outdoor golf course," something

Formal dinner in The Davenport Hotel's Hall of Doges, ca. 1918. (Courtesy of NWMAC, L87-1-2379-10)

that was popular on the roofs of New York hotels. The area included a small putting green and a tee for driving. Considering the elevated location, the entire area was wisely enclosed with netting to keep golf balls from going over the edge.

Rooftop garden, putting green, incredible service and stunning beauty – the Davenport Hotel had it all, and the people of Spokane embraced it whole-heartedly. Word spread around the country about the incredible hotel in Spokane, Washington. A year after opening, the Davenport was featured in *The Hotel Monthly* with a description that let its entire readership know exactly how impressive of a hotel it was. "The lobby of the Davenport Hotel is an institution. We do not have words to adequately describe it…Travelers from all over the world recognize at first glance upon entering the lobby of the hotel a 'something different.' There is an individuality expressed that compels admiration."

"In conversation with Mr. Davenport, regarding his ideal in the matter of hotel he said in substance: 'I consider first utility, second life, third beauty. I place utility first, for the reason that service is the keynote of successful hotel keeping. I put life next because I look upon this structure and its mission as an investment for all time. I consider beauty after the other qualities, for the reason that, when you have accomplished the useful and the lasting, it is largely a matter of taste to produce the harmonies – the restful, relaxing home-like atmosphere. And when you get that 'home' feeling in the hotel, you get all that can be obtained.'"

Through years of fine-tuning his trade, attending to detail and serving the people of Spokane, Louis Davenport indeed got all that could be attained, and so, too, did the people of Spokane. They got an elegant hotel, a legendary citizen and a rich lineage of history that continues to this day in the hotel that Spokane loves so much. ●

22

There's Something About A Soldier

Gonzaga University's Military History

Cadets 1st year, 1899-1900. (Courtesy of Gonzaga University, University Archives & Special Collections (USAC))

THE U.S. ARMY HAD AN ADVERTISING CAMPAIGN IN THE 1970s WITH THE catchphrase "There's something about a soldier!" Maybe it should have been changed to "There's something about a Gonzaga soldier." For over 114 years, Gonzaga University, in Spokane, has had a proud and strong connection to the military, producing some of the finest soldiers and military men and women around.

It all started back in 1899, when Fr. George de la Motte became the seventh president of Gonzaga. He was said to have been, "reared as an 'army brat', French style. He carried with him to the grave a soldierly bearing and a deep appreciation for the military virtues," according to *Gonzaga University: Seventy-five Years, 1887-1962,* written by Wilfred P. Schoenberg, S.J.

One of Fr. de la Motte's prefects was a student named James Kennelly, who had attended Gonzaga High School in Washington D.C., which was known for its cadet corps. "It would be difficult to decide which of these two, the president or the prefect, took the initiative in proposing a military at Gonzaga," wrote Schoenberg. Perhaps it was neither one above the other, but their combined interest and passion for the military that inspired Fr. de la Motte to reach out to retired Capt. Gerhard Luhn for a meeting to discuss the potential of offering military discipline and courses for the students.

Capt. Luhn and Fr. de la Motte met on November 21, 1899. Luhn, who had been stationed at forty different army posts throughout his career, was well known by those in the Jesuit community, according to Schoenberg. "Capt. Luhn was a familiar figure to many Gonzaga Jesuits. With his great white flowing beard, like an Old Testament prophet, he was easily recognized in any congregation from the altar, as well as from the choir loft,

Capt. Luhn leads the cadets, 1903. (Courtesy of Gonzaga University, USAC)

and his many gracious benefactions connecting with Masses on army posts had placed him in the category of a very special friend of the priests."

It was proposed that Capt. Luhn direct a cadet program — an offer he accepted with so much enthusiasm that he didn't waste any time getting started, enrolling students that very day. "He explained to them the end and aim of the corps and what was to be expected from each member. He then proceeded to enlist or enroll members. There were about sixty-five who signed their name(s). This was all done with solemnity and ceremony in order to make an impression on the boys. After the enrollment, Capt. Luhn lined them up in the yard and gave some instructions in drilling." Beginning that day, Capt. Luhn was solely responsible for running the program until he resigned, six years later, in 1905.

Both Fr. de la Motte and Capt. Luhn felt it was important for the corps to be officially recognized by the government, so they filed an application with the United States War Department. The application was accepted and Gonzaga's military department was officially established on January 9, 1900.

There were eighty cadets in two companies: A and B. Guns arrived in mid-May, but some of the cadets were too small to shoulder them. Much to the embarrassment of these young chaps, they were supplied with wooden guns to use during the drill, a fate far more hurtful to their pride than the heavy guns ever could have been to their small shoulders and muscles.

A statement in the Gonzaga end of the year catalogue for 1899-1900 promoted the cadet program, saying, "A cadet corps similar in aim, management and equipment to the military companies existing in many of the best colleges and academics of the country, is an important addition to the list of societies at Gonzaga College."

"In the casual days before the two great World Wars, the Fathers didn't take military training as a serious

Commissioned and non-commissioned officers, 1903. (Courtesy of Gonzaga University, USAC)

commitment…they apparently looked upon it as a kind of disciplinary program for gentleman boys," wrote Schoenberg. This observation was apparent to Maj. H.E. Tutherly, 11th Cavalry, who was sent to inspect the cadets. He wrote a scathing report, dated June 4, 1902, which was sent to the Inspector General:

"The majority of the students are too young to participate in military instruction such as is contemplated to be given under the supervision of an officer detailed by the War Department. I should judge that there were only about fifty students of an age suitable for drill," he wrote. "While the president and authorities seem very much interested to have these boys drill, take an interest in it, and do the best they can to promote it, I hardly think such exercises should be conducted under government supervision…While all this (drill) is done with good intention on the part of the authorities, I think it is a military farce, and worse for the service than to have no drill at all. I am therefore compelled to recommend that the officer be relieved from duty here, and the arms turned in. Capt. Luhn, the retired officer in charge of the military department, commanded the battalion drill dressed in obsolete uniform – braided blouse and chasseur cap – not in the present form of a captain of Infantry, and his whole uniform was soiled and worn beyond what an officer is suitable to appear in at a ceremony."

Such harsh words were no doubt unwelcome by Capt. Luhn, who, though he had a passion for the military, did not get much support from the school. He was provided housing, but no pay for his services. Despite multiple requests on his part to be paid for his services, the school denied it, reasoning the government should pay for his services, as he was preparing the young men for service in the military. Though he had a passion for his work, the lack of pay may have contributed to his decision to leave the school, and Spokane, in 1905, and move to St. Louis.

When Capt. Luhn left, the school had difficulty finding a replacement, so they picked a recent graduate, named Hugh Winder, who had become a captain in the cadet program. The War Department notified the school it could hire Winder, but the government would no longer officially recognize the program. At a loss of what to do without another instructor, they hired Winder and lost their official standing and, therefore, financial support of the government. As a result, the government wanted their supplies – guns, uniforms and etc. – returned to them, or purchased. The school stalled for over two years as they tried to raise enough money to pay for their supplies. Then, in the nick of time, they hired Capt. Edmund Butts, a member of the U.S. Army attached to Ft. George Wright, to take over the program. This allowed them to once again be officially recognized by the government and, therefore, cancelled their debt.

Capt. Butts' reign did not last long. In 1908, Gonzaga's then-president, Fr. Herman Goller, called for the dissolution of the cadet program after teachers complained that the amount of drill time required by the War Department interfered with the studies of the students.

An interest in a military program at Gonzaga resurfaced in1917, a few years after WWI broke out. Young men on campus were eager to enlist in the Army, but they knew Gonzaga's president, Fr. James Brogan, wanted to keep them in school as long as possible. As a compromise, Fr. Brogan persuaded officers from Ft. George Wright to provide drill instructors who formed a full company that would practice drills beginning April 23, 1917.

This whet the whistle of those young men who were eager to serve, but it far from satiated their hunger to be a part of the military glory and action. Many young men wanted to contribute to the war effort, and Gonzaga's campus began hemorrhaging students during the summer of 1917 when, free from school, they decided to enlist.

Other colleges were facing a similar problem, but a potential solution was found in the organization of the Student Army Training Corps (SATC). In a letter from Secretary of War Newton D. Baker, he explained that the SATC "aims to accomplish a two-fold object: first, to develop as a great military asset the large body of young men in colleges; and second, to prevent unnecessary and wasteful depletion of the colleges through indiscriminate volunteering by offering to the students a definite and immediate military status."

The object of the SATC was to allow men between the ages of 18 and 21 to continue their schooling and at the same time, prepare themselves for the nation's service.

An article in the May 21, 1918, *Spokane Chronicle* declared, "U.S. will take over Gonzaga: Gonzaga is to be, in effect, a military school next year under the direction of the government. The students at the university, between the ages of 18 and 21 years of age will be given military training by the government. All cadets will have the standing of enlisted men in the United States Army and will be subject to the call of the government at any time."

"The details of the arrangement are yet to come from Washington D.C.," Fr. Reid, who worked on the program, shared with the paper. "The change is assured, however. We will have in effect a military post here."

An article in the July 16, 1918, *Spokane Chronicle* stated that all Gonzaga students age 18 and older would spend summer vacation of 1919 at a student army training camp. "The boys enrolled in the student's army training corps will be enlisted for the duration of the war, with the understanding, however, that they will not be called to active duty until they reach draft age, unless urgent military reasons compel an earlier call."

The excitement about the SATC program and the meaning for the school was evident throughout the campus and city. Spokane was proud of the Gonzaga students who were embarking on a military career while at school.

Two days earlier, on July 14, 1918, U.S. Attorney Francis A. Garrecht was at Gonzaga to present a flag with 187 anchors and stars, representing the 187 Gonzaga students who had gone on to serve in the military, and said, "Gonzaga has taught her sons how to die well and her prayer is that in the moment of supreme test, none may falter. For while those in doing their bit for their country sacrifice their lives are not martyrs in the strict sense of the term, yet are they martyrs to duty, martyrs to their love of humanity..."

The SATC course of instruction consisted of fifty-three hours of instruction per week in military science and allied subjects with the curriculum resembling that of West Point.

Schools with any form of drill programs were instructed by the Secretary of War to send representatives to the Presidio in San Francisco for training during the summer of 1918. Select students from Gonzaga were sent to receive military training, so they could serve as military instructors at Gonzaga.

Fr. Brogan went as well, and met with the West Coast college presidents to learn the specifics of the SATC program. Students, age 18 and up, would be inducted on registration and would receive, besides uniforms

President Truman presents ROTC colors, 1950. (Courtesy of Gonzaga University, USAC)

and equipment, the pay of a private, which was $30. They would also receive housing and sustenance, ranging between one and two dollars per day.

While the interest in SATC was bountiful, supplies were not. Beds and bedding for up to forty students had to be borrowed from Ft. George Wright until additional supplies could be delivered by the Army.

The September 28, 1918, *Spokane Chronicle* reported, "At 9 a.m. Tuesday morning, simultaneously with 500 similar institutions all across the country, Gonzaga, which volunteered its facilities for a government military school, will be officially sworn into the federal service." A message from President Woodrow Wilson was read at all of the schools.

Less than a month after school began, the SATC faced its first battle, though it was not of the war variety; rather, they battled the Spanish Flu, which hit Gonzaga and Spokane quite hard. Beginning October 18, 1918, SATC students were forbidden to attend theaters, moving picture shows or any other places of amusement as precaution against the Spanish Flu. The school threatened expulsion as a penalty for violation of the rule. Though attempts were made to keep students from contracting the illness, sixty members of Gonzaga's SATC became ill.

The SATC began to feel rumbles of demise when on November 27, 1918, it was reported in the *Spokane Chronicle*, "The SATC at Gonzaga will be demobilized in the very near future according to war department inspectors…The University of Nebraska has received orders from the war department to demobilize their SATC immediately."

U.S. Victory Ship, Gonzaga Victory, 1945. (Courtesy of Gonzaga University, USAC)

By December 1918, the SATC was disbanded. WWI was over, and despite the enthusiasm and joy that brought, the young men had never been able to get the program up and running due to the flu epidemic that had caused them to cancel drills and instructions, and that was disheartening for them.

Military training at Gonzaga would not resurface again for nearly twenty years, but when it did, it was the beginning of a continual military presence on campus. In December 1938, President Franklin D. Roosevelt authorized the use of $100,000 of government funds to train college students as airplane pilots, after the passing of the Civil Aeronautics Act, which focused on the concern of the lack of pilots, both for military and private transportation purposes. The program was set up to train college students as airplane pilots and flight teachers, and to provide refresher courses for licensed pilots. With fears of war simmering ever stronger though, the objective soon transitioned to an emergency defense measure.

Gonzaga president, Fr. Leo Robinson, offered Gonzaga's facilities for government use in these military training programs. He wrote to the Civil Aeronautics Authority expressing a desire for Gonzaga to become a training center for young aviators. "I am deeply interested, and want to do all within my power to make our institution one of the many throughout the United States for the training of 20,000 young flyers next year. I am confident we can handle the courses required, and that Spokane has skilled aviators for the actual flying instruction."

Seventy-five men began training July 1, 1942, at Gonzaga. The men were trained as Army flying specialists and were housed at Gonzaga at the expense of the Army. It wasn't just students who participated; the program was open to men ages 18 to 37 who could pass the CAA mental and physical tests. The classes they took at

Members of the V-5, Navy officer training program at Gonzaga, 1945. (Courtesy of Gonzaga University, USAC)

Gonzaga included meteorology, navigation and civil air regulations, mathematics, physics, military science, drill and physical exercise. Each course lasted two months. Six teachers were added to the Gonzaga staff to teach the extra classes and students.

In March 1942, noticeable numbers of teachers and students had left campus to join the war effort in Europe. Their spaces were quickly filled with new arrivals. With Gonzaga's military connections to the land and air, it was no surprise that the sea was next, as witnessed by the arrival of Naval cadets in 1942. Lt. Com. Lyle L. Morris was the commanding officer of the Gonzaga Navy unit. Students took educational courses at Gonzaga while preparing to join the Navy. The program only lasted for two years but made quite the impact on the school.

The July 6, 1943 *Spokesman-Review* reported, "At Gonzaga, DeSmet Hall has become a naval station. Each floor is a deck. The hospital is sickbay. Cadets log out to go ashore, which means to go on leave to the city, log in to return aboard, which means returning to the hall...In short, if they had a hammock and an ocean, they might be at sea for all the nautical atmosphere."

On June 6, 1945, Oregon Shipbuilding Corporation slid the United States Victory ship, S.S. Gonzaga Victory, into the Willamette River. "We are doubly proud to see this great ship go down the ways, bearing the proud name of Gonzaga," said Gonzaga president Fr. Francis E. Corkery. "Out there somewhere in her voyaging, this ship will cross the paths of 1,500 of Gonzaga's loyal sons, fighting the battle for freedom."

In its time, 686 men received training in Gonzaga's Navy's V-12 program, and 1,780 men were trained in its civil aeronautics war training program, which included the Navy V-5.

Members of the V-5, Navy officer training program at Gonzaga, 1945. (Courtesy of Gonzaga University, USAC)

The October 19, 1945 headline in the *Gonzaga Bulletin* declared "It's Anchors Aweigh as Navy Shoves Off; Bluejackets leave Gonzaga campus Monday, October 22." The Navy officer-training unit terminated that week with the departure from campus of 150 men who spent two years and four months in the program. Seventy of them were V-12 trainees, with remaining men in the V-5 flight-training program. The V-12s reported to the University of Washington's Naval ROTC program on November 1, 1945, and the V-5 trainees reported to UC Berkley.

Wan Seegmiller, a member of the V-12, wrote this in the *Gonzaga Bulletin*. "The Army and Navy, long recognizing the need for capable educated officers, began to give the dwindling schools a transfusion of picked service personnel…Sounds of shouted commands and marching feet resounded over the peaceful campus, men in blue and cadets in tan filled the corridors and classrooms…But sometimes it was difficult to realize it was all part of the war. It seemed a far cry from the business of killing to be studying mathematics and history and English, but the men who were studying looked forward to a day when this training would furnish the leadership necessary to the winning of the war…The past is a tribute; the present, a reward; the future, a promise. Gonzaga looks at the past with pride; the present with thankfulness; the future with hope. Semper Fidelis."

With the pilot training program and the Navy gone, it was time for a new era in Gonzaga's military history. On February 4, 1947, in a letter to the adjunct general, Gonzaga submitted an application for the establishment of an Infantry unit of the Reserve Officers Training Corps (ROTC) at Gonzaga.

A return letter arrived from the Headquarters Sixth Army on April 23, 1947 stating that the War Department

Gonzaga's Loyola Guard, 1960. (Courtesy of Gonzaga University, USAC)

approved the application for the establishment of an Infantry ROTC unit for the 1947-1948 school year. The agreement, signed by Gonzaga president, Fr. Corkery, stated there had to be a minimum of 100 physically fit male students to maintain an ROTC program. Reaching the 100 mark was not a problem, as ROTC was required for all freshman and sophomore male students.

"In early September 1947, tons of ROTC equipment began to arrive," wrote Schoenberg. "Jeeps, 400 M-1 army rifles, side arms and so forth piled up behind the administration building, seemingly without end, an appalling contrast with the meagerness of equipment supplied to Gonzaga's last peace-time military program, the renowned cadets of 1900."

That first year, there were four companies made up of 250 students. They attended military classes three times per week and the entire corps attended marching drill from 11:10 until noon every Tuesday.

In 1949, ROTC was academically recognized as the department of military science and tactics; an ROTC band and rifle team were organized, and "thus, the unit became an established feature of campus life," wrote Schoenberg.

With the success of the ROTC Infantry unit, on December 19, 1950, an application for the establishment of an Ordnance unit was submitted by Fr. Corkery, and was quickly accepted.

In 1950, President Harry Truman came to campus to accept an honorary citation from Gonzaga (he opted for a citation over an honorary degree, saying he felt uncomfortable earning an honorary degree from any college other than the one at which he had studied.) The ROTC standard, with the university's coat of arms in the center, had

Distinguished military students, 1963-1964. The author's father, Jeff Thimsen, is third from the right. (Courtesy of Gonzaga University, USAC)

been designed and was expected to take six months to embroider and complete, but "providentially, the standard was finished a few days before President Truman's arrival."

President Truman agreed to present the colors to the ROTC unit during the ceremony for his honorary citation. This was the first time an American president had presented military colors to an ROTC unit. "I was highly interested and highly pleased at the work the ROTC did, and it gives me great pleasure to present this flag," said President Truman.

This description of the ROTC program, from 1959, explained to the public its goal and purpose: "The object of the ROTC program is to provide in peacetime, a yearly quota of highly qualified Second Lieutenants to meet, in the order stated, the annual needs of the Regular Army, the Active Army, the early deployed Reserve Component Troop Program units, and the annual and emergency leadership requirements of the Active Army and Reserve Components for replacement and expansion of the Army."

The popularity of the ROTC program continued to grow over the years, even as the program changed a bit. In the 1964-1965 school year, it became a volunteer program for the first two years. For those who were accepted into the program their junior year, an added incentive of 90 cents per day sweetened the deal and provided additional income. Many young men used this income to pay for their off-campus housing, which, due to a housing shortage, was required for most male students after their sophomore year. Another change came in 1976, when women were welcomed into the ROTC program.

Despite the changes over the years, one thing remained the same: Gonzaga's commitment to supporting the military, and producing educated and exemplary officers. It is true, there's something about a soldier – especially a Gonzaga soldier.

23

Where the Treetops Glisten

Bing Crosby And Spokane's White Christmas

"I'm dreaming of a white Christmas, just like the ones I used to know, where the treetops glisten and children listen to hear sleigh bells in the snow…"

– White Christmas

Bing Crosby and Rosemary Clooney in White Christmas.
(Courtesy of Gonzaga University, University Archives & Special Collections (USAC))

AN IMAGE OF AN IDYLLIC snow-covered town is surely painted in the mind of anyone who hears the words of the beloved Christmas song, *White Christmas*, made famous by Bing Crosby. With his clear, smooth voice, Bing paints a picture of a snow globe village in which many would like to live. If it sounds a bit like beautiful Spokane, it's no coincidence; Spokane happens to be the hometown of Bing.

Born May 3, 1903, in Tacoma, Washington, Harry Lollis Crosby (Bing) was named after his father as a consolation for not being the daughter for which his father hoped. He was the fourth of seven children born to parents Harry and Kate, with three older brothers, and eventually, two younger sisters and a younger brother.

After coming into tough financial times in Tacoma, Bing's father, Harry, found a job as a bookkeeper at Inland Brewery in Spokane. Harry moved east across the mountains to begin his job, while Kate, who was close to the end of a pregnancy, stayed behind with the children. He found a home for rent in an area of Spokane that was referred to as "Holy Land" because it was a dominantly Catholic neighborhood. With his father settled into the home and his job, and the new sibling born, the rest of Bing's family moved to Spokane in the summer of 1906.

They settled into a yellow, two-story house located at 303 E. Sinto Avenue. This was the first house the Crosbys lived in that had both indoor plumbing and electric lights. On the second floor were three bedrooms housing two children per room (the youngest child was not yet born). Bing and his older brother Edward (Ted) were put together in a room. Bing was outgoing and jovial, while his brother had a quiet, introverted personality. He found solace in writing, while Bing found his spot in singing and performing.

While the house was comfortable, they were not a wealthy family. Bing's father came from a well-to-do family and had been raised with servants and luxuries,

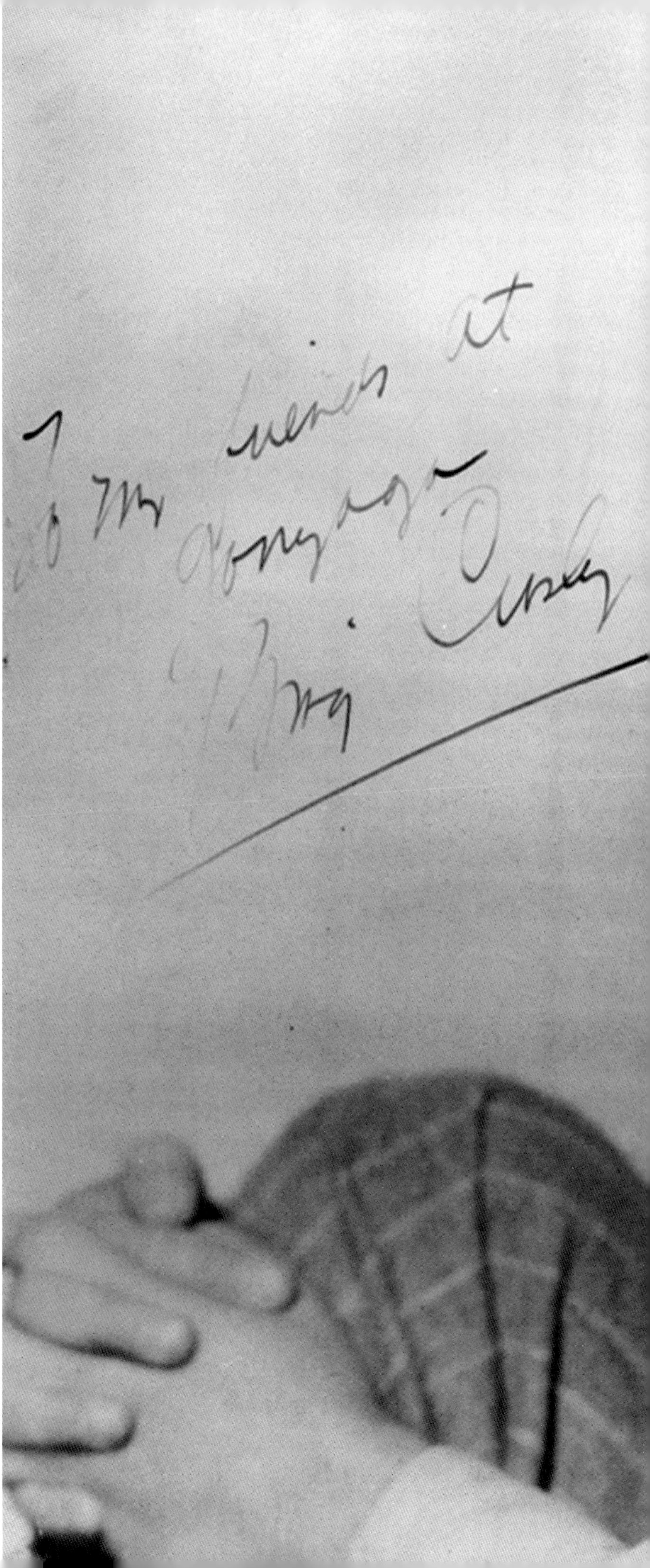

Bing Crosby portrait with pipe and autograph for GU. (Courtesy of Gonzaga University, USAC)

Bing Crosby, graduation day, 1920. (Courtesy of Gonzaga University, USAC)

never having to worry about finances. Without a strong work ethic, he dropped out of college during his senior year, taking odd jobs, mainly in bookkeeping. Harry had a tendency to spend ample amounts of money, despite the fact that he did not make much. This was a great source of stress for Bing's mother, who ran the family with an iron fist. One of the purchases Harry made was an Edison Phonograph on which music could be played. A member of a men's choir, Harry also played the mandolin and four-string guitar. His love of music was passed along to the entire family, but particularly to Bing. The family sang together on Sunday afternoons and evenings, gathering in their living room while Harry played the mandolin.

Bing's love of music was equally matched by his love for mischief. As a young boy, he and his group of friends called themselves the Boone Avenue gang. They got into a few scrapes, with Bing even being arrested on occasion for petty crimes.

According to author Gary Giddins' book, *Bing Crosby: A Pocketful of Dreams—the Early Years, 1903-1940*, "He was given more leeway than his brothers," his father conceded. "We were both so lenient that it's no wonder our other boys call Bing 'Mother's and Dad's pet.' Not that he was spoiled; he got his tannings. But he – well, he was different in a way. Made it sort of hard to spank him much."

When the summer of 1908 drew to an end, Bing joined his siblings at Webster Grade School, where, despite being only five years old, he was enrolled in first grade. Though there was not a kindergarten program available, Giddins suggests that Kate was "impatient to get him out from under her feet" and enrolled him in school despite his young age.

Kate was a strong-willed mother who always held high hopes for her children to attain "greatness." According to Giddins, "When Bing was young, Kate was the powerful center of his life. Her will ultimately helped drive him from Spokane, but he left with an armor of independence and raw nerve."

While the greatness of his talent was not yet know, his nickname, Bing, was emerging by 1910. The then seven year-old Harry would pester others to read him the *Bingville Bugle,* a parody newspaper, which was an insert in each Sunday issue of the *Spokesman-Review*. He would chant "Bing! Bing! Bing!" until someone would read it to him. The nickname stuck when a neighbor boy, Valentine Hobart, who also liked the *Bingville Bugle*, took to calling him "Bingo from Bingville." Others caught on, and it was shortened to Bing, which he was called by everyone – including his parents and siblings.

In 1911, the Crosbys built a family home, after having spent five years renting their house. The finished home was a two-story clapboard house located on East Sharp Avenue. That modest backyard and the surrounding neighborhood gave Bing plenty of space in which to run and play sports. He served as the captain of the

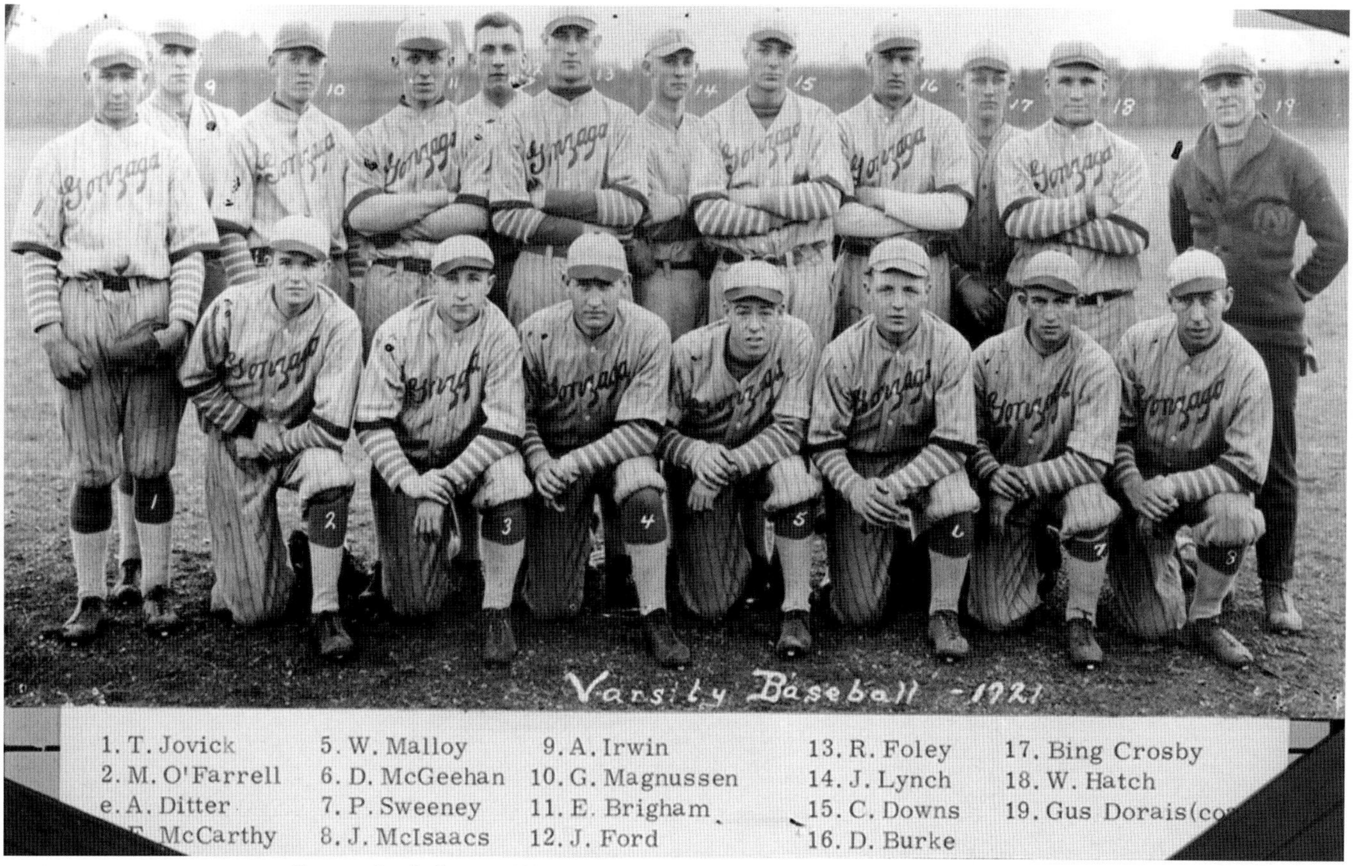

Gonzaga Baseball team, 1920. Bing Crosby is listed as "17." (Courtesy of Gonzaga University, USAC)

Dreadnoughts, his Junior Yard Association Midget Football League team, which had an impressive record. Later, at Gonzaga, he played third baseman on the school baseball team.

Bing also used his love of different sports to find himself employment. An avid swimmer who won seven medals in a citywide swimming contest, he worked as both a towel boy and a lifeguard at Mission Pool, starting in 1915. In 1916, he started caddying at local golf courses. Intrigued by the game, he scraped together some old clubs and learned how to play. This started a life-long love affair with golf, one that lasted literally until his dying day (on which he played eighteen holes of golf minutes before suffering a fatal heart attack).

His employment was not limited to the sports realm. The summer of 1917, Bing worked as a prop boy at the Auditorium, one of Spokane's most impressive theaters. It was there, while watching entertainer Al Jolson perform, that many think he first got the itch to perform publicly and professionally.

Bing also worked as a paperboy, delivering early morning editions of the *Spokesman-Review.* It was said that you could hear Bing coming, as he whistled and sang while he delivered the news. "Everyone who knew young Harry would speak of his constant singing and whistling that heralded his arrival," wrote Giddins. One of Bing's best friends from Gonzaga was Ray Flaherty, who later went on to play and coach in the NFL. Flaherty said of Bing, "He was always a happy kid and was always singing a song. Even though he was a little kid, he was singing. He just was full of music and he was a great whistler. He could really whistle....hell, he could sing like nobody else, sing and whistle. He had a hell of a whistle."

That whistling and singing was put to use when Bing, Flaherty and their friend, Francis Corkery (who later became a president of Gonzaga University) were the charter members of the Gonzaga Glee Club in 1914.

In 1920, Bing reached a milestone when he and fifty-one members of the High School Department of Gonzaga University graduated on June 9, 1920. Bing was one of two students from his class selected to speak at graduation, giving a speech entitled "The Purpose of Education."

The summer after graduation, before he started at Gonzaga University, proved to be a summer of fun for Bing and his good friend, Paul Teters. That summer they signed on to work as laborers on a farm in Cheney. From Spokane, it was a half-hour train ride and a two-dollar daily fare, so they planned on staying in Cheney the entire summer. Growing disillusioned with the work after two weeks, though, they abandoned their jobs, taking a train

Bing and Miss Spokane, 1950. (Courtesy of Gonzaga University, USAC)

Bing at a GU alumni event, 1951. (Courtesy of Gonzaga University, USAC)

to Portland where Bing's oldest brother, Everett, was working. Not able to find him immediately, they snuck onto a train headed for Los Angeles, but were caught and sent back to Portland on a cattle car. After getting arrested in Portland for sneaking out of a restaurant without paying for their meal, the boys were sent by Bing's Uncle George to work at a logging camp, operated by Bing's cousin.

While that original summer job did not work out, Bing found plenty of other ways to employ himself while in school. He worked part-time for his father's employer, Inland Brewery (which, because of prohibition, no longer produced beer, but pickles, among other things), as an office worker for local attorney Charles Albert, as a part-time night watchman for the Great Northern Railway, and as a janitor at Everyman's Club. He wanted to work hard because his parents were sacrificing in order to send him to school, and he didn't want to waste their money.

As a student at Gonzaga University, Bing was part of the group of students known as "townies." These were students who lived in town and did not reside at the school. As such, they were often looked down upon, and "townies" were not allowed on campus after 4:30 p.m. Despite his "townie" status, Bing's gentle and spirited personality won him many friends.

A total of eight years of Bing's life were spent at Gonzaga. After graduating from Webster Grade School, he attended four years at Gonzaga High School, and then another four years at Gonzaga University. Bing's mother was a devout Catholic, and his father converted to Catholicism in order to marry her. Kate's deep faith played a role in the way she and Harry raised their children. That, combined with his eight years spent around the Jesuit priests, gave Bing a solid background from which to draw when it came to developing his character, Fr. O'Malley, who appeared in both *Going My Way* and *The Bells of St. Mary's.*

Even with his wild streaks, Bing understood the importance of church and his faith. Long after the years of fame

Groundbreaking for the Crosby Library, 1956. (Courtesy of Gonzaga University, USAC)

and success began, he still attended mass every Sunday. In a radio interview with a priest, he said, "I get a great deal of consolation from my religion, Father, and I think it was firmly embedded in me somehow back there at Gonzaga High and Gonzaga University by the good Fathers."

His experience at Gonzaga not only strengthened his faith, but also his skills speaking and performing in public. "We had a lot of experience in public speaking and debating societies, standing on your feet and talking, and doing plays," he later said, "and if I have ability as an actor, that's where I got it."

He had plenty of chances to demonstrate that ability while in school. Among his performances, he played the role of Max, the crooked Mayor's man "Friday" in *Seven Keys to Baldpate,* and Ambrose Peale in the sophomore class play, *It Pays to Advertise.* An article in the April 1922 issue of the *Gonzaga Chronicle* stated, "Making the most of the play, replete with comical situations, the cast time and time again caused gales of laughter to sweep through the house. Harry Crosby, as the genial press agent Ambrose Peale kept the audience in a constant uproar."

More productions came over the next few years, but it was music that was taking up most of Bing's attention. In 1924, Bing had saved enough for a set of drums. Hearing of this, a North Central student named Alton Rinker asked Bing to join his music group. Though the other members were in high school, Bing was excited to be in a band and jumped at the chance. The band grew, added a few members, and named themselves the Musiclanders. They were fairly successful, holding steady gigs around Spokane until 1925, when most of the band members went off to college, except for Al and Bing. The two of them ended up developing an act and performing it at the Clemmer Theatre in downtown Spokane. This was a chance for Bing to showcase his voice and become a local fan-favorite.

Buoyed by their success, on October 15, 1925, at the age of 22, Bing and Al left for Los Angeles in a Model T, for what turned out to be an incredible journey. Within weeks of arriving in Los Angeles, they landed small gigs, which grew to larger ones, and soon they were on traveling circuits, making a name for themselves. Within a few months, they received an invitation to perform with one of the most famous entertainers of the time, Paul Whiteman, and his orchestra. In the fall of 1926, before they started touring with him, they traveled back

Bing and his second wife, Kathryn, on Gonzaga's campus, for graduation. (Courtesy of Gonzaga University, USAC)

to Spokane for a visit and to perform in front of their hometown. After this visit, it was an eleven-year stretch before Bing would return to Spokane. For the next three years, they toured with Whiteman developing a great reputation. It was just the tip of the iceberg.

Record deals, radio shows and eventually movie roles all came Bing's way, securing him as a Hollywood favorite. In 1937, he returned to Spokane to host a talent search called the Bing Crosby – Fox Theatre Talent Quest, which was sponsored by the *Spokesman-Review*. On October 21st, Bing visited Spokane and the four finalists. The winning male and female got to go to Hollywood with Bing for screen tests. In 1944, Bing himself was the winner of a contest of sorts; he won an Oscar for his role in *Going My Way*.

What the crooner's sweet, clear voice may be best known for, though, is the classic holiday song *White Christmas*. The song first premiered in Bing's 1942 film *Holiday Inn*. Not expected to be the breakout song of the movie, it was a huge hit, topping the charts and staying at number one for eleven weeks. It was so popular, a movie entitled *White Christmas*, based on the song and starring Bing, came out in 1954. This only increased Bing's popularity.

"There was a time, not so long ago, when it was truthfully said that no hour of the day or night, year after year, passed without the voice of Bing Crosby being heard somewhere on this earth," wrote Gilbert Seldes in *The Public Arts*.

Though Bing was a huge star by this time, he never forgot his home, Spokane, nor his deep gratitude toward the Jesuits and Gonzaga. Returning to Spokane on May 26, 1951, for homecoming weekend at Gonzaga University, the *Spokesman-Review* reported, "A rousing cheer from the several hundred alumni and their wives greeted Bing as he entered the union building. Stepping up on stage, he thanked them and recalled that he made his first public

Bing and his second wife, Kathryn, on campus, 1974. (Courtesy of Gonzaga University, USAC)

appearance from that very stage…Bing was nattily attired."

Bing's love for Gonzaga was not limited to appearances; he also supported the school financially and with other donations. He appeared as a spokesman on behalf of 3M Corporation, and persuaded them to donate a microfilm research center to Gonzaga. Proud of their famous alumnus, and appreciative of his generosity, a newspaper article proclaimed, "Regent Bing Crosby of Gonzaga University…will donate a Microfilm Research Center to Gonzaga." In all, Bing's donations to Gonzaga University were just shy of $1 million, demonstrating his devotion to the school and the Spokane community.

Walking on Gonzaga's campus, 1974. (Courtesy of Gonzaga University, USAC)

In the closing scene of *White Christmas*, Bing, dressed in a red velvet Santa suit, along with his similarly dressed co-stars Danny Kaye, Vera Ellen and Rosemary Clooney, sings the title song as a barn door opens, revealing a snow-globe scene of gently falling snowflakes. As Bing sings "*I'm dreaming of a white Christmas, just like the ones I used to know…,*" it is easy to imagine he was thinking back to Christmases-past in Spokane, where the snow would fall softly upon the streets and sidewalks of the place he loved, where he was born and raised. It is easy to image him singing the final verse of the song to the people of his great Spokane, *"And may all your Christmases be white…"* ●

24

Spokane's Masonic Temple

The Cornerstone of Spokane

President Theodore Roosevelt standing in Spokane Masonic Temple. (Courtesy of Library of Congress)

IT WAS JUST A PLOT OF LAND WHEN PRESIDENT THEODORE "TEDDY" ROOSEVELT turned the first shovelful of dirt in 1904, but now it holds one of the oldest and most beautiful buildings in all of Spokane. Tucked along a curving tree-lined boulevard, just west of downtown Spokane, the beautiful and historic Masonic Temple has reigned over Riverside Avenue for over 100 years.

Known as the "Cornerstone of Spokane," the Masonic Temple was where all of the social events in town took place. The nickname also refers to the cornerstone which was laid by President Theodore "Teddy" Roosevelt on October 6, 1904.

Crowds gathered outside of the Masonic Temple during the dedication ceremony, 1905. (Courtesy of NWMAC, L97-19.130)

The Masonic Temple's location was selected after the Masonic organization dreamed of constructing a building that would not only house all of their organizational events, but one which would also provide the people of Spokane with a public building to be used as a civic center.

"The building was designed for public service," said Gordon Vails, a member of the Masonic organization and a citizen associated with the building since 1948. "It has served that purpose, and it continues to serve that purpose today."

The eyes of the Masonic organization fell upon a piece of land located on Riverside Avenue, which was owned by James N. Glover, one of the founding fathers of Spokane. Negotiating a deal, the land was purchased for a reported $5,000. Building the actual temple, however, was a far pricier project.

With estimates for the cost of the building running at $42,500, the association knew they would have to gather donations to cover expenses. Several fundraisers were launched, including selling "subscription notes to the Masonic Temple Fund" and selling lifetime memberships to the Temple – to those within the Masonic organization only – for $180 each.

President Roosevelt, an avid fan of the Pacific Northwest and a Mason himself, returned to Spokane for the building's dedication in 1905. This new building, which was considered beautiful and a major addition to the city, did not stay untouched for long. Quickly outgrowing the space, a second portion was added to the building in 1925, creating the large building that now stands on Riverside Avenue.

According to Jon Wyss, former Vice President of the temple and an avid supporter of the building, when the second half of the building was added in 1925, it was accomplished by cutting off the end of the building at the point where a sphinx statue was located. The second half of the building was built over a massive basalt rock that could not be moved from the ground. As a result, the sidewalks running in front of the building are "vaulted sidewalks" that are hollow underneath, and the building connected to underground tunnels, which traveled south

The Masonic Temple's entry, along1108 W. Riverside Avenue, during construction. (Courtesy of NWR, SPL)

to the Steam Plant. The vacant areas were used for storage by rolling items on logs over the rock into the storage area. It is rumored that while building the second half of the current building, a worker fell into the hole near the rock and was killed.

For Spokane residents in the early 1900s, the Masonic Temple was one of the most popular venues in town, providing a place for socialization, entertainment and in some cases, information.

Wrestling matches, dinners, dances, proms, political debates, concerts and graduations from schools around Spokane took place in the various rooms of the Masonic Temple. The Lewis and Clark class of 1940 accepted their diplomas on a stage at the Masonic Temple. Kinman Business College, along with the nursing schools from St. Luke's and Deaconess, all held their graduations in the Masonic Temple as well.

"There wasn't an opera house, so the Masonic Temple was used," said Lawrence Morgan, a longtime affiliate of the Masonic organization, and a descendant of Dr. E. D. Olmstead, who was an organizational charter member of the Masonic Temple Association, as well as a mayor of Spokane. "It is the most beautiful building in Spokane!"

With a built-in projection booth in both the Auditorium and the Commandary, two of the most elegant rooms in the building, the Masonic Temple was the first place in Spokane to have a double theater. Dressing

The north side of the Masonic Temple building. (Courtesy of NWR, SPL)

in their finest – dresses, hats and gloves for the ladies, and suits and top hats for the men – Spokane residents would descend upon the Masonic Temple on Saturday evenings for a double feature of news and entertainment. News reels would play downstairs in the Auditorium, providing the latest news from far and wide, while upstairs in the Commandary, silent films would show on the stage screens.

As the newsreels and silent movies were projected onto the stages of each room, patrons occupied built-in wooden and leather theater seats that wrapped around the room from one side of the stage to the other. Hidden on the bottom of each chair was an attached metal rack specifically built to hold the top hats that gentleman would wear to the events.

Other popular events that drew crowds of Spokane residents to the Masonic Temple were boxing matches, which were known as "smokers." Boxing rings would be set up in the middle of the Auditorium, while guests gathered in the seats circling the room, and judges stationed themselves on the stage. As spectators made their way into the building, men were handed cigars to smoke throughout the evening.

Jan Danker, who served as a former events coordinator for the Masonic Temple, recalled the times she spent in the Auditorium from 1953 to 1954 as a cast member in the plays that Washington Water Power employees put on for the community. "We put on charity aid shows and held them once a year," she said. "We did *HMS Pinafore* and *French Can-Can Girls*."

Employees took advantage of the two-story tall stage with twenty-five hand-painted backdrops hanging on a pulley system ready to descend onto the stage, as well as an old theater crank handle lighting system, which was still in use as of 2004.

When opening night of the charity shows came, nearly every one of the 1,400 built-in seats, along with the 400 wooden theater chairs set up in the center of the room, were filled. "The water company was huge," said Danker. "Everyone who worked there brought family, friends and neighbors."

The wooden stage upon which performers danced and sang was unique at the time it was built because it had

The Auditorium in the Masonic Temple had seats with racks underneath them for top hats. (Courtesy of NWMAC, L87-1-28984-25)

pop-up flood lighting, as well as a hand crank stage that could be lowered to create an orchestra pit.

Below the stage, in the bowels of the building, were dressing rooms where the actors prepared for their entrance onto the large stage. Small rooms, complete with a toilet, a sink and a mirror, offered privacy while actors changed and prepared for their roles. After the performances, they were able to wash in one of two showers, which sit below and behind the stage area.

Even further below the underground dressing rooms, a hallway lead to a long dark tunnel, which opened into a cavernous sub-basement, designated as one of Spokane's bomb shelters during WWII. Fifty-five gallon drums, filled with water and food rations were still down there in the early 2000s, according to Wyss.

Hovering three floors above the Auditorium on the backside of the building was the beloved Blue Room. Teddy Roosevelt stood in this room to have his picture taken during the building's dedication ceremony. Standing with one hand on a table and staring straight ahead, Roosevelt was surrounded by the same furniture that occupied the room for over 100 years. Visitors looking for a unique experience could stand in the same spot where Roosevelt stood, and rest their hand on the table he is touching in the picture.

It was also possible for a visitor to stand on the original Davenport Hotel carpet while in the Blue Room. Louis Davenport was a strong supporter of the Masonic Temple, recognizing the role it played in the community as a civic center, so when re-carpeting the Davenport Hotel, he decided to donate the hotel's old, yet still excellently preserved carpet to the Blue Room at the Masonic Temple. Despite the numerous years and countless feet that shuffled, stepped and trod on the carpet, it remained in good condition, gracing the floor in all of its splendor.

The Blue Room once served as the main funeral parlor for the city of Spokane. Caskets were placed for viewing in a side room once visible from the Blue Room through a large picture window. A curtain behind the basket created a private area for families. Guests entered the Blue Room and streamed past the picture window in order to view the body and pay their last respects. Once everyone was seated, the casket would be closed and wheeled out a back door onto the stage of the Blue Room so that the service could be conducted. Because the Temple was

A 1943 Kaiser Aluminum event at the Masonic Temple, which was considered a civic center. (Courtesy of NWMAC, L87-1-29748-43)

a public building, funeral services for people of any faith could be conducted there.

On the very top floor of the Masonic Temple was the Falls Room, which was a massive cave-like room with brick walls, exposed rafters and sturdy metal braces. With fourteen-foot ceilings, it was one of the few rooms in town tall enough to accommodate marching groups practicing their drills. In addition to hosting the drill practices of the Masonic organizations, local ROTC military groups would come to this room to practice during the cold winter months. They would march in formation across the open floor, turning, pivoting and hoisting their flags until their movements were perfectly in sync.

Every room in the Masonic Temple played host to numerous civic events throughout the history of Spokane. Whether it was a performance by Bing Crosby or the Spokane Symphony, the pep-rally for the 1962 basketball game between Gonzaga Prep and Lewis & Clark, garden club floral shows or the final Congressional debate between Nethercutt and Foley two days before the 1994 election, the Masonic Temple was at the heart of Spokane's history for much of its existence as a city.

Standing tall above the Spokane River for over 100 years, the Masonic Temple accomplished its goal by providing the people of Spokane with a public building and civic center. Walking through the grand meeting halls and rooms within the building, one couldn't help but feel that history was spilling out from every corner, weaving the present through the past. Cascading down through the years, the history of the building entwined itself around the citizens of Spokane in the form of memories. These memories will remain with those who experienced them and they will forever live on through the history of the building that created them. ●

25

Spokane's Shriners Hospital

A Legacy of Love and Hope

Chief of Surgery, Dr. Eikenbary, with patients in 1924. (Courtesy of Spokane Shriners Hospital)

IN 1920, WHEN THE SHRINERS GATHERED FOR THEIR NATIONAL CONVENTION, they were searching for a way to give back and to make a difference in the communities in which they lived. After discussing how to do this, they decided to open and support a system of hospitals for children with orthopedic problems. The first Shriners Hospital for Crippled Children opened in 1922 in Shreveport, Louisiana. Two years later, on November 15, 1924, a Shriners Hospital opened in Spokane.

Spokane was the seventh Shriners Hospital for Crippled Children, but was the first "mobile unit," hospital. The mobile unit did not have a permanent, stand-alone structure; rather, it was a 20-bed ward in a rented section of St. Luke's Memorial Hospital. The initial unit was known as "the biggest little Shriners Hospital" in the Shriners system because it served so many children; patients came from Montana, Northern Idaho, Washington, Alaska, British Columbia and Alberta.

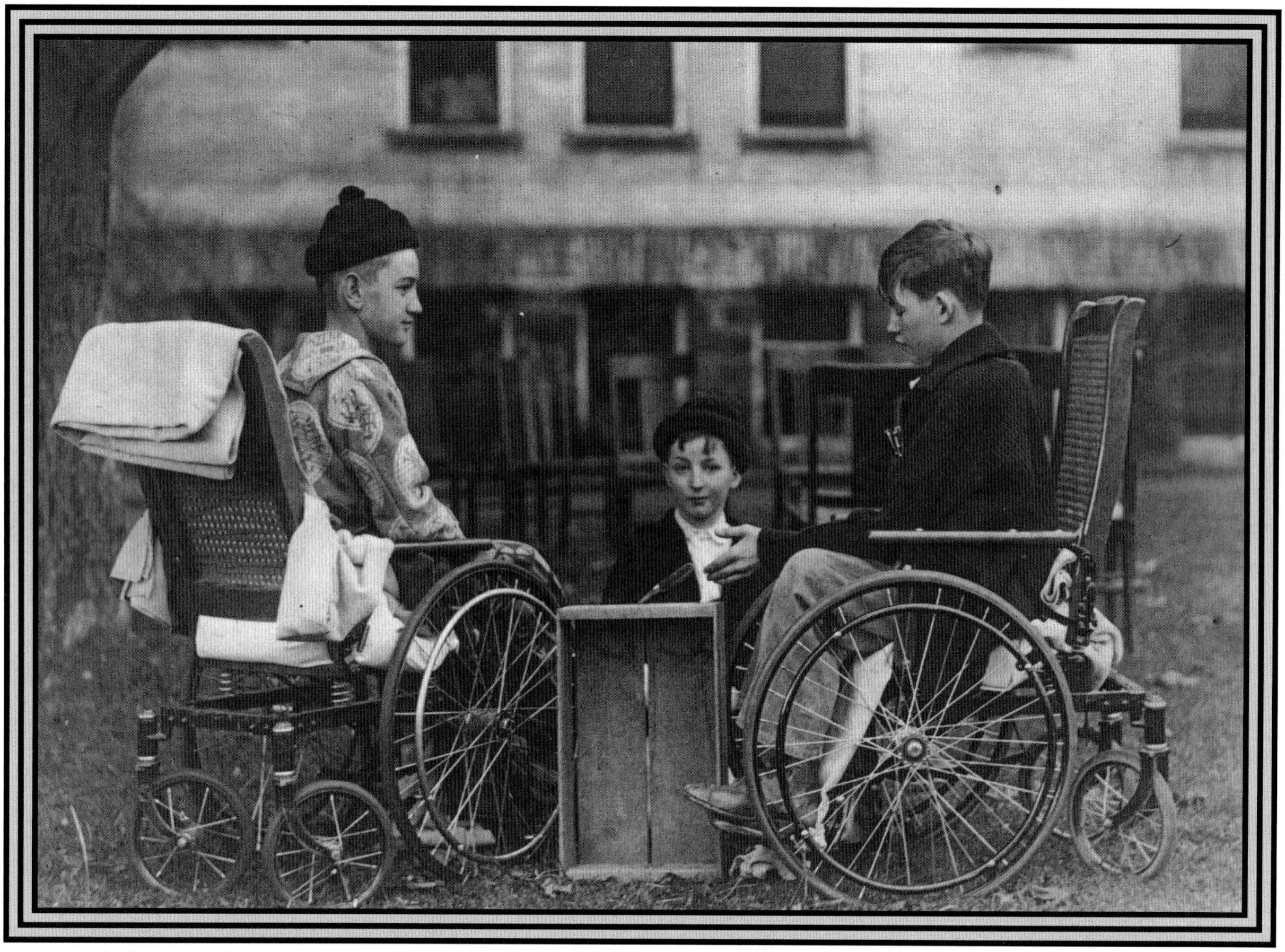

Children enjoyed time outside, playing games. These children were at the hospital in the early 1920s. (Courtesy of Spokane Shriners Hospital)

The mission of Spokane's mobile unit of Shriners Hospital was declared, "To provide free and skilled attention to crippled children whose parents or guardians are unable to pay for such service, and whose disabilities can be sufficiently improved to enable them to be self- supporting in after life."

Patients never paid for services at Shriners Hospitals. All costs for the hospitals were financed by a five-dollar annual fee paid by each member of the Shrine, as well as by bequests, endowments and donations, and later, by money raised through events such as the annual Shrine circuses, rodeos, horse shows and football games.

When opened as a mobile unit, the cost per patient, per day, was three dollars, though patients were never charged. By 1956, that cost would rise to $11.11 per day. Despite what seemed like rising expenses, the cost per patient for all expenses at Spokane's Shriners Hospital was the lowest of all Shriners Hospitals.

In his message to the El Katif Temple's Spring Ceremonial on May 18, 1926, Henry A. Pierce, chairman of the Governing Board, said this in his assessment of the importance of Spokane's Shriners Hospital. "When one realizes that these children are reconstructed from helpless cripples to useful citizens, able to make their own way in the world, at an average expense of less than $300.00 per patient, it looks like the greatest humanitarian work ever conceived by man."

The first year the hospital was open, 115 patients were treated. Polio was a major affliction of patients, as were clubfeet, bone infections and tuberculosis of the joints.

One of the first patients was June Penney, an 11 year-old girl from Kalispell, Montana. Her story was told in an unmarked 1927 newspaper clipping. "Two years ago on Christmas Eve, June was stricken with infantile paralysis – the most dreaded of all children's diseases. The malady left her paralyzed from her arms down. She could neither walk, dress nor feed herself." After surgeries by Dr. C. F. Eikenbary, chief surgeon, and physio-therapy treatments, June grew better, and "the morning following the Halloween parade, June was placed aboard a Great Northern train for Kalispell, able to walk, able to dress herself and able to use her hands and arms."

Children on the playground in 1935, under the watchful eye of nurses. (Courtesy of Spokane Shriners Hospital)

Inspired by great tales of medical success for the children, the Shriners wanted to reach even more children, making it a mission to bring them to Spokane to provide medical care. "We are desirous of ferreting out every needy case in your district and getting them on our waiting list. We only accept cases of crippled children up to 14 years of age, which are entirely charity cases. In other words, we do not accept part pay for any of the medical service. Neither do we accept mental defectives," read a letter from Spokane Shriners Hospital to P.O. King of LaCrosse, Wisconsin.

On Thursdays at the mobile unit, patients from Spokane and outlying communities who were able to walk could be seen at an outpatient clinic, the first of its kind in the area.

Dr. Mitchell Langworthy was the beloved chief surgeon for the mobile unit from March 1926 until October 1929, when he was "the victim of a bullet from an unhappy industrial patient in his private practice."

One thing that Dr. Langworthy saw the beginnings of, but did not live long enough to see come to fruition, was the building of a permanent structure. There was interest among the Shriners, as well as the community, to build a permanent stand-alone hospital, rather than continuing with a mobile unit, but it would take a great deal of money.

In 1926, as a way to raise money, H.P. Flickinger, the City of Spokane's plumbing inspector, and also a member of El Katif temple, created a foil committee. Local residents saved and collected tin foil to raise money. The collected foil came mainly from the wrapping on cigarettes and cigars, and donation boxes were set up in most cigar stores in the city. The popularity of the drive spread from Spokane and became a nationwide phenomenon. The foil was shipped from Spokane to Chicago, where it was melted into tin-alloy bars. The last load, shipped to Chicago in 1933, filled an entire Northern Pacific train car with over 100,000 pounds of foil. A large sign was painted onto the side of the car, letting people know it was full of foil to benefit the local Shriners Hospital.

Though the foil drive had been successful for seven years, the 1933 load was one of the last that was sent from

Old postcard. (Courtesy of Spokane Shriners Hospital)

Spokane, as there was a decline in the amount of tin foil being used, because foil was being replaced with cellophane in cigarette and cigar wrappers. The foil was worth six cents per pound, and originally, Mr. Flickinger hoped to raise $100 to $200 at the most. By 1933, the campaign had raised close to $1,500.

According to an article in the *Spokane Chronicle* in 1933, "The best part of the idea, however, remains to be told. The collecting of foil gave Shriners and others interested in the hospitals for crippled children an incentive to raise money from other sources. Indirectly, the foil idea has been responsible for money raising campaigns that have poured thousands of dollars into the hospital funds. So, though tin foil does die a natural death, it will have served a good purpose; it will have been the means of restoring hundreds of crippled children to usefulness."

The Shriners Hospital's governing body was growing increasingly serious about wanting to put a permanent hospital in Spokane, estimating the cost to be between $50,000 and $75,000. They were held back from beginning the project, though, because they did not have the funds to pay for both the labor and material.

J.B Felts was chairman of the Board of County Commissioners in 1933 and was a vocal advocate of the push to build a permanent, stand-alone Shriners Hospital. Part of his "campaign" for the construction project was that it could be considered an "unemployed project," meaning that it would provide job opportunities to local craftsman who would be hired to work on the project. Mr. Felts suggested that if local suppliers offered their products at cost, it would be affordable, and in the process would provide jobs for the laborers.

Felts argued that a Shriners Hospital "is not an institution that calls for assistance from the Community Chest nor, ever will it be an additional burden on a presently overloaded community. By giving needy men work now, it would not alone provide cash for food and clothing, but it would tend to raise the morale of those who would rather work than remain idle and be fed at city and county expense."

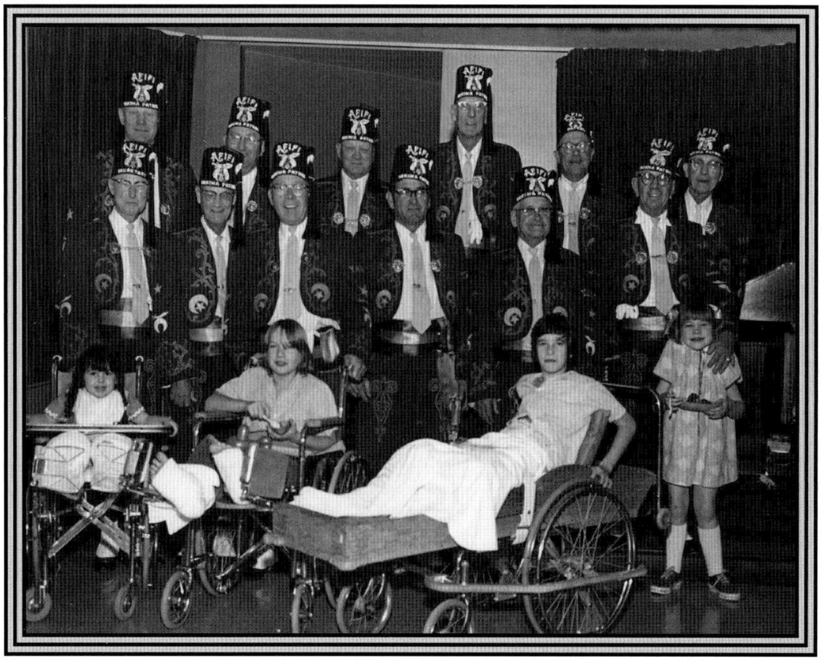
Shriners often visited the patients. (Courtesy of Spokane Shriners Hospital)

The following article by C. A. Bartleson, president of Building Supplies, Inc., appeared in the February 7, 1933 edition of the *Spokane Chronicle* and was a major show of support for the project:

"*Having noticed several articles in your recent editions relative to building the Shriners Hospital at the present time, we wish to commend the fine spirit which animated Mr. Felts and the other proponents of this plan for giving work to some of our unemployed.*

It is probably well known to you that building laborers and craftsmen have suffered abnormally during this depression to the extent that 80 percent of those normally employed in the building trades are now without work, according to department of labor figures as of January 1, 1933.

Naturally, any project, which can give jobs to a part of these men would be most opportunely welcome.

In the Spokane Chronicle of February 2, we read with approval the letter from Mr. Georg of the firm of Alloway & Georg offering to aid in the construction of the Shrine Hospital without fee. Our company would like to place itself on record as being anxious to cooperate to the end that the proposed building could be erected. We offer to furnish common bricks for use in the Shrine Hospital at cost. We do not manufacture any other building materials, so are limiting our offer to products of our own make."

Nurses with children on the lawn, in the 1920s. (Courtesy of Spokane Shriners Hospital)

It wasn't just people from Spokane who were assisting with the cost of building the Spokane Shriners Hospital. A freewill collection was taken at the Masonic and Eastern Star picnic in Coeur d'Alene's city park on July 18, 1933.

"Our picnic was a real success and, if we had no other success than the collection for use in the Shrine Hospital, that in itself would be very gratifying," wrote Herbert F. Minister, master of Kootenai Lodge No. 24 A.F. & A.M. of Coeur d'Alene, in a note that accompanied a $128 check. Similarly, the Western Montana Shrine Club presented an $800 check, which was raised at a dance in Missoula. Montana had a great interest in the success of Shriners Hospital because 20 to 25 percent of the patients were from Montana.

The *Spokane Chronicle's* 18th annual baking contest earmarked all money raised from selling baked goods, which in 1934 totaled $802, to the hospital's building fund. In 1936, local schools rallied to help with the hospital building fund. The annual football game, played between North Central High School and Gonzaga Prep, held on Armistice Day 1936, brought in $1,600, all of which was donated to the building fund.

All of the financial support made the proposed building a reality. In March of 1939, the hospital moved into its new building. The four-ward Spokane Shriners Hospital for Crippled Children was constructed for $85,000. Amazingly, the entire building was completely paid for by the time it was dedicated. According to archives, "The architecture was of a mosque design with a copper dome, in remembrance of the Mystic Shrine. It stood on the triangular plot just south of the main entrance to the original St. Luke's Memorial Hospital."

Children were transported to St. Luke's Memorial Hospital for surgery, via an underground tunnel. This route was used for 32 years, until 1971, when St. Luke's built a new hospital across town (its current location). The old hospital was leveled, and the land was purchased by a local charitable foundation. Charitable indeed; they gave the deed for the land to the Shriners.

Old Shriner's Hospital, Spokane Washington Unit. (Courtesy of Spokane Shriners Hospital)

The hospital, located on its own patch of land on Summit Boulevard, became a home-away-from-home for its young patients who often stayed for months on end. Hospital rules stated, "While the child is in the hospital doing well, if parents or relations are not present, they will receive one postcard a week, telling of its progress. If he is old enough to write himself, he will be encouraged to write as often as possible. If he is to be operated upon, you will be notified in advance, and one card each day, reporting on his condition until he is

Celebrating her100th day in the hospital, with a big piece of pie. (Courtesy of Spokane Shriners Hospital)

again convalescent will be sent… There will be no accommodation for parents or others to remain at the hospital."

Children were not able to bring anything personal with them—none of their clothes, blankets, toys or stuffed animals from home. They were given all new things once inside the hospital. Hand-carved wooden toys were distributed to each patient once they arrived, and hand-sewn clothing was provided for them.

Polio and tuberculosis were such common and frightening diseases in the 1930s, that when children were admitted, they were put into isolation cubicles for 72 hours, to monitor and ensure they were not carrying the diseases. While these diseases are serious, but nowhere near as frightening nowadays, this was before the appropriate vaccines and antibiotics were available, and a disease like polio or tuberculosis could be fatal.

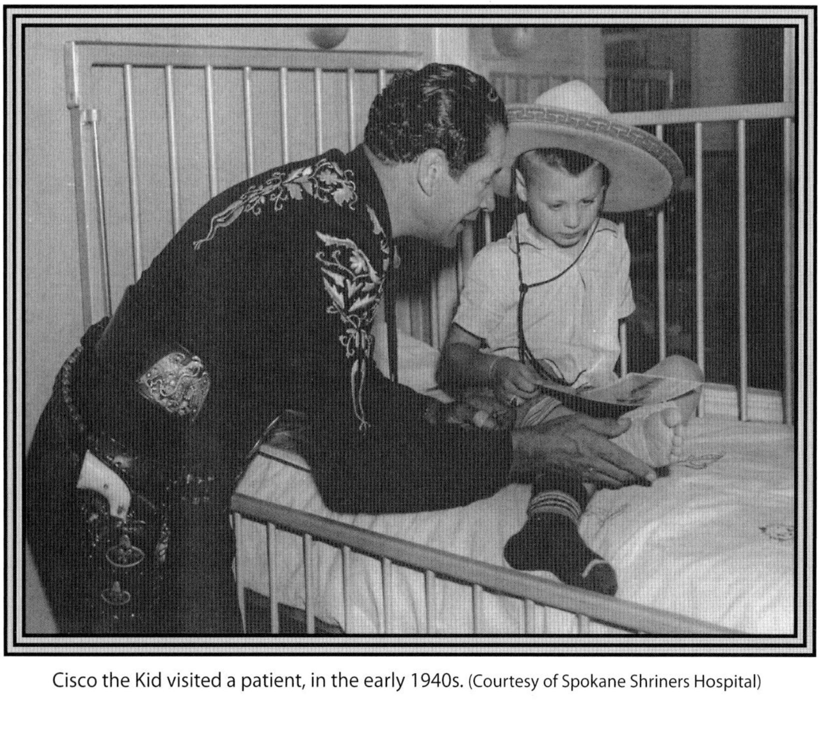

Cisco the Kid visited a patient, in the early 1940s. (Courtesy of Spokane Shriners Hospital)

Because there were no antibiotics, children underwent "elaborate skin preparations involving a surgical scrubbing and covering with sterile towels 48 hours before surgery, then again 24 hours before."

The average hospital stay for patients admitted during the 1930s was four months, most of which time they were away from their family. Visits were strictly limited to Sunday afternoons. This strict rule helped to ensure no communicable diseases were spread to the children. As a result of spending so much time together, without their families, there was a sense of camaraderie among the children.

A patient receiving her personal birthday cake and a visit from a Shriner. (Courtesy of Spokane Shriners Hospital)

Though the patients were removed from their loved ones, there was still plenty of love in the hospital, according to Mrs. Margery Livingston, the second superintendent of Spokane's Shriners Hospital. "I'll never forget one little girl whose face was severely burned," she wrote in *Shriners Hospital for Children – Spokane, 75 Years of Caring*. "Despite the fact that her face was terribly scarred, I knew she felt loved and beautiful when she was there. All the children were loved."

There were celebrations for the children to make their time at the hospital enjoyable. Holidays were a special occasion for the children. Each year at Christmas, Santa Claus came to visit, and on all holidays there was a special dinner, for which they would gather together to eat. On a patient's 100th day in the hospital, they got a special celebration, similar to a birthday. And when it came to birthdays, each child received their own personalized birthday cake.

There were special visitors, as well. Vice President Charles Curtis (vice president for President Hoover) was on a train heading to Spokane for a speaking engagement, and on the train ride he was given so many gifts of apples and bouquets of flowers, that he didn't know what to do with them, so he requested they be donated to the Shriners Hospital as gifts to the children. Years later, the original Lassie came to visit, and other visitors, including Red Skelton, members of the Harlem Globetrotters, Mickey Mouse and local sports stars would stop in to visit the children.

In 1951, a new wing was added to the

El Katif Shriners in front of their train car. (Courtesy of Spokane Shriners Hospital)

Away from their families, patients formed strong bonds while living at Shriners, spending their days playing together. (Courtesy of Spokane Shriners Hospital)

hospital, adding 15 more beds, an isolation room and a formula room connected to the area for babies. According to a report, the hospital had many modern marvels, including an "X-ray and photographic room; outpatient department with cast room; laundry; library and conference rooms on the second floor; nurses' quarters; a dental office with the very latest equipment; resident surgeon's quarters; chief surgeon's office; a large glass enclosed sun porch; two large deepfreeze and cold storage units; new laundry equipment." The hospital also was one of the few buildings with both heat and air conditioning.

Two teachers from the Spokane public school system were provided without charge to the patients, so that as they spent long stays in the hospital they were able to keep up with their schoolwork.

Spokane's Shriners Hospital stood on Summit Boulevard as a sign of hope and help for children for over 52 years. In 1991, a new, modern hospital was built high upon the hill, on the corner of Monroe Street and Fifth Avenue. This hospital is again connected to one of the city's major hospitals, this time Deaconess, providing access to additional medical service if needed.

Things are much different nowadays, in part because the risk of infection is so much less, the technology and advancements in medicine and the psychology of healing have advanced, and the duration of hospital stays have been reduced dramatically. When the current hospital was built in 1991, "on-site family rooms and inpatient room parent beds were added so parents could remain close to their children."

The one thing that has not changed is Shriners Hospitals' unwavering determination to help children in need. A statement that was part of the dedication for the 1939 hospital, may say it best:"To the Glory of God and to all humankind, regardless of race, creed or color, Shriners Hospitals for Crippled Children are dedicated. No man stands more erect than when he stoops to help a crippled child." ●

26

Gem Of The City

The Fox Theater

Theater patrons lined up under the Fox Theater's marquee for a 1945 Greer Garson and Gregory Peck movie. (Courtesy of NWMAC, L87-1.44834-45)

IN 1931, THE COUNTRY WAS IN THE MIDDLE OF THE GREAT DEPRESSION. WITH MOST people's thoughts focused on how to stretch their money to cover expenses, and where their next meal was coming from, things of frivolity, glamour and elegance were not a part of people's lives. Then, in the fall of 1931, a little bit of joy was brought to the residents of Spokane when the Fox Theater, one of the most glamorous and elegant theaters of all time, opened its doors.

For the residents of Spokane, the theater was an oasis. Outside, the economy may have been crumbling, times were tough and there were problems aplenty, but once you crossed the threshold of the theater's double doors, those problems were forgotten as you escaped into a world of elegance and glamour.

Children wait outside of the Fox Theater for a parade in 1932. (Courtesy of NWMAC, L87-1-984-32)

Plans for the theater were first announced in the May 12, 1927 issue of the *Spokesman-Review*, which splashed the news of the land purchase for the theater across the pages. "The theater will be built for the West Coast Company, which has many millions invested in theatrical enterprises on the Pacific coast. The company has taken a thirty-five-year lease on the structure, in which they will operate the highest character of motion pictures and musical revues, similar to the way they give in the Deluxe Famous Players Theater. Mr. Rosenbaum (purchaser) is building for them in Seattle. There is no theater superior to what is planned by Mr. Rosenbaum and associates for Spokane anywhere in California or western America. As real estate investors and operators, Mr. Rosenbaum and associates feel that Spokane is at the point of an upward swing that will last for years and bring about a decided and unforgettable revival and prosperity."

The story ran two years before the Great Depression began with the Stock Market crash of 1929. Despite the downward turn in prosperity for the nation, the decision was made to continue with the plans to build the theater. In fact, plans were rushed, and construction began on August 1, 1930.

The town held its breath with excitement over the theater, which became a regular topic in the newspaper, and was referred to as the "$1,000,000 Fox West Coast Theater." Those one million dollars were expected to be used

Three actresses pose inside of the Fox Theater, which was one of the most elegant theaters in which to perform. (Courtesy of NWMAC, L87-1-844-32)

to help create one of the most breathtaking theaters ever built. "No expense will be spared in equipment and decorations," said Fox West Coast Theaters.

Mr. John Eberson, a New York architect specializing in theaters and public buildings, who was also in charge of design and construction for the Fox, was brought to Spokane in August 1927, to help publicize the theater. He gave a presentation at The Davenport Hotel, explaining all of the architectural elements of the Fox that would set it apart from any other theater. When Eberson arrived at the hotel, he took immediate notice of the light fixtures in the building. Years before, he had worked on a project, designing the lights for a "hotel in Washington," but he never knew which hotel it was. As he entered The Davenport, he recognized the light fixtures and saw his work for the first time. It must have been flattering and gave Eberson a fondness for The Davenport and Spokane.

"This [theater] is designed to offer the amusement-loving public a restful interior that will put them in a proper frame of mind to receive the entertainment," said Eberson. "In most of the finer theaters there is a glitter of silks, satins and glass, which is not restful. The atmospheric interior, carried out in an artistic and consistent fashion is becoming popular. In our execution, we take no chances of being grotesque or deviating from the artistic.

"The auditorium proper will represent an Italian garden under a moonlit sky. The illusion will be created with

The sixty-foot wide sunburst on the ceiling represented sunlight illuminating a quiet forest. (Courtesy of NWMAC, L94.24.40)

the brush and lighting arrangements, which are original and create a natural atmosphere. Rough texture plasters and a great deal of polychrome will be used. The whole scheme will be Hispano-Italian, carried out in the antique fashion. The whole building will allow theater patrons to forget their immediate surroundings under the charm of the old country Mediterranean influence."

By the time the theater was built, this original Mediterranean design had been replaced by an Art Deco style, which was unlike anything people in Spokane had seen before. Few people were privileged enough to travel around the country, much less the world, so the artistic style made popular in metropolitan areas was something new to many.

Norwegian-born muralist Anthony Heinsbergen, who had a reputation as one of the best designers of theater interiors, was hired to create an amazing underwater world upon the walls and ceiling of the Fox. Starting from the ground and moving up to the ceiling, Heinsbergen's mural transitioned from underwater floral patterns to a landscape of castles, rivers and clouds that morphed into a sky with a stunning sixty-foot wide sunburst showing sunlight spreading out across the ceiling and illuminating a quiet forest resting under a sky full of stars.

As many local workers as possible were used in the construction of the Fox, which was a major undertaking.

The transition of the murals, from underwater to castles and sky, is visible in this picture of the lobby area. (Courtesy of NWMAC, L94.9.94)

Built to seat 2,500, it was two stories tall at the front, and soared to seven stories within the main portion of the building. At the top of the building stood the Fox sign, which was made from letters three feet high, one on top of another, and was illuminated with neon lighting costing $9,000.

The plumbing throughout the building cost $15,000 and was contracted to James Smythe Plumbing and Heating of Spokane. It took two train carloads to transport all of the plumbing supplies needed for the job.

Because it was so new, the term "air conditioning" was meaningless to most people, but they knew enough to get excited when they heard a about a ventilating machine that was being installed in the theater. The apparatus, made by York Ice Machinery, cost $43,000 to install, but the cost was worth the buzz it created. It took in six cubic feet of washed fresh air per minute, per person, with a total circulation of 66,000 cubic feet of air per minute.

The cool air wasn't the only planned source of physical comfort for patrons. The coral colored, velour-backed green leather box spring seats were designed to be thirty-four inches apart and were promoted with the promise that "the longest legs can be cared for without banging the knees against the back of the seat ahead."

Even the restrooms were elegant and offered all of the comforts for which one could hope. The men's restroom was decorated with murals of sports and athletics, while the women's restroom was an oasis of elegance.

A total of 3,578 incandescent bulbs were used for interior lighting in addition to two neon strips bordering a grand mirror in the foyer, and a diamond neon illumination in the foyer ceiling. Forty-eight spotlights and 108 reflector lamps ensured everything on the stage was easily visible.

Equipped with a grand three-dimension screen for motion pictures, the stage was set up for all types of entertainment. Thirty feet deep and eighty feet high, it was fully equipped for motion pictures as well as vaudeville and musical entertainments.

The foyer extended the entire width of the building, opening onto First Avenue. Offices occupied the Sprague side of the building on the second floor, and there were shops on the ground floor on the Monroe and Sprague frontages. West End Pharmacy, Lee Frame Shop, Earl's Lunch, City Transfer and Storage, Inland Electric and the Royal Apartments, which had occupied the space before, all had to be moved to make room for the theater.

After watching the construction take place for over a year, the town was on edge with excitement when opening night finally arrived. The crowds that came out in their finest to line the streets and celebrate the opening of the theater were unlike anything the city had seen.

On September 3, 1931, lights were placed on the street for the opening celebration. Fifty-thousand people crowded into the neighboring streets, all hoping for a glimpse of the corner of Sprague and Monroe, where Mitzi Green, George O'Brien, Anita Page, Victor McLaglen and Ed Brendel, five of Hollywood's leading actors of the time, were brought in for the grand opening of the Fox Theater.

It was expensive to get a ticket for the opening night gala, meaning it was mainly the wealthy in their fine clothing that filled the interior of the theater. The common folk had to settle for a glimpse from the crowded street or the picture painted by the following report, which ran in the September 3, 1931 edition of the *Spokesman-Review.* Readers were mesmorized as they read the details:

"Ornamental metal doors swing open and project him [the patron] at once into a veritable fairyland of chased glass, gleaming aluminum, warmly colored walls, flaming sunbursts of light, shimmering mirrors, floral mural decorations and thick, warm, rich carpets of blue and red.

"The foyer itself seems almost as large as many theaters. Broad easy staircases above the checkroom lead to the lounge, the restrooms and the balcony.

"Overhead is a star-like centerpiece in aluminum and gold that covers most of the ceiling and conceals the lights. The walls meet the ceiling with a fluted border done in silver. Floral decorations on walls and ceiling are sparsely used in keeping with the chaste expanses of metal and glass.

"The great sidewall, which contains the exquisite metal doors leading to the auditorium on the lower floor, is a thing of rare beauty. It is divided into panels that extend from the floor to the ceiling.

"This is not idle phrase. The Fox Theater hopes to and should attract thousands of Inland Empire residents as regular patrons. Good roads in all directions and automobiles will be factors in attaining this result.

"Spokane residents already have become familiar with the modernistic exterior of the new theater. Its great, bare dust-colored walls with incidental ornamental devices and fleetings to give a play of light and shade bizarre and so futuristic that the casual passerby catches his breath in surprise and wonder. Certainly Spokane has seen nothing like it before.

"Patrons should save their gasps of amazement for the thrill that sheer beauty affords when they reach the auditorium, a spacious place with 1,450 seats downstairs and 900 in the balcony, 240 of which are loge seats.

"The correctly operated theater of today, displaying a definite interest in the welfare, pride, domestic and conventional conveniences and the development of the community in which it operates, can be classed as a community institution in which public ideas and expressions are given proper voice."

One person who truly believed the Fox Theater should be a community institution was Dr. David C. Cowen, a local physician. As his "contribution to the prevention of juvenile delinquency," he leased the Fox Theater every Saturday morning from June 14 to September 13, 1947, and offered free shows for Spokane and surrounding areas' children during their summer vacations. He had room for 4,000 children per performance; however, if there were more than that who wanted to attend, he would provide accommodations for them at another theater: the State.

In a May 14, 1947 story in the *Spokesman-Review*, he explained what motivated him to offer such a service. "I want to make it possible for all children to enjoy clean, wholesome entertainment during the vacation months,"

The art deco style of the theater was a first in Spokane. Even the staircase to the restrooms was rich in detail. (Courtesy of NWMAC, L94.24.41)

he said, "where they will be off the streets and away from the influences which contribute to juvenile delinquency." Free buses were provided to transport children from city orphanages to the theater for the free shows. At each showing, two to three portable radios were given away, and every other week he gave a bicycle to one child. "If this experience keeps one child from harm or temptation during the summer months, it will be more than worth what it costs," said Cowen.

For each of the children who attend those shows, the Fox became an oasis, and earned a special spot in their hearts. This was true for nearly every patron who passed through the doors.

"When my brother and I were treated to movies at the Fox in the middle 1930s, it was about as old as we were," said patron Jean Fowler. "The sweeping staircase to the second level looked like a castle. At either side of the lady's lounge sat two lovely sand-filled urns, which served as ash trays. With all the wonder of a four-year-old, my brother asked if these were for cats when they came to the Fox."

Employees were active members of the promotions of the theater. Dick Hazelmyer, who worked in promotions and as a stagehand at the Fox Theater, recalled one assignment where he dressed up in a space suit to promote the movie *Destination Moon*. It wasn't all costumes and promotions for him, though; Hazelmyer got to meet some of

The refreshment counter at the Fox Theater, 1959. (Courtesy of NWMAC, L87-1-1550-59)

the celebrities who came to the Fox, including Bing Crosby and Katherine Hepburn. He even got to sit and have coffee with Crosby once, and recalled, "The waitress was so flustered that she spilled coffee on Crosby."

The Fox was a coveted spot for young girls to land a job as an usherette. Each season brought with it new uniforms that demonstrated the glamour of Spokane's spacious Fox Theater. For their new fall uniforms, one year the usherettes wore bright colors that matched the art deco style of the walls. The uniforms consisted of bolero jackets of purple pastel, over green sateen blouses and green sharkskin trousers. "I was an usherette at the Fox in 1952, and I saw *South Pacific* eleven times," said Roberta Croase.

With time and age, the elegance of the Fox began to diminish, especially as multiplex, suburban theaters popped up, and going out to the movies became a more common and casual event. In 1975, the balcony at the Fox was walled off, creating two additional screening rooms, making the Fox a tri-plex. It was sold to Tom Moyer Luxury theaters of Portland, Oregon, in 1977, and was controlled by management in another city. Another slap in the face to this once regal and grand theater came in 1989, when it was turned into a discount, second-run theater.

The downhill slide continued for the Fox as it fell further and further into disrepair. It looked like the end was in sight for what was once one of Spokane's most unique and glamorous feathers in its cap. Plans were tossed around for the future of the theater and included everything from tearing it down to turning the theater into a parking lot. Then the sweet sound of salvation came from the Spokane Symphony. Setting out on a massive fundraising campaign, they bought the theater and saved the Fox.

The fruits of their labor were shown on November 17, 2007, when seventy-six years, two months and two weeks to the day after it first opened, the Fox, the only remaining Art Deco theater north of San Francisco, held its grand re-opening, once again bringing glamour and elegance to a town that again holds its breath with excitement.

27

Spokane Army Air Depot

The Beginning of a Military Legacy at Fairchild Air Force Base

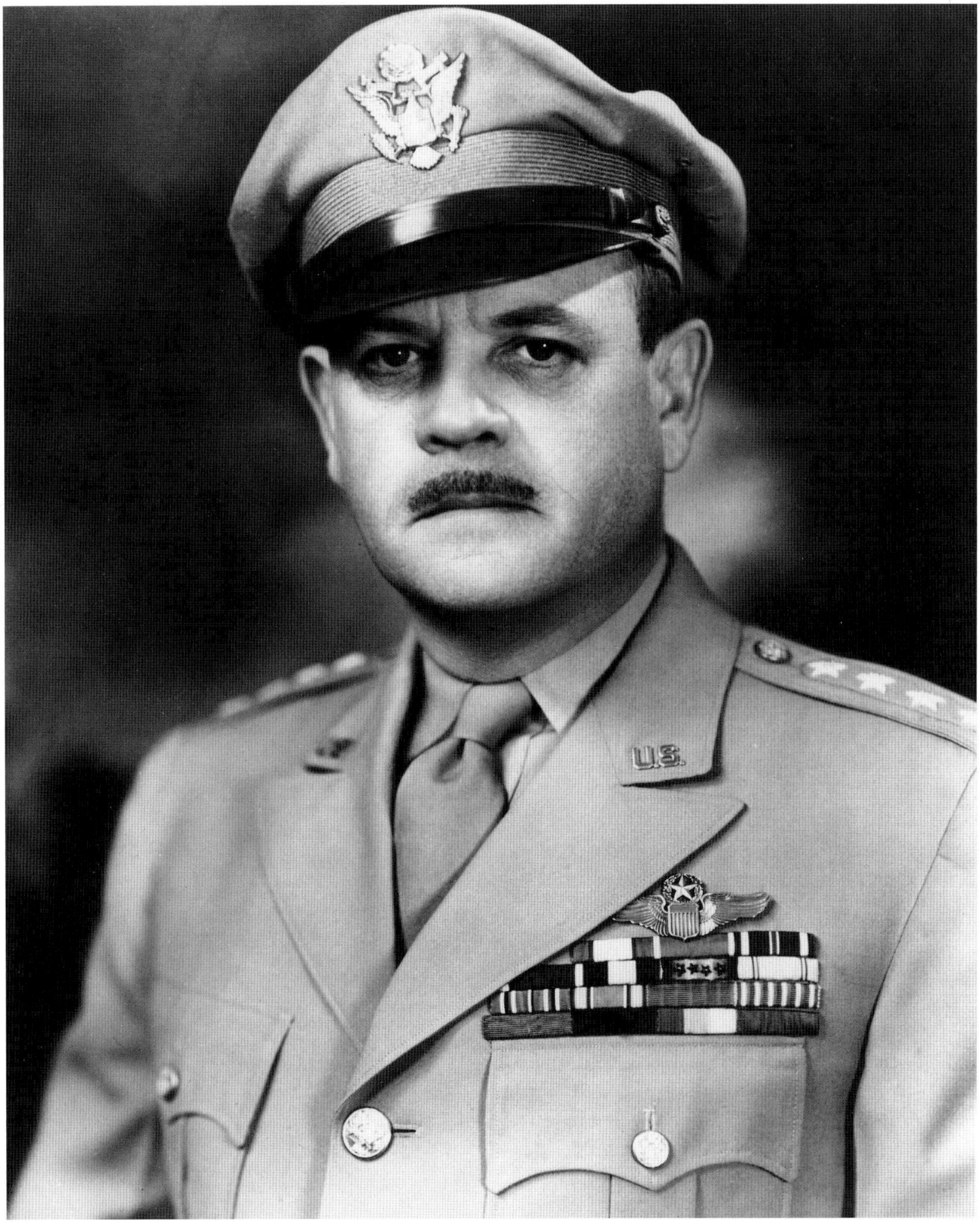

General Muir S. Fairchild. (Courtesy of Fairchild AFB)

IN 1919, A MONTANA PILOT MADE AN EMERGENCY LANDING IN A FIELD WEST OF Spokane, known as White Bluff Prairie. People flocked from town to see the airplane, something that most at that time had never seen, staring at its strange shape and the daring pilot who had dipped through the sky in the contraption. While a plane in that area was so rare it was reason for excitement, airplanes soon became a regular sight on White Bluff Prairie, thanks to the arrival of the Spokane Army Air Depot.

General Fairchild, third from right, and other Pan American Flyers receiving their DCF certificates. (Courtesy of Library of Congress)

Due to the economic depression gripping the nation and Spokane in the 1930s, the Spokane Chamber of Commerce felt they needed to find a way to boost the local economy, which radiated with despair. They figured one of the best ways to pump enthusiasm and dollars into the local economy was to attract a military installation to the area.

A congressional party set out to tour Washington in 1935, in an effort to find a location in the Pacific Northwest in which to establish an Army Air Corps supply and maintenance depot. According to *Fairchild AFB 1942-1982; Sentinel of the Pacific Northwest* by the 92BWM History office, "Records indicate that one of the prime factors considered in selection of Spokane was the strategic location for the defense of Alaska." The process of selection took several years, but the group soon narrowed their choices to Salt Lake City, Utah, and Spokane.

A military presence would have been nothing new in Spokane. Ft. George Wright, which was an old Army post north of the Spokane River, was established in 1892. Additionally, Felts Field and the later-built Spokane International Airport served as airfields used by the military.

General Muir S. Fairchild (Courtesy of Fairchild AFB)

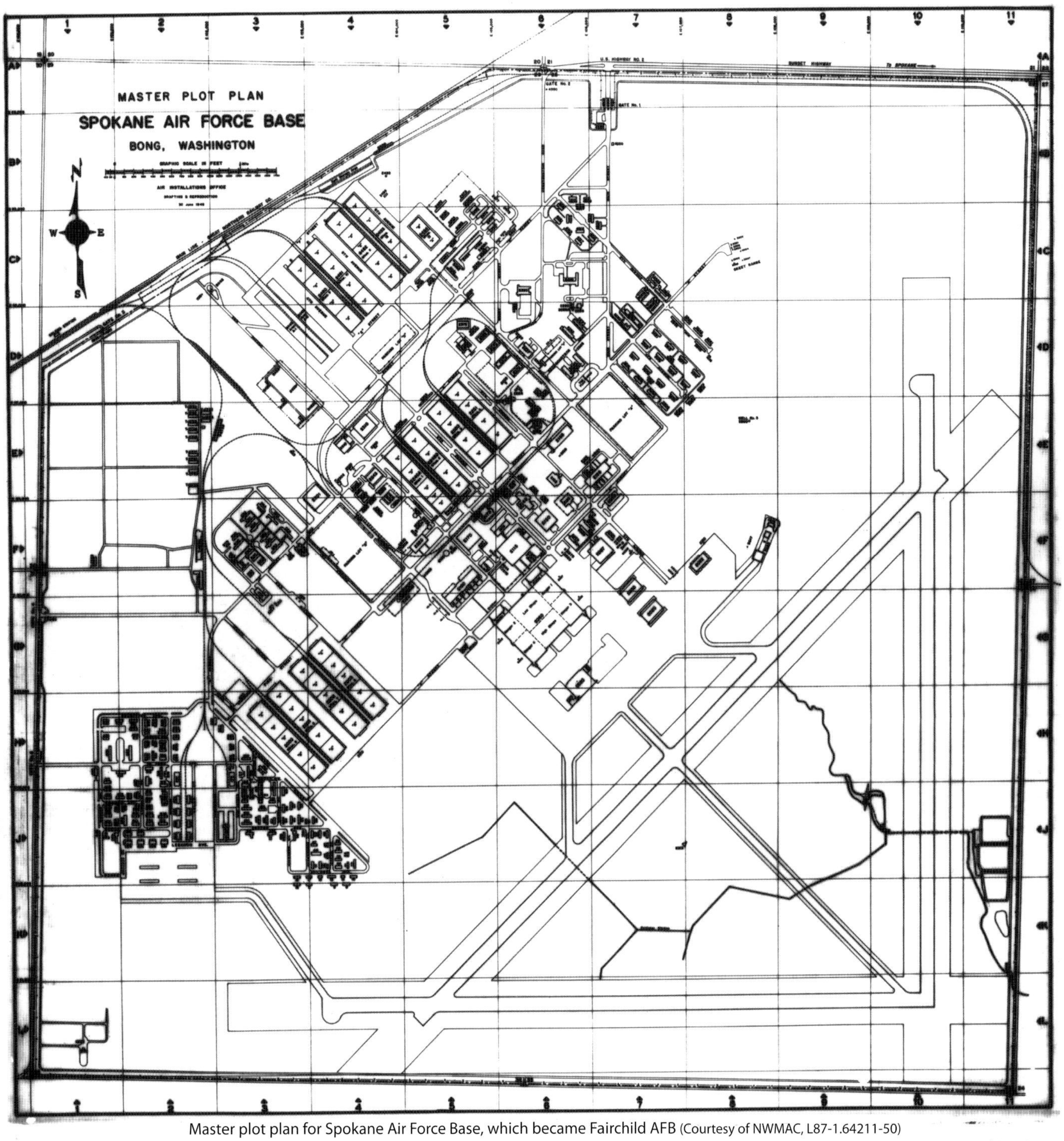

Master plot plan for Spokane Air Force Base, which became Fairchild AFB (Courtesy of NWMAC, L87-1.64211-50)

By 1940, the government's interest in Salt Lake City had been replaced by an interest in Everett, Washington. This set up a competition between two Washington cities. According to *Sentinel of the Pacific Northwest*, "Competition between the industrial and commercial west and the agricultural east had long been an element in the growth picture of the state of Washington. The location of this defense complex became another area in which the interest of the factions conflicted."

While Everett offered close proximity to McChord Field and the Boeing Plant, which would make repairs and supplies for military airplanes more accessible, Spokane was attractive because it was inland, which made it less susceptible to air attacks. Northern Pacific Railroad stepped in, providing an extra benefit that made Spokane more desirable. They worked with Spokane city officials to create priority-shipping schedules and guaranteed equipment and line construction, ensuring the depot would be able to quickly and efficiently move supplies to service the planes.

General Fairchild leading a staff meeting. (Courtesy of Fairchild AFB)

It wasn't just business voices in Spokane that were rallying for the depot; Congressman Charles M. Leavy, from Spokane was back in Washington D.C. rallying on behalf of his constituents, explaining to Congress why a depot in Spokane was a great decision.

Not everyone was excited to see the possible arrival of the depot, though. Most noticeably opposed were the farmers who lived and made their livelihood on White Bluff Prairie, the land that was the proposed site for the depot. Eight families took legal action to stop the sale of their land, but "opposing the government during wartime was not looked upon favorably," noted the authors of *Sentinel of the Pacific Northwest.*

In the end, their legal action was no match for the voices of the city leadership and of Congressman Leavy. The depot was awarded to Spokane on September 12, 1941.

Before construction could begin, though, the War Department had to receive the title for the land, which financially fell on the shoulders of the citizens of Spokane. The land had to be provided to the government free of charge, so it was up to the citizens of Spokane to purchase the land for the depot. To purchase 1,500 acres, the city needed to raise around $110,000. While that amount could have been a daunting amount of money to raise during an economy that was slumped, the people of Spokane saw the benefit of having the depot and were willing to put their money where their goals were. In two days they raised $76,000, and by the end of the week, they reached their goal, plus they raised an additional $15,000. In total, the city raised $124,996.77.

Knowing they would have to sell and abandon their land, the landowners that had opposed the depot grudgingly accepted a proposed offer of $70 per acre. They were outraged when the final sale went through and they only received $40 per acre. The discrepancy came about because the final sale included 2,400 acres, rather than the 1,500 originally sought by the government.

Personnel of the Main Guard, 92nd Air Police, photographed at the main entry gate, Spokane AFB ,1950. (Courtesy of Fairchild AFB)

The property on which the depot would be built was purchased by public subscription by citizens of Spokane for a total of $101,078.66, in January 1942, and the title for the land was officially transferred to the U.S. Government.

Construction of the depot took more than a year. At one point, 2,500 workers were employed on the construction project. The workforce erected 262 buildings, the largest of which was a twelve-acre repair hanger. Construction also resulted in eight miles of railroad track traveling throughout the depot and twelve warehouses that were each larger than a city block.

There was a great deal of administrative work to be done before the completion of the construction process; however, there were no completed buildings at the depot, nor space available at Ft. George Wright or at Felts Field, both of which saw military activity. As a result, administrative and headquarters were based in downtown Spokane in the Hutton Building, later moving to the Kemp & Herbert Building, also downtown.

Finally, in March 1942, the first buildings were completed and were available for occupation by Army engineers. The depot was to be home to the Spokane Air Technical Service Command (the maintenance portion of the depot), and Spokane Air Material Command (the supply portion). Although the newly constructed depot would go through ten different names over the years, and was often called "Galena," by locals, the first official name was Spokane Army Air Depot.

The depot not only provided an economic boost for employees but for the city as well, as demonstrated in *Sentinel of the Pacific Northwest.* "Unlike the usual defense industry which operated in the suburbs of cities and drew their workers from its population, early Spokane Depot operations actually revived the economy of the inner city. Buildings like the Cowley School and the Kemp & Herbert Building, which had been vacant for three

A line of B-17s, known as the Flying Fortress, await repair. (Courtesy of Fairchild AFB)

Workers maintain and repair B-17 engines. (Courtesy of Fairchild AFB)

years prior to the arrival of the Service Area Command, were put back into use, thus increasing their value. The population grew in the city and the tax base of the city increased monthly."

The goal for the city was to bring a military installation in order to pump money in to the local economy, and that was exactly what happened. As noted in *Sentinel of the Pacific Northwest*, "Expectations for the depot were overwhelmingly surpassed. The government spent more than $25 million in construction of the installation; the civilian workforce was more than double the anticipated level; and the expected payroll of $8 million a year was nearly tripled by the fall of 1943."

In June 1943, Service Area Command (SAC) moved onto the depot, occupying forty-four buildings and employing over 700 civilians. Those employees were just the tip of the iceberg. A constant supply of trained employees was needed. Unfortunately, most of the jobs that needed to be filled were skilled labor in areas like aircraft maintenance and other defense-oriented trades, and there

Women Depot workers check aircraft parts on an assembly line. (Courtesy Fairchild Air Force Base)

were not enough people trained in these professions. The government created a solution that was too good to pass up. Men and women could go to school to learn these trades, and get paid $75 a month to be students. This had roughly the same buying power that $1,031 did in 2014. Whey they graduated, many of them could look forward to jobs at the depot that paid $125 per month, which was the equivalent of $1,718 in 2014. Men and women both took advantage of this offer, with women eventually composing twenty-five percent of the work force at the depot. They partook in all forms of work, including welding, sheet metalwork and making wooden boxes for shipping supplies.

B-17 and B-29 planes lined up for repairs. (Courtesy of Fairchild AFB)

The spring and summer of 1943 brought much activity to the depot.

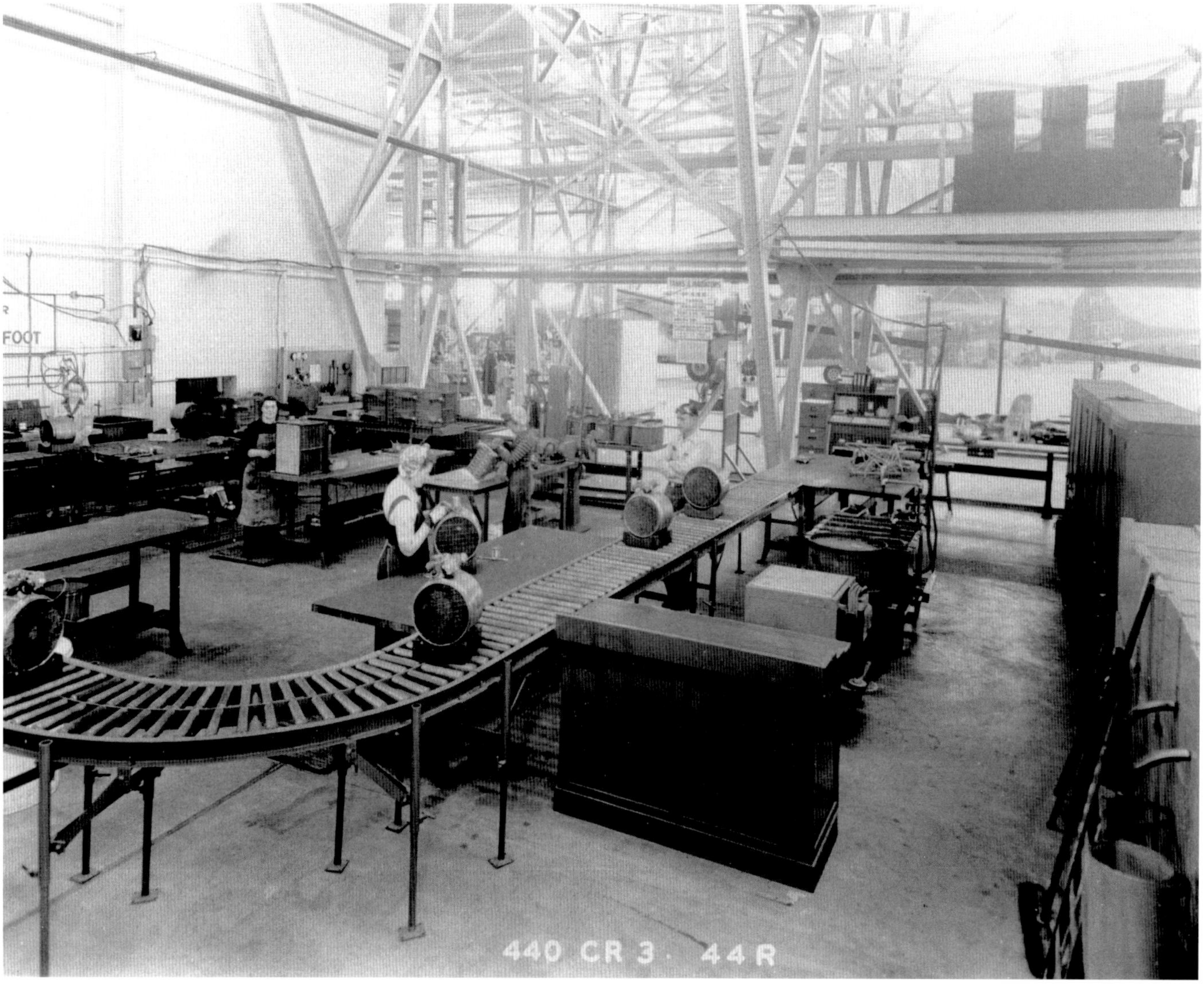

Women were a major part of the workforce at the Spokane Army Air Depot. Here they check aircraft parts on an assembly line. (Courtesy of Fairchild AFB)

General Fairchild's portrait unveiling. (Courtesy of Fairchild AFB)

May 14, 1943, marked the arrival of the first Women Army Air Corps (WAAC) contingent, and on July 5, 1943, one day after Independence Day, the first official aircraft to land at the depot was a B-17 Flying Fortress, flown by Brigadier General Jacob H. Rudolph, the commanding officer for the depot.

That month, the recently trained graduates of the aircraft maintenance program put their skills to work, performing the first aircraft maintenance on a B-17 bomber, which they nicknamed "Junior." By the end of November 1944, 1,250 B-17 aircraft had been repaired at the depot, and by June 1945, 10,000 engines had been repaired. It wasn't just the number of aircraft that were repaired that was impressive; the turn-around time for repairs was a point of pride for those

Maintenance crews work on a B-29 Superfortress. At one point the largest fleet of B-29s was located outside of Spokane. (Courtesy Fairchild AFB)

who worked at the depot. Aircraft were repaired and back in the air within three days thanks to the skill, efficiency and pride taken by the employees at the depot.

While the depot was a spot to which injured aircraft came for maintenance, it was also a supply station from which aircraft supplies could be sent anywhere in the world. "Fifteen-thousand tons of supplies and aircraft parts were processed through the depot each month. In less than two years, a total of 150,000 tons of material was supplied from the airfield, with nearly twenty percent of that sum going overseas," *Sentinel of the Pacific Northwest* noted.

The end of the war was good, in the sense that the end of any war is good for those who are involved and touched by its devastating events, but it also marked the bittersweet beginning of the end for the depot. By August 1945, seventy-five percent of the aircraft maintenance department had been let go and the number of employees dropped from 10,000 down to 7,536. By the fall of 1945, that number was reduced again, leaving only 744 maintenance employees. The supply portion of the depot felt the

A B-29's artwork is touched up. (Courtesy of Fairchild AFB)

The Women Army Air Corps arrived at the Depot on May 14, 1943, with a marching band welcome. (Courtesy of Fairchild AFB)

cuts too, losing over fifty percent of its ranks, due to decreased demand.

The Air Service Command, which provided the supply portion of the depot, was officially inactivated in March 1947, bringing the Spokane Air Depot to a close. With the closure of the depot came another name change, from Spokane Air Depot to Spokane Army Air Field.

Six months later, on September 18, 1947, the United States Air Force was formed as a separate branch of the military, and in 1948, the Spokane Air Depot officially became Spokane Air Force Base. The airfield was transferred to the Fifteenth Air Force (15AF) Strategic Air Command (SAC) and the 92nd and 98th Bombardment groups were assigned with their B-29 bombers. At one point, the largest B-29 organization was ten miles outside of Spokane.

The two bombardment groups were deployed to Okinawa, Japan in response to the hostile situation in Korea, and, according to *Sentinel of the Pacific Northwest,* "The 92nd returned after only two months, but the 98th remained in the Far East for the duration of the conflict and never returned."

By 1950, the Air Force had created a policy to name its installations after fallen, heroic aviators, preferably ones who hailed from areas near each base. Needing to change the name from Spokane Air Force Base, a committee met to select a heroic, fallen and local aviator who fit the bill. After much consideration they selected General Muir S. Fairchild.

A native of Bellingham, Washington, Fairchild was a member of the Washington National Guard from 1916 to1917, at which time he transferred to the Aviation Cadets. After training stateside and in Europe, he was commissioned in the Aviation Section of the Signal Reserve. In 1918, he began a career as a flight instructor; however, he "was separated from the Army in October 1919." The separation was short lived as he was back in the Army July 1, 1920. For the next twenty-eight years he held a variety of distinguished positions, including an Air Corps representative to the Douglas Aircraft Company, administrative roles in the Office of the Chief of the Air Corps, and his last role was Air Force Vice-Chief of Staff at the Pentagon. He died while serving in this position, on March 17, 1950. A little over one year after his death, in July 1951, a dedication ceremony was held, changing the name of Spokane Air Force Base to Fairchild Air Force Base, which it remains today.

Though the names and exact assignments have changed, one thing that has remained constant is the presence of a military installment on White Bluff Prairie, and the continued dedication to our community and our nation by the men and women who have served there. ●

28

Full Bloom Celebration

Spokane's Lilac Festival

A Lilac Festival Queen, ca. 1940. (Courtesy of Spokane Lilac Festival Association)

Garden Club parade float, 1910. (Courtesy of Spokane Lilac Festival Association)

MUCH HAS CHANGED IN SPOKANE SINCE 1938. BUSINESSES HAVE COME AND gone, city leadership has changed, roads have been widened, houses have been built, beloved sites like Natatorium Park and the East Sprague drive-in movie theater have exited to stage-left while newer favorites like Riverfront Park's pavilion and the AMC multiplex theater have made their home in our hearts. Lives have been lived, loved and lost; memories have been made and the population has grown. One thing that has not changed, however, is the spirit of pride Spokane residents feel in their town. One of the best examples of that spirit and pride is the annual Lilac Festival, which began in 1938.

There are differing stories on how the lilac, which is named after the Arabian word for blue, made its way to Spokane. Many sources credit J.J. Browne with having first introduced the Lilac to Spokane in 1906; however, the lilac is also said to have first come to Spokane by way of the first settlers in the area who brought shoots to plant in their gardens. One such shoot seems to have found its way to the Monroe Denman homestead near Hillyard in 1883. An article in the May 10, 1957 *Spokesman-Review* quoted A.M. Denman as saying, "My aunt, Clara Denman, brought the lilac in her trunk from Morristown, Minnesota, and gave it to my father." Later, in 1906, one of Spokane's well-known, high-society residents, J.J. Browne, ordered and planted two lilacs in his yard in Browne's Addition at 2226 E. Second Avenue.

It wasn't until years later that more lilacs made their way to Spokane, which would one day become known as the "Lilac City." During the late 1930s, Spokane resident John W. Duncan traveled back east, where he met John Dunbar of Rochester, New York. Dunbar was considered an authority on lilacs, and he showed Duncan his collection of the flowers, sharing his deep knowledge of the flower with him. Lured by the beauty of the cultivated gardens and thick lush lilac bushes, what Duncan saw must have made him yearn for something equally beautiful and exotic in his own garden. Deciding that the beauty should not be limited to gardens in New York, Duncan brought 128 named lilac varieties back to Spokane with him when he returned. Wanting to share the beauty of the flower with his fellow residents, Duncan donated his lilacs to the city of Spokane. They were planted throughout the city, and by 1938, 200 lilac bushes were blooming in the area.

Spokane enjoyed a hearty national reputation for its fine parks. The Spokane Parks Department, under the direction of Aubrey White and the aforementioned John Duncan, and with guidance from Dr. S.E. Lambert and

The 1941 Lilac Court, at The Davenport Hotel. (Courtesy of Spokane Lilac Festival Association)

Queen Diane Hausken and Maj Gen Charles Eisenhart.
(Courtesy of Spokane Lilac Festival Association)

The Lilac Court makes an appearance with local servicemen.
(Courtesy of Spokane Lilac Festival Association)

The 1956 Lilac Court receives corsages from local servicemen. (Courtesy of Spokane Lilac Festival Association)

W.T. Triplett, began promoting Spokane as the "Lilac City." Local garden clubs began their campaign to plant lilac bushes throughout the city of Spokane. In 1938, there was an inventory of thirty lilacs in Coeur d'Alene Park and 144 at Manito Park alone. Fragrant lilacs had taken root.

What better way to promote Spokane as the "Lilac City," and to celebrate the beauty of the flowers than to have a festival – specifically a Lilac Festival? It came to fruition, or dare we say, "blossomed," thanks to the work of the Associated Garden Clubs of Spokane and the Spokane Floral Association.

The first Lilac Festival was held for eight days, from May 17 to 24, 1938. A flower show at The Davenport Hotel and a small parade with seven cars and one float made up most of the festival that first year. The flower show at The Davenport Hotel included displays of lilac bushes and lilac blooms that were entered in a contest for prizes. The judging for the event was held at the Civic Building, but the exact date for the judging had to be put on hold until a sunny day was available, during which time the lilacs could bloom and be seen in their full glory.

During this first Lilac Festival, the entire city got into the spirit. The Davenport Hotel and The Crescent department store featured fresh lilacs in their displays for the entire week, and it was urged that lilacs be sent to shut-ins and those sick in the hospital during the festival week. How beautiful the city must have looked and smelled during this celebration.

In 1939, the festival added a slogan contest, a tea and a card party to the week's activities. These ideas were suggested by Polly M. Judd, the then-president of the Garden Clubs of Spokane, and the namesake of one of Spokane's city parks. Many participants entered Judd's suggested slogan contest, which was won by Mrs. F. P. Montieth, who suggested, "Spokane is Best When Lilac Drest." This is perhaps the most well-remembered and beloved Lilac Festival slogan of all time.

For the 1940 Lilac Festival, there was an addition to the events with the selection of Lilac Royalty and the Lilac Festival Queen. This coveted title was given to a young woman who represented Spokane and the festival through attendance at community events, luncheons and more. The crowning glory of the title came in the glamorous parade ride. The first Lilac Festival Queen was Shannon Mahoney. She rode through the streets of the city during a parade in an elegant flower bedecked carriage with a canopy of flowers overhead. Residents who lined the streets

The Audubon Garden Club's parade float, 1950. (Courtesy of Spokane Lilac Festival Association)

to view the parade cheered as their queen came into sight. They also cheered to see and hear the high school marching bands, which were added to the parade in 1940. With a parade, royalty and marching bands, along with the flower shows, the festival was becoming one of the city's brightest and most beloved celebrations.

Despite the glamorous and somewhat scene-stealing addition of royalty and marching bands, the festival's flower show with multiple varieties of lilacs continued to be a hit, drawing large numbers of both entrants and those who came out simply to see the splendor of the displays. The lilac truly was the crowning glory.

Five years into its existence, just as the festival was reaching new heights of popularity and becoming one of the city's most anticipated events, life interrupted the fun with the start of WWII. With our boys fighting overseas, rations a daily norm, and most people focusing on being as frugal and conservative as possible, holding a frivolous festival seemed inappropriate, so the festival was put on hold in 1942. It was not until 1946, after the end of WWII, that it was considered appropriate to resume the festival in all of its glory.

Despite the cancellation of the parade, royalty and excessive festivities, there were still a few signs of the festival during those bleak years. The lilacs were still blooming, so the flower show was still held. Additionally, lilacs were dispensed to the soldiers who came through Spokane on troop trains, as the city's way of cheering them upward and onward. Parades, floats, marching bands and royalty would all have to wait to shine their light until the war was over though.

In 1946, with the war over and life looking up, the festival returned to Spokane. That year also marked the official formation of the Spokane Lilac Festival Association. This group of community members joined together volunteering their time to coordinate, organize, finance, promote and produce the event. Among the Association's charter members were several well-known names belonging to families that were pillars in the community, including Mrs. Wm H. Cowles Jr., and Joel Ferris.

Having the power of an organization behind it boosted the festival's size. The parade grew noticeably as the years went by and as the organization got behind the event. The first floats were buggies and carriages decorated with lilacs and garden flowers. Pick-up trucks were used, and some of them were driven backwards down the parade route so the bed of the truck, decorated with flowers, was seen first. The big round wheels of the buggies

1960 Lilac Court, with actor John Vivyan.
(Courtesy of Spokane Lilac Festival Association)

and carriages, and the wheels of the automobiles, were decorated with flowers, turning wheels into rotating bouquets.

The elegance of the event extended beyond the parade. In 1942, the first Lilac Festival Coronation Ball was held and was well promoted in the newspaper beforehand and for years after. A *Spokesman-Review* article captured the excitement surrounding the Ball. "Saturday night… the Coronation Ball will be held as a prelude to Lilac Festival week. Queen Gail Jackson will receive her crown 'amid pomp and grandeur reminiscent of age old royal ceremonies,' according to Lloyd Anderson, president of the Spokane Lilac Festival Association. The coronation will be held at the Spokane Hotel, beginning at 9 p.m."

By 1948, there were forty bands and thirty floats participating in the parade, and 40,000 bystanders soaking it all in from the streets of downtown Spokane. Visiting royalty from forty surrounding towns in Washington, Idaho and British Columbia came for the parade. Every town had a queen and royal court.

The belles of the ball, or of the parade in this case, were always the Lilac Royalty. With the queen in her lilac colored gown, and the accompanying military personnel in their dress uniforms, it was a grand parade indeed!

Traditionally, there were two parades held in May of each year: the Lilac Festival Community Parade, celebrating lilacs and the city, and the Armed Forces Day Parade, celebrating our community military men and women. In 1951, a third parade, the Junior Lilac Parade began. With three parades, the streets were crowded and something needed to change. As a result, in 1955, the Lilac Festival Community Parade and the Armed Forces Day parades merged and were held on Saturday morning.

In 1960, a nighttime parade known as the Torchlight Parade began. The fun of gathering in the evening, listening to the bands under the darkened sky, and watching the lights on the floats was a huge draw. Soon thereafter, the number of spectators for the evening parade surpassed those of the morning parade, and in 1967, the two parades were combined into one and became known as The Lilac Festival Armed Forces Torchlight Parade, a name it still bears today. Despites the changes in time and name, the parades consistently drew crowds and were a huge hit.

Realizing the popularity of the Armed Forces addition to the parade, festival organizers decided to expand the festival to include more of the local military in the planned activities. In the 1960s, festival organizers added Fairchild Air Force Base Aerospace Day as the finale to the festival week. It turned out to be a huge success. Visitors poured onto the base to see airplanes, how the base ran and to experience the usually unattainable views behind the gates.

If one doubts the power of one little flower, guess again. The Lilac Festival became so successful and popular that it began drawing big names to Spokane to celebrate the event, including Ed Sullivan, Peggy Lee and Hopalong Cassidy. These entertainers performed in the Lilac Time Night Show, which was added to the festival line-up in the 1950s and lasted through the 1970s.

The Lilac Festival Queen, at The Davenport Hotel.
(Courtesy of Spokane Lilac Festival Association)

Nowadays, the Lilac Festival is still an important a part of our community. Young women are still selected to serve as Lilac Royalty, the week of festivities draws out the best of our great city's spirit, and the parade draws thousands of visitors for whom the sound of the marching bands resonates in their hearts. As the years have passed, the Lilac Festival continues as a vibrant event, celebrating Spokane's blooming civic pride. ●

Acknowledgements

GREAT THINGS DO NOT HAPPEN ON YOUR OWN OR in your own strength. It takes a village to raise a child. It takes 600 to 800 grapes to make a bottle of wine. And it definitely takes more than one person to publish a book. Thank you to everyone who has helped me in this process:

Every writer needs a great editor, and I had that in Pia I. Longinotti. In addition to being an incredible professional educator, she has a mastery of commas and the English language that helped me greatly. Her countless hours of reading, reviewing and editing my writing helped fine-tune this book.

Finding the right pictures to accompany the stories in this book was essential. Thank you to all who put in time, effort and patience, helping in the process: Stephanie Plowman, Chair, Special Collections Librarian at the Foley Library at Gonzaga University; Frank Oesterheld, MA, Assistant Archivist at the Joel E. Ferris Library and Archives at the Northwest Museum of Arts and Culture; Jeff Creighton, Northwest Museum of Arts and Culture; Kristin Monasmith, Director of Public Relations at Spokane Shriners Hospital; Spokane Lilac Festival Association; Charles V. Mutschler, Ph.D, Archives & Special Collections Department, Eastern Washington University Library.

Thank you to Mike McCoy, at Jostens Inc. for nearly a full year of patiently answering questions and assisting with printing decisions.

Thank you to Greg Johnson, for his legal wisdom, and for encouragement along the way to pursue my dream.

Thank you to David Crary, my colleague of ten years, for his great talent, creativity and vision in the layout and creative design of this book. His skill, enthusiasm and commitment to producing a beautiful product reassured me the book was in the best hands possible.

Thank you to my family and friends for their support, encouragement and enthusiasm for this project over the past three and a half years. A special thanks to my dad, who, before his death, greatly encouraged me to see this project through, and to my mom, who has continued steadfastly where he left off.

Thanks be to God, for the blessings, care and love He has so graciously provided to me, and for the future that awaits. ●